DIGITAL VIDEO PROCESSING PROJECTS USING PYTHON AND TKINTER

VIVIAN SIAHAAN
RISMON HASIHOLAN SIANIPAR

Copyright © 2024 BALIGE Publishing

All rights reserved. No part of this book may be reproduced, stored in a retrieval system, or transmitted in any form or by any means, without the prior written permission of the publisher, except in the case of brief quotations embedded in critical articles or reviews. Every effort has been made in the preparation of this book to ensure the accuracy of the information presented. However, the information contained in this book is sold without warranty, either express or implied. Neither the authors, nor BALIGE Publishing or its dealers and distributors, will be held liable for any damages caused or alleged to have been caused directly or indirectly by this book. BALIGE Publishing has endeavored to provide trademark information about all of the companies and products mentioned in this book by the appropriate use of capitals. However, BALIGE Publishing cannot guarantee the accuracy of this information.

Published: MARCH 2024
Production reference: 0100324
Published by BALIGE Publishing Ltd.
BALIGE, North Sumatera

ABOUT THE AUTHOR

Vivian Siahaan is a highly motivated individual with a passion for continuous learning and exploring new areas. Born and raised in Hinalang Bagasan, Balige, situated on the picturesque banks of Lake Toba, she completed her high school education at SMAN 1 Balige. Vivian's journey into the world of programming began with a deep dive into various languages such as Java, Android, JavaScript, CSS, C++, Python, R, Visual Basic, Visual C#, MATLAB, Mathematica, PHP, JSP, MySQL, SQL Server, Oracle, Access, and more. Starting from scratch, Vivian diligently studied programming, focusing on mastering the fundamental syntax and logic. She honed her skills by creating practical GUI applications, gradually building her expertise. One particular area of interest for Vivian is animation and game development, where she aspires to make significant contributions. Alongside her programming and mathematical pursuits, she also finds joy in indulging in novels, nurturing her love for literature. Vivian Siahaan's passion for programming and her extensive knowledge are reflected in the numerous ebooks she has authored. Her works, published by Sparta Publisher, cover a wide range of topics, including "Data Structure with Java," "Java Programming: Cookbook," "C++ Programming: Cookbook," "C Programming For High Schools/Vocational Schools and Students," "Java Programming for SMA/SMK," "Java Tutorial: GUI, Graphics and Animation," "Visual Basic Programming: From A to Z," "Java Programming for Animation and Games," "C# Programming for SMA/SMK and Students," "MATLAB For Students and Researchers," "Graphics in JavaScript: Quick Learning Series," "JavaScript Image Processing Methods: From A to Z," "Java GUI Case Study: AWT & Swing," "Basic CSS and JavaScript," "PHP/MySQL Programming: Cookbook," "Visual Basic: Cookbook," "C++ Programming for High Schools/Vocational Schools and Students," "Concepts and Practices of C++," "PHP/MySQL For Students," "C# Programming: From A to Z," "Visual Basic for SMA/SMK and Students," and "C# .NET and SQL Server for High School/Vocational School and Students." Furthermore, at the ANDI Yogyakarta publisher, Vivian Siahaan has contributed to several notable books, including "Python Programming Theory and Practice," "Python GUI Programming," "Python GUI and Database," "Build From Zero School Database Management System In Python/MySQL," "Database Management System in Python/MySQL," "Python/MySQL For Management Systems of Criminal Track Record Database," "Java/MySQL For Management Systems of Criminal Track Records Database," "Database and Cryptography Using Java/MySQL," and "Build From Zero School Database Management System With Java/MySQL." Vivian's diverse range of expertise in programming languages, combined with her passion for exploring new horizons, makes her a dynamic and versatile individual in the field of technology. Her dedication to learning, coupled with her strong analytical and problem-solving skills, positions her as a valuable asset in any programming endeavor. Vivian Siahaan's contributions to the world of programming and literature continue to inspire and empower aspiring programmers and readers alike.

Rismon Hasiholan Sianipar, born in Pematang Siantar in 1994, is a distinguished researcher and expert in the field of electrical engineering. After completing his education at SMAN 3 Pematang Siantar, Rismon ventured to the city of Jogjakarta to pursue his academic journey. He obtained his Bachelor of Engineering (S.T) and Master of Engineering (M.T) degrees in Electrical Engineering from Gadjah Mada University in 1998 and 2001, respectively, under the guidance of esteemed professors, Dr. Adhi Soesanto and Dr. Thomas Sri Widodo. During his studies, Rismon focused on researching non-stationary signals and their energy analysis using time-frequency maps. He explored the dynamic nature of signal energy distribution on time-frequency maps and developed innovative techniques using discrete wavelet transformations to design non-linear filters for data pattern analysis. His research showcased the application of these techniques in various fields. In recognition of his academic prowess, Rismon was awarded the prestigious Monbukagakusho scholarship by the Japanese Government in 2003. He went on to pursue his Master of Engineering (M.Eng) and Doctor of Engineering (Dr.Eng) degrees at Yamaguchi University, supervised by Prof. Dr. Hidetoshi Miike. Rismon's master's and doctoral theses revolved around combining the SR-FHN (Stochastic Resonance Fitzhugh-Nagumo) filter strength with the cryptosystem ECC (elliptic curve cryptography) 4096-bit. This innovative approach effectively suppressed noise in digital images and videos while ensuring their authenticity. Rismon's research findings have been published in renowned international scientific journals, and his patents have been officially registered in Japan. Notably, one of his patents, with registration number 2008-009549, gained recognition. He actively collaborates with several universities and research institutions in Japan, specializing in cryptography, cryptanalysis, and digital forensics, particularly in the areas of audio, image, and video analysis. With a passion for knowledge sharing, Rismon has authored numerous national and international scientific articles and authored several national books. He has also actively participated in workshops related to cryptography, cryptanalysis, digital watermarking, and digital forensics. During these workshops, Rismon has assisted Prof. Hidetoshi Miike in developing applications related to digital image and video processing, steganography, cryptography, watermarking, and more, which serve as valuable training materials. Rismon's field of interest encompasses multimedia security, signal processing, digital image and video analysis, cryptography, digital communication, digital forensics, and data compression. He continues to advance his research by developing applications using programming languages such as Python, MATLAB, C++, C, VB.NET, C#.NET, R, and Java. These applications serve both research and commercial purposes, further contributing to the advancement of signal and image analysis. Rismon Hasiholan Sianipar is a dedicated researcher and expert in the field of electrical engineering, particularly in the areas of signal processing, cryptography, and digital forensics. His academic achievements, patented inventions, and extensive publications demonstrate his commitment to advancing knowledge in these fields. Rismon's contributions to academia and his collaborations with prestigious institutions in Japan have solidified his position as a respected figure in the scientific community. Through his ongoing research and development of innovative applications, Rismon continues to make significant contributions to the field of electrical engineering.

ABOUT THE BOOK

The first project is a video player application with an additional feature to compute and display the MD5 hash of each frame in a video. The user interface is built using Tkinter, a Python GUI toolkit, providing buttons for opening a video file, playing, pausing, and stopping the video playback. Upon opening a video file, the application displays metadata such as filename, duration, resolution, FPS, and codec information in a table. The video can be navigated using a slider to seek to a specific time point.

When the video is played, the application iterates through each frame, extracts it from the video clip, calculates its MD5 hash, and displays the frame along with its histogram and MD5 hash. The histogram represents the pixel intensity distribution of each color channel (red, green, blue) in the frame. The computed MD5 hash for each frame is displayed in a label below the video frame. Additionally, the frame hash along with its index is saved to a text file for further analysis or verification purposes.

The class encapsulates the functionality of the application, providing methods for opening a video file, playing and controlling video playback, updating metadata, computing frame histogram, plotting histogram, calculating MD5 hash for each frame, and saving frame hashes to a file. The main function initializes the Tkinter root window, instantiates the class, and starts the Tkinter event loop to handle user interactions and update the GUI accordingly.

The second project is a video player application with additional features for frame extraction and visualization of RGB histograms for each frame. Developed using Tkinter, a Python GUI toolkit, the application provides functionalities such as opening a video file, playing, pausing, and stopping video playback. The user interface includes buttons for controlling video playback, a combobox for selecting zoom scale, an entry for specifying a time point to jump to, and buttons for frame extraction and opening another instance of the application.

Upon opening a video file, the application loads it using the imageio library and displays the frames in a canvas. Users can play, pause, and stop the video using dedicated buttons. The zoom scale can be adjusted, and the video can be navigated using scrollbar or time entry. Additionally, users can extract a specific frame by entering its frame number, which opens a new window displaying the extracted frame along with its RGB histograms and MD5 hash value.

The class encapsulates the application's functionalities, including methods for opening a video file, playing/pausing/stopping video, updating zoom scale, displaying frames, handling mouse events for dragging and scrolling, jumping to a specified time, and extracting frames. The main function initializes the Tkinter root window and starts the application's event loop to handle user interactions and update the GUI accordingly. Users can also open multiple instances of the application simultaneously to work with different video files concurrently.

The third project is a GUI application built with Tkinter for calculating hash values of video frames and displaying them in a listbox. The interface consists of different frames for video display and hash values, along with buttons for controlling video playback, calculating hashes, saving hash values to a file, and opening a new instance of the application. Users can open a video file using the "Open Video" button, after which they can play, pause, or stop the video using corresponding buttons.

Upon opening a video file, the application reads frames from the video capture and displays them in the designated frame. Users can interact with the video using playback buttons to control the video's flow. Hash values for each frame are calculated using various hashing algorithms such as MD5, SHA-1, SHA-256, and others. These hash values are then displayed in the listbox, allowing users to view the hash values corresponding to each algorithm. Additionally, users can save the calculated hash values to a text file by clicking the "Save Hashes" button, providing a convenient way to store and analyze the hash data. Lastly, users can open multiple instances of the application simultaneously by clicking the "Open New Instance" button, facilitating concurrent processing of different video files.

The fourth project is a GUI application developed using Tkinter for analyzing video frames through frame hashing and histogram visualization. The interface presents a canvas for displaying the video frames along with control buttons for video playback, frame extraction, and zoom control. Users can open a video file using the "Open Video" button, and the application provides functionality to play, pause, and stop the video playback. Additionally, users can jump to specific time points within the video using the time entry field and "Jump to Time" button.

Upon extracting a frame, the application opens a new window displaying the selected frame along with its histogram and multiple hash values calculated using various algorithms such as MD5, SHA-1, SHA-256, and others. The histogram visualization presents the distribution of pixel values across the RGB channels, aiding in the analysis of color composition within the frame. The hash values are displayed in a listbox within the frame extraction window, providing users with comprehensive information about the frame's content and characteristics. Furthermore, users can open multiple instances of the application simultaneously, enabling concurrent analysis of different video files.

The fifth project implements a video player application with edge detection capabilities using various algorithms. The application is designed using the Tkinter library for the graphical user interface (GUI). Upon execution, the user is presented with a window containing control buttons and panels for displaying the video and extracted frames.

The main functionalities of the application include opening a video file, playing, pausing, and stopping the video playback. Additionally, users can jump to a specific time in the video, extract frames, and open another instance of the video player application. The video playback is displayed on a canvas, allowing for zooming in and out using a combobox to adjust the scale.

One of the key features of this application is the ability to perform edge detection on frames extracted from the video. When a frame is extracted, the application displays the original frame alongside its edge detection result using various algorithms such as Canny, Sobel, Prewitt, Laplacian, Scharr, Roberts, FreiChen, Kirsch, Robinson, Gaussian, or no edge detection. Histogram plots for each RGB channel of the frame are also displayed, along with hash values computed using different hashing algorithms for integrity verification. The edge detection result and histogram plots are updated dynamically based on the selected edge detection algorithm.

Overall, this application provides a convenient platform for visualizing video content and performing edge detection analysis on individual frames, making it useful for tasks such as video processing, computer vision, and image analysis.

The sixth project is a Python application built using the Tkinter library for creating a graphical user interface (GUI) to play videos and apply various filtering techniques to individual frames. The application allows users to open video files in common formats such as MP4, AVI, and MKV. Once a video is opened, users can play, pause, stop, and jump to specific times within the video.

The GUI consists of two main panels: one for displaying the video and another for control buttons. The video panel contains a canvas where the frames of the video are displayed. Users can zoom in or out on the video frames using a combobox, and they can also scroll horizontally through the video using a scrollbar. Control buttons such as play/pause, stop, extract frame, and open another video player are provided in the control panel.

When a frame is extracted, the application opens a new window displaying the extracted frame along with options to apply various filtering methods. These methods include Gaussian blur, mean blur, median blur, bilateral filtering, non-local means denoising, anisotropic diffusion, total variation denoising, Wiener filter, adaptive thresholding, and wavelet transform. Users can select a filtering method from a dropdown menu, and the filtered result along with the histogram and hash values of the frame are displayed in real-time.

The application also provides functionality to open another instance of the video player, allowing users to work with multiple videos simultaneously. Overall, this project provides a user-friendly interface for playing videos and applying filtering techniques to individual frames, making it useful for tasks such as video processing, analysis, and editing.

CONTENT

COMPUTING HASH VALUE OF EACH FRAME IN VIDEO — 1
- Importing Libraries — 1
- The Class and Constructor — 2
- Creating Widgets — 2
- Opening Video — 5
- Playing Video — 6
- Updating Video Frame — 7
- Saving Frame Hash to File — 9
- Pausing Video — 10
- Stopping Video — 11
- Updating Metadata Table — 12
- Extracting Metadata Information — 13
- Computing Histogram of Color Channels — 15
- Visualizing Histogram — 16
- Computing Hash Value for a Given Frame — 18
- Entry Point of Program — 18
- Running Program — 19
- Full Source Code — 22

COMPUTING HASH VALUE OF EACH FRAME IN VIDEO AND DISPLAYING ITS RGB HISTORGAM — 27
- Importing Libraries — 28
- The Class and Constructor — 29
- Creating Widgets — 31
- Opening Video — 33
- Playing Video — 34
- Stopping Video — 35
- Toggling Video — 36
- Updating the Zoom Level — 36
- Displaying Video Frames — 37
- Handling Mouse Wheel Events — 38
- Handling Mouse Button Press Events — 39
- Handling Mouse Drag Events — 40
- Handling Horizontal Scrolling in Scrollbar — 41

Navigating to Specific Time Points	42
Extracting and Displaying Specific Frame	43
Displaying Extracted Frame and Its Histogram	44
Creating Another Instance	46
Entry Point of Application	47
Running Program	48
Full Source Code	50

COMPUTING HASH VALUE OF A VIDEO FILE — 55

Importing Libraries	56
Structure and Behavior of GUI	57
Opening and Selecting Video File	59
Displaying Video	60
Playing, Pausing, and Stopping Video	61
Calculating Hash Values	62
Saving Hash Values	64
Opening Another Instance of Application	65
Entry Point For Running Program	66
Running Program	67
Full Source Code	68

COMPUTING HASH VALUE OF EIGHT DIFFERENT HASH FUNCTIONS ON EACH FRAME IN VIDEO AND DISPLAYING ITS RGB HISTORGAM — 71

Importing Libraries	72
Class and Its Constructor	74
Creating Widgets	75
Opening, Playing, Stopping, and Toggling Video	78
Updating Zoom Level	80
Showing Frame	80
Enhancing User Interaction	82
Jumping to a Specific Time in Video	83
Extracting Frame	84
Showing Extracted Frame	85
Opening Another Instance of Application	87
Entry Point of Application	88
Running Program	89
Full Source Code	91

DETECTING EDGES ON EACH FRAME IN VIDEO — 97

Importing Libraries	98
Class and Its Constructor	99
Creating Widgets	101
Opening, Playing, Stopping, and Toggling Video	103
Showing Frame	104

Handling Mouse Events	106
Jumping to a Specific Time	107
Showing Extracted Frame	108
Applying Canny, Sobel, Prewitt, and Laplacian Edge Detectors	111
Applying Scharr Edge Detector	112
Applying Roberts Edge Detector	114
Applying FreiChen Edge Detector	115
Applying Kirsch Edge Detector	116
Applying Robinson Edge Detector	118
Applying Gaussian Edge Detector	119
Applying Various Edge Detection Algorithms	120
Updating Histogram Plots and Hash Values	123
Displaying Edge Detection Result	125
Open Another Instance of The Application	126
Entry Point for Application	126
Running Program	127
Full Source Code	129

FILTERING EACH FRAME IN VIDEO   **139**

Importing Libraries	140
Class and Its Constructor	141
Creating Widgets	142
Opening, Playing, Stopping, and Toggling Video	145
Showing Frame	146
Handling Mouse Events	147
Extracting and Showing Frame	148
Gaussian Filtering	151
Mean Filtering	152
Median Filtering	153
Bilateral Filtering	154
Non-Local Means Denoising	155
Anisotropic Diffusion	156
Total Variation Denoising	158
Wiener Filtering	159
Adaptive Filtering	161
Wavelet Filtering	162
Applying Filters	163
Combining Image Channels	165
Updating Histogram and Hash Values	166
Showing Filtering Result	167
Entry Point for Application	168
Running Program	169
Full Source Code	170
Bibliography	186

COMPUTING HASH VALUE OF EACH FRAME IN VIDEO

CALCULATING AND SAVING MD5 HASH OF EACH FRAME

This Python code creates a simple video player application using Tkinter, a Python GUI library, allowing users to open video files, play them, pause, stop, and seek through frames. It also calculates and saves the MD5 hash of every frame in the video.

Importing Libraries

```
import tkinter as tk
from tkinter import filedialog, ttk
from PIL import Image, ImageTk
import moviepy.editor as mp
import numpy as np
import os
import hashlib
```

- tkinter: This library provides GUI functionality.
- filedialog: It allows the user to interact with the file system to open files.
- ttk: This module provides themed widgets for tkinter.
- PIL: Python Imaging Library, used for image processing.
- moviepy.editor: A library for working with video files.
- numpy: A library used for numerical operations on arrays.
- os: Provides operating system functionality for file operations.

- hashlib: Used for generating hash values.

The Class and Constructor

Let's dive into the VideoPlayerApp class's __init__() method step by step:

```python
class VideoPlayerApp:
    def __init__(self, master):
        self.master = master
        self.master.title("MD5 HASHING OF EVERY FRAME IN VIDEO")

        self.create_widgets()
```

1. Class Definition:
    - class VideoPlayerApp: defines a new class named VideoPlayerApp. This class encapsulates the behavior and properties of a video player application.
2. __init__() Method:
    - def __init__(self, master): declares the constructor method for the VideoPlayerApp class. It takes master as a parameter, which typically represents the main window or frame in Tkinter applications.
    - self.master = master: This line assigns the master parameter to an instance variable self.master, allowing access to the main window throughout the class.
    - self.master.title("MD5 HASHING OF EVERY FRAME IN VIDEO"): Sets the title of the main window to "MD5 HASHING OF EVERY FRAME IN VIDEO". This title appears in the window's title bar.
    - self.create_widgets(): Calls the create_widgets() method, which is responsible for creating and placing all the GUI elements within the main window.

In summary, the __init__() method initializes an instance of the VideoPlayerApp class by setting up the main window title and calling a method to create the GUI elements. This method ensures that when a VideoPlayerApp object is created, it starts with a properly configured main window.

Creating Widgets

The create_widgets() method is responsible for setting up and placing all the GUI elements within the main window of the video player application. Let's break down each part of this method:

1. Open Button:
```python
self.open_button = tk.Button(self.master, text="Open Video", command=self.open_video)
self.open_button.pack(pady=10)
```

- This creates a button labeled "Open Video" using the Button widget from Tkinter.
- When clicked, it calls the open_video() method.
- The button is then packed into the main window with some vertical padding (pady) to provide spacing between elements.

2. Video Frame Label:

```
self.video_frame = tk.Label(self.master)
self.video_frame.pack()
```

- This creates a label widget (Label) named self.video_frame. This label will be used to display video frames.
- It is packed into the main window without any additional padding.

3. Metadata Table:

```
self.metadata_table = ttk.Treeview(self.master, columns=('Property', 'Value'))
self.metadata_table.heading('#0', text='Property')
self.metadata_table.heading('#1', text='Value')
self.metadata_table.pack(pady=10)
```

- This creates a treeview widget (Treeview) named self.metadata_table. This table will display metadata information about the video.
- It consists of two columns: "Property" and "Value".
- The table is packed into the main window with some vertical padding.

4. Button Frame for Controls:

```
self.button_frame = tk.Frame(self.master)
self.button_frame.pack()
```

- This creates a frame (Frame) named self.button_frame to hold control buttons (play, pause, stop).
- The frame is packed into the main window.

5. Play, Pause, and Stop Buttons:

```
self.play_button = tk.Button(self.button_frame, text="Play", command=self.play_video)
self.play_button.pack(side=tk.LEFT, padx=5)
```

```python
self.pause_button        =       tk.Button(self.button_frame,       text="Pause",
command=self.pause_video)
self.pause_button.pack(side=tk.LEFT, padx=5)

self.stop_button = tk.Button(self.button_frame, text="Stop", command=self.stop_video)
self.stop_button.pack(side=tk.LEFT, padx=5)
```

- These create buttons (Button) for controlling video playback (play, pause, stop).
- Each button is packed into the button frame (self.button_frame) with some horizontal padding (padx) to provide spacing between buttons.
- They are packed from left to right (side=tk.LEFT) within the button frame.

6. Seek Slider:

```python
self.seek_slider = tk.Scale(self.master, from_=0, to=100, orient=tk.HORIZONTAL,
command=self.seek_video)
self.seek_slider.pack()
```

- This creates a slider (Scale) named self.seek_slider for seeking through the video.
- It ranges from 0 to 100 and is oriented horizontally.
- When the slider value changes, it calls the seek_video() method.
- The slider is packed into the main window.

7. Frame Hash Label:

```python
self.frame_hash_label = tk.Label(self.master, text="Frame Hash:", font=("Helvetica",
30))
self.frame_hash_label.pack()
```

- This creates a label (Label) named self.frame_hash_label to display the hash value of the current frame.
- It uses a larger font size (Helvetica, 30) to make the text more prominent.
- The label is packed into the main window.

8. Canvas Widgets:

```python
self.canvas = tk.Canvas(self.master, width=600, height=300)
self.canvas.pack(side=tk.LEFT)

self.frame_canvas = tk.Canvas(self.master, width=600, height=300)
self.frame_canvas.pack(side=tk.RIGHT)
```

- These create canvas widgets (Canvas) for displaying video frames and specific frame displays.
- Each canvas widget has a width of 600 pixels and a height of 300 pixels.
- They are packed into the main window, with the first canvas (self.canvas) placed on the left side and the second canvas (self.frame_canvas) placed on the right side.

In summary, the create_widgets() method sets up various GUI elements required for the video player application, including buttons for controlling playback, a slider for seeking through the video, labels for displaying metadata and frame hashes, and canvas widgets for displaying video frames and histograms. Each element is appropriately packed into the main window to create the desired layout.

Opening Video

This open_video() method handles the functionality when the user clicks the "Open Video" button to select a video file. Let's go through it step by step:

```
def open_video(self):
    self.video_filename = filedialog.askopenfilename(filetypes=[("Video files", "*.mp4;*.avi;*.mpeg")])
```

- filedialog.askopenfilename() opens a file dialog window for the user to select a video file.
- filetypes parameter specifies the types of files that can be selected. In this case, it filters files with extensions .mp4, .avi, and .mpeg and displays only video files in the dialog window.
- The selected file's path is stored in self.video_filename.

```
if self.video_filename:
    self.video_clip = mp.VideoFileClip(self.video_filename)
    self.update_metadata_table(self.video_filename)
    self.seek_slider.config(to=self.video_clip.duration)
```

- If a video file is selected (self.video_filename is not empty), the code proceeds.
- mp.VideoFileClip(self.video_filename) loads the selected video file using moviepy.editor. It creates a VideoFileClip object named self.video_clip representing the video.
- self.update_metadata_table(self.video_filename) calls the update_metadata_table() method to display metadata information about the selected video file in a table.

- self.seek_slider.config(to=self.video_clip.duration) updates the seek slider's maximum value (to) to the duration of the loaded video (self.video_clip.duration). This ensures that the slider's maximum value corresponds to the total duration of the video, allowing users to seek through the entire video duration.

In summary, the open_video() method allows users to select a video file, loads the selected video file, displays its metadata, and updates the seek slider's maximum value based on the video's duration. This functionality is essential for initializing the video player application with the chosen video file.

Playing Video

This play_video() method is responsible for starting the playback of the loaded video when the user clicks the "Play" button. Let's break down its functionality:

```
def play_video(self):
    if self.video_clip is not None and not self.playing:
```

- This condition checks whether self.video_clip is not None (i.e., a video is loaded) and whether the video is not already playing. This ensures that the video playback can only start if there is a loaded video (self.video_clip) and if the playback is not already in progress (not self.playing).

```
        self.playing = True
        self.update_video_frame()
```

- If the condition is met, it sets the playing flag to True, indicating that the video is now playing.
- Then, it calls the update_video_frame() method to start updating and displaying video frames continuously, effectively playing the video.

In summary, the play_video() method initiates video playback if a video is loaded and playback is not already in progress. It sets the playing flag to True and starts updating and displaying video frames by calling the update_video_frame() method. This method is crucial for allowing users to start playing the loaded video in the video player application.

Updating Video Frame

This update_video_frame() method is crucial for continuously updating and displaying video frames during playback. Let's break down its functionality step by step:

```
def update_video_frame(self):
    if self.playing:
```

- This checks if the video is currently playing (self.playing is True). If the video is not playing, this method won't proceed, effectively pausing the frame updates.

```
        frame_np    =    self.video_clip.get_frame(self.video_frame_idx    /
self.video_clip.fps)
```

- self.video_clip.get_frame() retrieves the video frame at the specified index. Here, self.video_frame_idx represents the current frame index, and self.video_clip.fps provides the frames per second of the video. By dividing the frame index by the frame rate, we get the time in seconds corresponding to the frame index. This is used to retrieve the frame.
- The retrieved frame is stored as a NumPy array in frame_np.

```
        frame_hash = self.calculate_frame_hash(frame_np)
```

- self.calculate_frame_hash() computes the MD5 hash of the frame (frame_np). The hash value represents a unique identifier for the frame.

```
        frame = Image.fromarray(frame_np)
        frame_tk = ImageTk.PhotoImage(frame)
```

- The NumPy array frame_np is converted to a PIL Image object using Image.fromarray(). PIL (Python Imaging Library) is used here for image processing.
- The PIL Image object is then converted to a Tkinter-compatible image using ImageTk.PhotoImage() and stored in frame_tk. This allows displaying the frame in a Tkinter canvas.

```
        self.canvas.create_image(0, 0, anchor=tk.NW, image=frame_tk)
        self.canvas.image = frame_tk
```

- The Tkinter canvas (self.canvas) is updated with the new frame image. The create_image() method places the image on the canvas at coordinates (0, 0) with the

anchor set to NW (northwest). This means the top-left corner of the image will be positioned at (0, 0) on the canvas.
- The self.canvas.image attribute is set to frame_tk to keep a reference to the image, preventing it from being garbage collected.

```
hist = self.get_frame_histogram(frame_np)
if hist:
    self.plot_histogram(hist)
```

- The method self.get_frame_histogram() calculates the histogram of the current frame (frame_np). If the histogram is successfully calculated (if hist:), the histogram is plotted using self.plot_histogram().

```
self.frame_hash_label.config(text=f"Frame {self.video_frame_idx}: Frame Hash: {frame_hash}")
```

- The label (self.frame_hash_label) displaying the frame hash is updated with the current frame number (self.video_frame_idx) and its corresponding hash value (frame_hash).

```
self.save_frame_hash_to_file(self.video_filename, self.video_frame_idx, frame_hash)
```

- self.save_frame_hash_to_file() saves the frame index, along with its hash value, to a text file associated with the loaded video.

```
self.video_frame_idx += 1
```

- Increment the frame index (self.video_frame_idx) to move to the next frame.

```
if self.video_frame_idx < self.video_clip.duration * self.video_clip.fps:
```

- Check if the current frame index is less than the total number of frames in the video (self.video_clip.duration * self.video_clip.fps). If so, there are more frames to display.

```
self.seek_slider.set(self.video_frame_idx / self.video_clip.fps)
```

- Update the position of the seek slider to reflect the current frame being displayed. This ensures that the slider moves along with the video playback.

```
self.master.after(33, self.update_video_frame)
```

- Use self.master.after() to schedule the update_video_frame() method to be called again after a certain delay (33 milliseconds in this case). This effectively updates the video frame continuously, achieving smooth playback.

```
else:
    self.stop_video()
```

- If the current frame index exceeds the total number of frames in the video, it means the video playback has reached the end. In this case, the stop_video() method is called to stop the playback.

In summary, the update_video_frame() method is responsible for continuously updating and displaying video frames during playback. It retrieves each frame, calculates its hash value, updates the GUI elements accordingly, and schedules itself to be called again to update the next frame. This ensures smooth and continuous video playback in the video player application.

Saving Frame Hash to File

The save_frame_hash_to_file() method is responsible for saving the index and hash value of a frame to a text file associated with the loaded video. Let's break down its functionality:

```
def save_frame_hash_to_file(self, video_filename, frame_idx, frame_hash):
```

This method takes three parameters:
- video_filename: The filename (including path) of the loaded video.
- frame_idx: The index of the frame being processed.
- frame_hash: The hash value corresponding to the frame.

```
# Extract video filename without extension
filename_without_extension = os.path.splitext(os.path.basename(video_filename))[0]
```

- os.path.basename(video_filename) extracts the filename from the full path of the video file.
- os.path.splitext() splits the filename into its base name and extension.

- filename_without_extension stores the base name of the video file (without the extension).

```
txt_filename = f"{filename_without_extension}_frame_hash.txt"
```

- txt_filename is constructed by appending "_frame_hash.txt" to the base name of the video file. This will be the name of the text file where frame index and hash values will be saved.

```
with open(txt_filename, "a") as file:
    file.write(f"{frame_idx}\t{frame_hash}\n")
```

- The method opens the text file specified by txt_filename in append mode ("a"). If the file does not exist, it will be created.
- It writes the frame index (frame_idx) and its corresponding hash value (frame_hash) to the file, separated by a tab (\t), and appends a newline character (\n) to move to the next line.
- The with statement ensures that the file is properly closed after writing, even if an exception occurs.

In summary, the save_frame_hash_to_file() method constructs a filename for a text file based on the loaded video's filename, and then appends the frame index and hash value of a frame to that file. This allows for the recording of frame hash values for subsequent analysis or verification. Each line in the text file corresponds to a frame, containing its index and hash value.

Pausing Video
The pause_video() method is quite straightforward. Let's break down its functionality:

```
def pause_video(self):
    self.playing = False
```

- When called, this method sets the playing attribute to False.
- This attribute (self.playing) is a flag that indicates whether the video is currently playing or paused. Setting it to False effectively pauses the video playback.

In summary, the pause_video() method is responsible for pausing the video playback by setting the playing flag to False, indicating that the video is no longer playing. This method is triggered when the user clicks the "Pause" button in the user interface.

Stopping Video

The stop_video() method is responsible for stopping the video playback altogether. Let's break down its functionality:

```
def stop_video(self):
    self.playing = False
    self.video_frame_idx = 0
```

- When called, this method first sets the playing attribute to False.
  - This attribute (self.playing) acts as a flag that indicates whether the video is currently playing or paused. Setting it to False halts the video playback.
- Then, it resets the video_frame_idx attribute to 0.
  - self.video_frame_idx represents the index of the current frame being displayed. By setting it to 0, the video playback is reset to the beginning.

In summary, the stop_video() method halts the video playback by setting the playing flag to False, indicating that the video is no longer playing, and resets the frame index to 0, effectively stopping the video at its initial frame. This method is triggered when the user clicks the "Stop" button in the user interface.

Seeking Spesific Position in Video

The seek_video() method is responsible for seeking to a specific position in the video when the user interacts with the seek slider. Let's break down its functionality:

```
def seek_video(self, value):
    if self.video_clip is not None:
```

- This method first checks if a video is loaded (self.video_clip is not None). If there is no loaded video, seeking is not possible, so the method exits.

```
        pos_in_seconds = float(value)
        self.video_frame_idx = int(pos_in_seconds * self.video_clip.fps)
```

- If a video is loaded, it converts the current slider value (value) to seconds (pos_in_seconds) by converting it to a float.
- Then, it calculates the corresponding frame index (self.video_frame_idx) by multiplying the seconds by the video's frames per second (fps) and converting the result to an integer.

```
        if not self.playing:
            self.update_video_frame()
```

- If the video is not currently playing (not self.playing), it calls the update_video_frame() method.
- This ensures that if the video is paused when seeking, the frame is updated immediately upon seeking.

```
        else:
            frame_np    =    self.video_clip.get_frame(self.video_frame_idx    /
self.video_clip.fps)
            hist = self.get_frame_histogram(frame_np)
            if hist:
                self.frame_canvas.delete('all')
                self.plot_histogram(hist)
                frame_number = int(self.video_frame_idx / self.video_clip.fps)
                self.frame_canvas.create_text(300,   20,   text=f"Histogram   for   Second
{frame_number}", font=("Helvetica", 16), anchor=tk.CENTER)
                self.frame_canvas.create_text(300,    280,    text="Pixel    Intensity",
font=("Helvetica", 10), anchor=tk.CENTER)
                self.frame_canvas.create_text(30,         150,         text="Frequency",
font=("Helvetica", 10), anchor=tk.CENTER)
```

- If the video is playing, it retrieves the frame corresponding to the calculated frame index (self.video_frame_idx) using self.video_clip.get_frame().
- It then calculates the histogram of the frame and plots it on the frame canvas.
- Additionally, it updates the frame histogram display with the corresponding frame number and labels for better visualization.

In summary, the seek_video() method allows the user to seek to a specific position in the video by updating the frame index based on the slider value. If the video is paused, it immediately updates the frame display. If the video is playing, it updates the frame display and histogram, providing a visual representation of the video content at the seeked position.

Updating Metadata Table

The update_metadata_table() method is responsible for populating a metadata table with information about the loaded video file. Let's examine its functionality:

```
def update_metadata_table(self, file_path):
    metadata = self.get_video_metadata(file_path)
```

- This method first calls the get_video_metadata() function with the provided file_path to retrieve metadata about the video file.

- metadata is a dictionary containing various properties of the video file, such as filename, duration, resolution, codec, etc.

```
for key, value in metadata.items():
    self.metadata_table.insert('', 'end', text=key, values=(value))
```

- It then iterates through the key-value pairs in the metadata dictionary.
- For each key-value pair, it inserts a new row into the metadata table (self.metadata_table).
- The insert() method is used to add a new item to the table. The first argument '' specifies the parent item (since this is a top-level item, it's an empty string), 'end' specifies that the new item should be inserted at the end of the table, text=key sets the text displayed in the first column (the property name), and values=(value) sets the value displayed in the second column (the corresponding property value).

In summary, the update_metadata_table() method retrieves metadata about the loaded video file and inserts this information into a metadata table. Each row in the table represents a property of the video file, with the property name displayed in the first column and its corresponding value displayed in the second column. This method is called when a video file is opened to update the metadata display in the user interface.

Extracting Metadata Information

The get_video_metadata() method is responsible for extracting metadata information from a given video file. Let's go through its functionality:

```
def get_video_metadata(self, file_path):
    metadata = {}
    video = mp.VideoFileClip(file_path)
```

- This method starts by creating an empty dictionary metadata to store metadata information.
- It then uses mp.VideoFileClip(file_path) from the moviepy.editor module to load the video file specified by file_path into a video object.
- The video object represents the loaded video file and allows access to various properties and attributes of the video.

```
metadata['File Name'] = os.path.basename(file_path)
metadata['Duration (s)'] = video.duration
metadata['Width (px)'] = video.size[0]
metadata['Height (px)'] = video.size[1]
```

```
metadata['FPS'] = video.fps
```

- Next, the method extracts specific metadata properties from the loaded video and adds them to the metadata dictionary.
- The file name of the video file is obtained using os.path.basename(file_path) and stored under the key 'File Name'.
- The duration of the video in seconds is stored under the key 'Duration (s)'.
- The width and height of the video frame in pixels are stored under the keys 'Width (px)' and 'Height (px)', respectively.
- The frames per second (FPS) of the video is stored under the key 'FPS'.

```
if 'video' in video.reader.infos:
    metadata['Codec'] = video.reader.infos['video']['codec_name']
    metadata['Bit Rate (kbps)'] = video.reader.infos['video']['bit_rate'] // 1000
else:
    metadata['Codec'] = "Unavailable"
    metadata['Bit Rate (kbps)'] = "Unavailable"
```

- The method checks if video metadata information is available. If available, it retrieves additional information such as codec and bit rate.
- It checks if 'video' key exists in video.reader.infos, which contains metadata information about the video stream.
- If metadata is available, it extracts the codec name and bit rate from video.reader.infos['video'] and stores them under the keys 'Codec' and 'Bit Rate (kbps)', respectively.
- If metadata is not available, it sets the values for codec and bit rate to "Unavailable".

```
return metadata
```

- Finally, the method returns the populated metadata dictionary containing information about the video file.

In summary, the get_video_metadata() method extracts various metadata information from a given video file, including file name, duration, frame size, FPS, codec, and bit rate (if available). This metadata is then returned as a dictionary, which can be used to populate a metadata table or display metadata information in the user interface.

Computing Histogram of Color Channels

The get_frame_histogram() method computes the histogram of color channels (Red, Green, and Blue) for a given frame. Let's break down its functionality:

```
def get_frame_histogram(self, frame):
    if len(frame.shape) == 3:
```

- This condition checks if the frame has three dimensions, indicating that it's a color frame with separate channels for Red, Green, and Blue.
- If the frame has three dimensions, it implies it's a color image, and the method proceeds to compute histograms for each color channel.

```
        hist_red, bins_red = np.histogram(frame[:,:,0].ravel(), bins=64, range=[0,64])
        hist_green, bins_green = np.histogram(frame[:,:,1].ravel(), bins=64, range=[0,64])
        hist_blue, bins_blue = np.histogram(frame[:,:,2].ravel(), bins=64, range=[0,64])
```

- The histograms for each color channel are computed using NumPy's np.histogram() function.
- frame[:,:,0], frame[:,:,1], and frame[:,:,2] access the Red, Green, and Blue channels of the frame, respectively.
- ravel() flattens the 2D array into a 1D array, which is then used to compute the histogram.
- bins=64 specifies the number of bins in the histogram, and range=[0,64] specifies the range of pixel values (from 0 to 63) for each color channel.

```
        return hist_red, hist_green, hist_blue
```

- The method returns the histograms for each color channel (hist_red, hist_green, and hist_blue).

```
    else:
        return None
```

- If the frame does not have three dimensions, it means it's a grayscale image or a single-channel frame. In such cases, the method returns None, indicating that no histogram could be computed.

In summary, the get_frame_histogram() method calculates histograms for the Red, Green, and Blue color channels of a given frame. It returns these histograms if the frame is a color image, and

None otherwise. This method is useful for visualizing the distribution of pixel intensities across different color channels in a video frame.

Visualizing Histogram

The plot_histogram() method is responsible for visualizing the histograms of the Red, Green, and Blue color channels on a canvas. Let's break down its functionality:

```
def plot_histogram(self, hist):
    hist_red, hist_green, hist_blue = hist
```

- The method takes the hist parameter, which is a tuple containing histograms for the Red, Green, and Blue color channels.
- It unpacks this tuple into three separate variables: hist_red, hist_green, and hist_blue, each representing the histogram for its respective color channel.

```
max_value = max(np.max(hist_red), np.max(hist_green), np.max(hist_blue))
scale = 500 / max_value   # Adjusted scale
```

- max_value is calculated as the maximum value among the maximum values of histograms for each color channel.
- The scale is calculated to normalize the histograms based on the maximum value. It ensures that the histogram bars fit within the specified canvas height.

```
bar_width = 8   # Lebar batang histogram
max_height = 300   # Tinggi maksimum batang histogram
```

- bar_width defines the width of each histogram bar.
- max_height specifies the maximum height of the histogram bars on the canvas.

```
for i in range(64):
```

- The method iterates over a range of 64, assuming there are 64 bins in each histogram.

```
x0 = i * 10
x1 = x0 + bar_width
```

- x0 and x1 represent the x-coordinates of the left and right edges of the histogram bar, respectively. They are calculated based on the current iteration index (i) and the bar_width.

```
    y0 = 500
    y1 = max(100, 500 - hist_red[i] * scale)    # Batasi tinggi maksimum batang histogram
```

- y0 and y1 represent the y-coordinates of the top and bottom edges of the histogram bar, respectively.
- y0 is set to 500, which represents the baseline for the histogram bars.
- y1 is calculated based on the histogram value (hist_red[i]) multiplied by the scale factor, ensuring the histogram bars are scaled proportionally to fit within the canvas height.

```
    self.frame_canvas.create_rectangle(x0, y0, x1, y1, fill="red")
```

- The create_rectangle() method of the canvas (self.frame_canvas) is used to draw a rectangle representing the histogram bar.
- The coordinates (x0, y0) and (x1, y1) specify the top-left and bottom-right corners of the rectangle, respectively.
- The fill parameter specifies the color of the rectangle, in this case, "red" for the Red channel histogram bar.

```
    # Similar operations are performed for the Green and Blue channels
```

- Similar operations are repeated for the Green and Blue channels, with appropriate adjustments for their respective histograms.

In summary, the plot_histogram() method generates a visual representation of the histograms for the Red, Green, and Blue color channels on a canvas. It iterates over the histogram bins and draws corresponding histogram bars with different colors on the canvas, ensuring that the bars are scaled proportionally to fit within the specified canvas height. This method is called to visualize the distribution of pixel intensities across different color channels of a video frame.

Computing Hash Value for a Given Frame

The calculate_frame_hash() method computes a hash value for a given frame. Let's break down its functionality:

```
def calculate_frame_hash(self, frame):
    return hashlib.md5(frame.tobytes()).hexdigest()
```

- This method takes a single parameter frame, which represents an image frame.
- It converts the frame data into bytes using the tobytes() method.
- The hashlib.md5() function from the Python standard library is then used to create an MD5 hash object.
- The update() method of the hash object could be used to update the hash with data from the frame bytes, but here, the hash is directly computed from the frame bytes by passing them to the md5() function.
- Finally, the hexdigest() method is called on the hash object to obtain the hexadecimal representation of the computed hash value, which is returned by the method.

In summary, the calculate_frame_hash() method computes the MD5 hash of the byte representation of a given frame and returns the hexadecimal representation of the hash value. This hash value can be used to uniquely identify the content of the frame. It is commonly used for tasks such as content verification, duplicate detection, and integrity checking.

Entry Point of Program

This snippet defines the main() function, which is the entry point of the program. Let's break down its functionality:

```
def main():
    root = tk.Tk()
    app = VideoPlayerApp(root)
    root.mainloop()
```

- The main() function is responsible for creating the main application window and running the event loop (mainloop()).
- It first creates an instance of the Tk() class from the tkinter library, which represents the main application window. This window is commonly referred to as the root window.
- Then, it creates an instance of the VideoPlayerApp class, passing the root window as an argument. This initializes the video player application within the main window.
- Finally, it calls the mainloop() method on the root window, which starts the event loop. This loop listens for user input, such as button clicks and keyboard events, and updates the application's display accordingly.

```
if __name__ == "__main__":
    main()
```

- This conditional block ensures that the main() function is only called if the script is executed directly, not if it's imported as a module into another script.
- When the script is run directly (__name__ is equal to "__main__"), the main() function is called, initiating the execution of the application.
- If the script is imported as a module elsewhere, the main() function won't be automatically executed, allowing the module to be reused without running the application.

In summary, the main() function sets up and runs the main application window for the video player. It creates the root window, initializes the video player application within it, and starts the event loop to handle user interactions and maintain the application's responsiveness. The conditional block ensures that the main() function is executed only when the script is run directly as the main program.

Running Program
Run program. You will see the tkinter GUI, as shown in figure below.

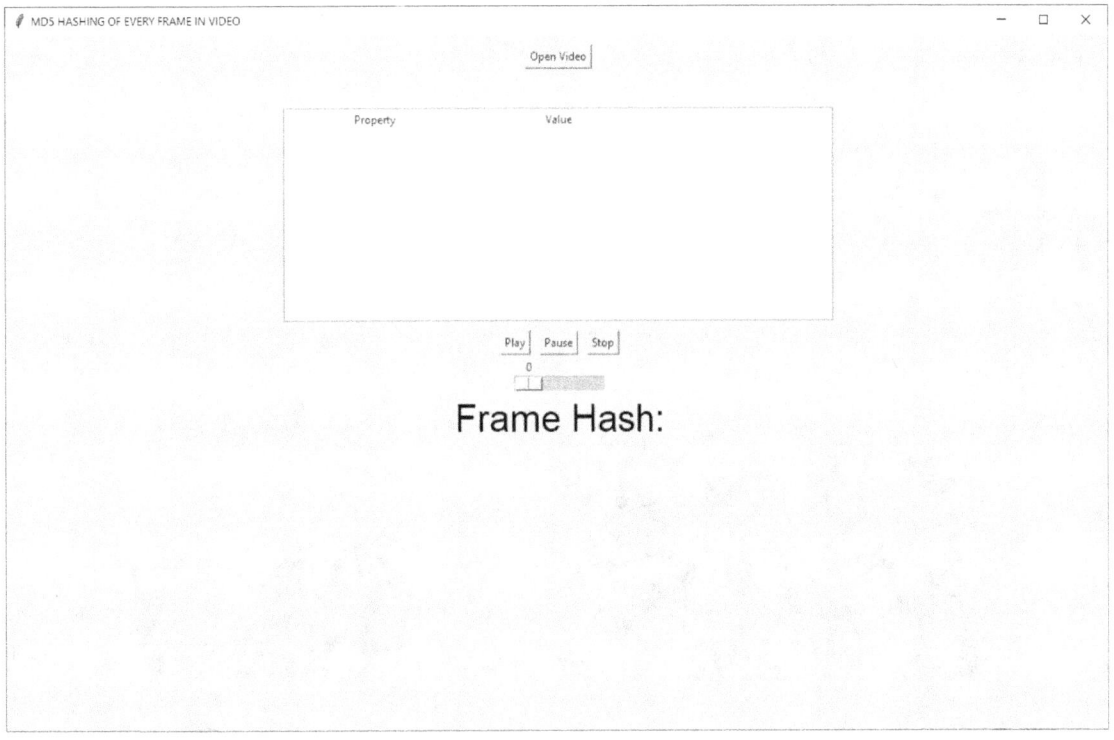

Then, click on Open Video button and choose a video file. You will see the metadata of the given video file in the table as shown in figure below.

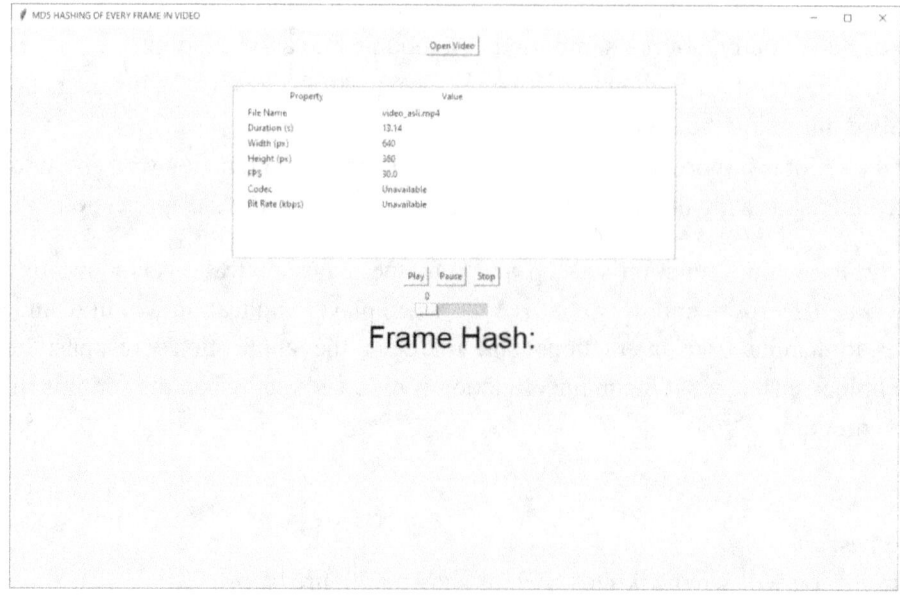

Then, click on Play button. Then, the video will run and its histogram and hash value of each frame is shown.

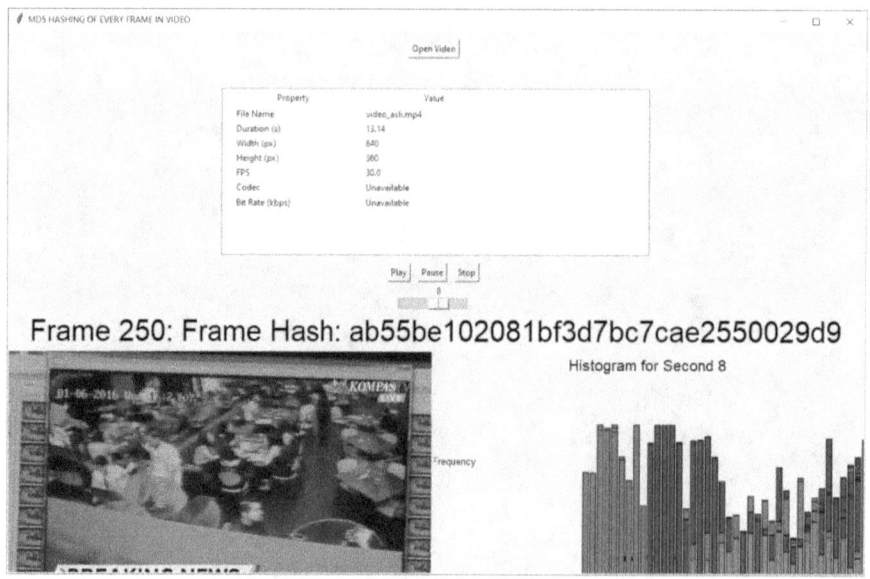

Open your working directory. You will see the hash value of each frame is saved in txt file.

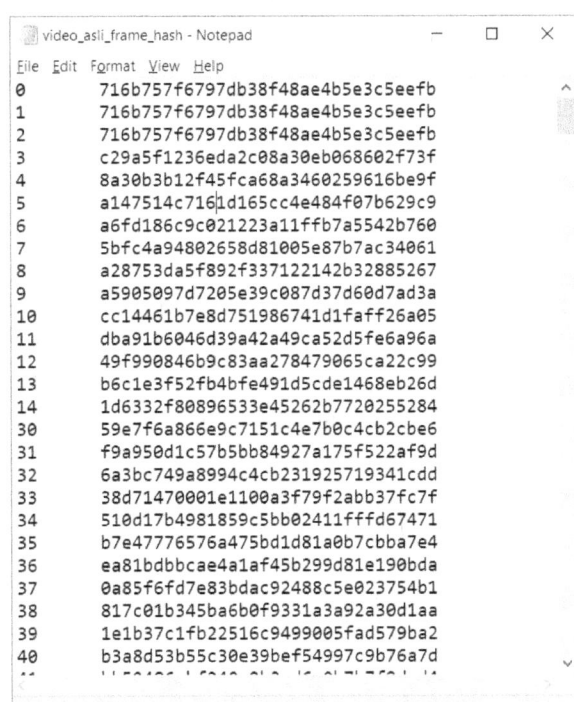

Conclusion

In this project, we've dissected a Python script designed to create a video player application with advanced functionalities such as frame hashing and metadata display. The script utilizes various libraries including Tkinter for GUI development, Pillow (PIL) for image processing, moviepy for video editing, numpy for numerical operations, and hashlib for hashing operations. The application allows users to open video files, visualize individual frames, display metadata, play, pause, and seek through videos, while also computing and saving MD5 hashes for each frame.

The VideoPlayerApp class serves as the backbone of the application. It's initialized with a master window and constructs various GUI elements such as buttons, labels, sliders, and canvases to create a user-friendly interface for interacting with video files. Each element is carefully crafted to serve a specific purpose, whether it's opening videos, controlling playback, displaying frames, or visualizing histograms.

The core functionality of the application revolves around processing video frames. The update_video_frame() method continuously updates the canvas with frames fetched from the video clip. For each frame, it calculates an MD5 hash representing its content and updates the frame hash label accordingly. This hash is then saved to a text file, providing a means for frame-by-frame content verification and integrity checking.

Furthermore, the application offers insights into the video's metadata. The get_video_metadata() method extracts essential information such as filename, duration, resolution, FPS, codec, and bitrate, which are then displayed in a metadata table. This feature enhances user experience by providing contextual information about the video being played, facilitating informed decision-making and understanding of the video's characteristics.

Lastly, the plot_histogram() method offers a visual representation of the pixel intensity distribution across different color channels (Red, Green, Blue) in a frame. By computing and plotting histograms, users gain insights into the color composition of video frames, enabling them to analyze visual patterns and make informed adjustments or observations during playback. Overall, the application combines intuitive user interface design with powerful backend functionality, offering users a comprehensive tool for video playback, analysis, and content verification.

Full Source Code

```python
import tkinter as tk
from tkinter import filedialog, ttk
from PIL import Image, ImageTk
import moviepy.editor as mp
import numpy as np
import os
import hashlib

class VideoPlayerApp:
    def __init__(self, master):
        self.master = master
        self.master.title("MD5 HASHING OF EVERY FRAME IN VIDEO")

        self.create_widgets()

    def create_widgets(self):
        self.open_button = tk.Button(self.master, text="Open Video", command=self.open_video)
        self.open_button.pack(pady=10)

        self.video_frame = tk.Label(self.master)
        self.video_frame.pack()

        self.metadata_table = ttk.Treeview(self.master, columns=('Property', 'Value'))
        self.metadata_table.heading('#0', text='Property')
        self.metadata_table.heading('#1', text='Value')
        self.metadata_table.pack(pady=10)
```

```python
        # Frame for play, pause, and stop buttons
        self.button_frame = tk.Frame(self.master)
        self.button_frame.pack()

        self.play_button = tk.Button(self.button_frame, text="Play", command=self.play_video)
        self.play_button.pack(side=tk.LEFT, padx=5)

        self.pause_button = tk.Button(self.button_frame, text="Pause", command=self.pause_video)
        self.pause_button.pack(side=tk.LEFT, padx=5)

        self.stop_button = tk.Button(self.button_frame, text="Stop", command=self.stop_video)
        self.stop_button.pack(side=tk.LEFT, padx=5)

        self.seek_slider = tk.Scale(self.master, from_=0, to=100, orient=tk.HORIZONTAL, command=self.seek_video)
        self.seek_slider.pack()

        # Label widget for displaying frame hash
        self.frame_hash_label = tk.Label(self.master, text="Frame Hash:", font=("Helvetica", 30))  # Modified font size
        self.frame_hash_label.pack()

        self.video_clip = None
        self.playing = False
        self.video_frame_idx = 0
        self.video_filename = None  # Store video filename

        # Canvas for video frame
        self.canvas = tk.Canvas(self.master, width=600, height=300)
        self.canvas.pack(side=tk.LEFT)

        # Canvas for specific frame display
        self.frame_canvas = tk.Canvas(self.master, width=600, height=300)  # Adjusted size
        self.frame_canvas.pack(side=tk.RIGHT)

    def open_video(self):
        self.video_filename = filedialog.askopenfilename(filetypes=[("Video files", "*.mp4;*.avi;*.mpeg")])
        if self.video_filename:
            self.video_clip = mp.VideoFileClip(self.video_filename)
            self.update_metadata_table(self.video_filename)
            self.seek_slider.config(to=self.video_clip.duration)

    def play_video(self):
        if self.video_clip is not None and not self.playing:
            self.playing = True
            self.update_video_frame()

    def update_video_frame(self):
        if self.playing:
            frame_np = self.video_clip.get_frame(self.video_frame_idx / self.video_clip.fps)
            frame_hash = self.calculate_frame_hash(frame_np)
            frame = Image.fromarray(frame_np)
```

```python
            frame_tk = ImageTk.PhotoImage(frame)

            self.canvas.create_image(0, 0, anchor=tk.NW, image=frame_tk)
            self.canvas.image = frame_tk

            hist = self.get_frame_histogram(frame_np)
            if hist:
                self.plot_histogram(hist)

            # Update frame hash label with frame number
            self.frame_hash_label.config(text=f"Frame {self.video_frame_idx}: Frame Hash: {frame_hash}")

            # Save frame hash to a text file
            self.save_frame_hash_to_file(self.video_filename, self.video_frame_idx, frame_hash)

            self.video_frame_idx += 1
            if self.video_frame_idx < self.video_clip.duration * self.video_clip.fps:
                self.seek_slider.set(self.video_frame_idx / self.video_clip.fps)
                self.master.after(33, self.update_video_frame)
            else:
                self.stop_video()


    def save_frame_hash_to_file(self, video_filename, frame_idx, frame_hash):
        # Extract video filename without extension
        filename_without_extension = os.path.splitext(os.path.basename(video_filename))[0]
        txt_filename = f"{filename_without_extension}_frame_hash.txt"

        with open(txt_filename, "a") as file:
            file.write(f"{frame_idx}\t{frame_hash}\n")

    def pause_video(self):
        self.playing = False

    def stop_video(self):
        self.playing = False
        self.video_frame_idx = 0

    def seek_video(self, value):
        if self.video_clip is not None:
            pos_in_seconds = float(value)
            self.video_frame_idx = int(pos_in_seconds * self.video_clip.fps)
            if not self.playing:
                self.update_video_frame()
            else:
                frame_np = self.video_clip.get_frame(self.video_frame_idx / self.video_clip.fps)
                hist = self.get_frame_histogram(frame_np)
                if hist:
                    self.frame_canvas.delete('all')
                    self.plot_histogram(hist)
                    frame_number = int(self.video_frame_idx / self.video_clip.fps)
                    self.frame_canvas.create_text(300, 20, text=f"Histogram for Second {frame_number}", font=("Helvetica", 16), anchor=tk.CENTER)
```

```python
                    self.frame_canvas.create_text(300, 280, text="Pixel Intensity", 
font=("Helvetica", 10), anchor=tk.CENTER)
                    self.frame_canvas.create_text(30, 150, text="Frequency", 
font=("Helvetica", 10), anchor=tk.CENTER)

    def update_metadata_table(self, file_path):
        metadata = self.get_video_metadata(file_path)
        for key, value in metadata.items():
            self.metadata_table.insert('', 'end', text=key, values=(value))

    def get_video_metadata(self, file_path):
        metadata = {}
        video = mp.VideoFileClip(file_path)
        metadata['File Name'] = os.path.basename(file_path)
        metadata['Duration (s)'] = video.duration
        metadata['Width (px)'] = video.size[0]
        metadata['Height (px)'] = video.size[1]
        metadata['FPS'] = video.fps

        if 'video' in video.reader.infos:
            metadata['Codec'] = video.reader.infos['video']['codec_name']
            metadata['Bit Rate (kbps)'] = video.reader.infos['video']['bit_rate'] // 1000
        else:
            metadata['Codec'] = "Unavailable"
            metadata['Bit Rate (kbps)'] = "Unavailable"

        return metadata

    def get_frame_histogram(self, frame):
        if len(frame.shape) == 3:
            hist_red, bins_red = np.histogram(frame[:,:,0].ravel(), bins=64, range=[0,64])
            hist_green, bins_green = np.histogram(frame[:,:,1].ravel(), bins=64, range=[0,64])
            hist_blue, bins_blue = np.histogram(frame[:,:,2].ravel(), bins=64, range=[0,64])
            return hist_red, hist_green, hist_blue
        else:
            return None

    def plot_histogram(self, hist):
        hist_red, hist_green, hist_blue = hist

        max_value = max(np.max(hist_red), np.max(hist_green), np.max(hist_blue))
        scale = 500 / max_value  # Adjusted scale

        bar_width = 8  # Lebar batang histogram
        max_height = 300  # Tinggi maksimum batang histogram
        for i in range(64):
            x0 = i * 10
            x1 = x0 + bar_width
            y0 = 500
            y1 = max(100, 500 - hist_red[i] * scale)  # Batasi tinggi maksimum batang histogram
            self.frame_canvas.create_rectangle(x0, y0, x1, y1, fill="red")

            y0 = y1
```

```python
            y1 = max(100, 500 - hist_green[i] * scale)  # Batasi tinggi maksimum batang histogram
            self.frame_canvas.create_rectangle(x0, y0, x1, y1, fill="green")

            y0 = y1
            y1 = max(100, 500 - hist_blue[i] * scale)  # Batasi tinggi maksimum batang histogram
            self.frame_canvas.create_rectangle(x0, y0, x1, y1, fill="blue")

    def calculate_frame_hash(self, frame):
        return hashlib.md5(frame.tobytes()).hexdigest()

def main():
    root = tk.Tk()
    app = VideoPlayerApp(root)
    root.mainloop()

if __name__ == "__main__":
    main()
```

COMPUTING HASH VALUE OF EACH FRAME IN VIDEO AND DISPLAYING ITS RGB HISTORGAM

CALCULATING MD5 HASH OF EVERY FRAME AND DISPLAYING HISTOGRAM

The following Python script implements a video player application with additional features including frame hashing, frame extraction, and histogram visualization. The application is developed using the Tkinter library for building the graphical user interface (GUI) and other libraries such as Pillow (PIL), imageio, matplotlib, and hashlib for various functionalities.

The VideoPlayerApp class encapsulates the main functionality of the application. It initializes the application window, sets up GUI elements such as canvas, buttons, labels, and entry fields, and defines methods for opening video files, playing, pausing, stopping, and extracting frames from videos. Additionally, it handles events such as mouse wheel scrolling, mouse dragging, and time jumping.

Upon opening a video file, the application displays the video frames on a canvas, allowing users to navigate through the frames using scrollbars or jump to a specific frame or time. Users can play, pause, stop the video playback, and extract frames for further analysis. The application also provides zoom functionality to adjust the size of the displayed frames according to user preferences.

The show_frame() method retrieves frames from the video file and displays them on the canvas. It dynamically adjusts the frame size based on the zoom scale selected by the user. Furthermore, the application calculates and displays histograms for each RGB channel of the extracted frames, offering insights into the color distribution within the frames.

The extract_frame() method enables users to extract and display individual frames in a separate window. It provides visualizations of the extracted frames along with their corresponding histograms and MD5 hash values for content verification purposes. Moreover, the application allows users to open multiple instances of the video player for simultaneous playback of different videos.

In conclusion, this Python script implements a versatile video player application with advanced features for frame manipulation, visualization, and content analysis. It combines user-friendly GUI elements with powerful backend functionality, offering users a comprehensive tool for viewing, analyzing, and extracting frames from video files.

Importing Libraries

```
import tkinter as tk
from tkinter import ttk
from tkinter import filedialog
from PIL import Image, ImageTk
import imageio
import matplotlib.pyplot as plt
from matplotlib.backends.backend_tkagg import FigureCanvasTkAgg
import hashlib
```

The code imports several Python libraries that are essential for building a graphical user interface (GUI), processing images, reading video files, visualizing data, and performing cryptographic hashing. Let's go through each import statement and its purpose in detail:
- import tkinter as tk: Tkinter is a standard GUI (Graphical User Interface) toolkit for Python. This statement imports the Tkinter module and aliases it as tk for easier access. Tkinter provides various widgets like buttons, labels, entry fields, and canvases that can be used to create interactive applications with graphical interfaces.
- from tkinter import ttk: The ttk module provides themed widgets in addition to the standard Tkinter widgets. Themed widgets have a more modern and consistent appearance

across different platforms. This statement imports the entire ttk module into the current namespace.
- from tkinter import filedialog: The filedialog submodule of Tkinter provides dialogs for opening and saving files. It allows users to browse files and directories on their system and select files for input/output operations. This statement imports the filedialog submodule for file-related operations.
- from PIL import Image, ImageTk: PIL (Python Imaging Library) is a powerful library for opening, manipulating, and saving many different image file formats. This statement imports both the Image and ImageTk modules from PIL. Image module is used for image processing tasks like resizing and converting images, while ImageTk module provides support for displaying images in Tkinter GUI applications.
- import imageio: Imageio is a Python library for reading and writing a wide range of image, video, and volumetric data formats. It supports many common video formats like MP4, AVI, and MKV. This statement imports the imageio module for reading video files in the application.
- import matplotlib.pyplot as plt: Matplotlib is a popular data visualization library in Python. It provides a MATLAB-like interface for creating static, animated, and interactive visualizations. This statement imports the pyplot module from Matplotlib and aliases it as plt. pyplot provides a simple and procedural interface for creating plots and charts.
- from matplotlib.backends.backend_tkagg import FigureCanvasTkAgg: Matplotlib's FigureCanvasTkAgg is a canvas widget for embedding Matplotlib figures into Tkinter applications. It allows Matplotlib plots to be seamlessly integrated into Tkinter GUIs, enabling interactive data visualization within Tkinter windows.
- import hashlib: Hashlib is a module in Python's standard library that provides interfaces to cryptographic hash functions. It supports secure hashing algorithms like MD5, SHA-1, SHA-256, etc. This statement imports the hashlib module for computing hash values, which can be used for various cryptographic and data integrity purposes.

The Class and Constructor

```
class VideoPlayerApp:
    def __init__(self, master):
        self.master = master
        self.master.title("FRAME HASHING AND HISTOGRAM---RISMON HASIHOLAN SIANIPAR")

        self.video = None
        self.video_path = None
        self.paused = False
        self.zoom_scale = tk.IntVar(value=1)
        self.frame_index = 0
```

```
        self.start_x = None
        self.start_y = None
        self.current_x = 0
        self.current_y = 0
        self.photo = None  # Save object reference to PhotoImage globally

        self.create_widgets()
```

This class, VideoPlayerApp, represents a video player application with features for displaying video frames, extracting frames, and visualizing frame histograms. Let's break down the __init__() method and its attributes:

1. def __init__(self, master): This is the constructor method for the VideoPlayerApp class. It initializes an instance of the class with the given master widget, typically a Tkinter root or Toplevel window.
2. self.master = master: This attribute stores a reference to the master widget passed to the constructor. It allows access to the root or parent window where the video player will be displayed.
3. self.master.title("FRAME HASHING AND HISTOGRAM---RISMON HASIHOLAN SIANIPAR"): Sets the title of the master window to "FRAME HASHING AND HISTOGRAM---RISMON HASIHOLAN SIANIPAR". This title will be displayed in the window's title bar.
4. self.video = None: This attribute stores the video data once a video file is opened. It will hold a reference to the video data loaded into the application.
5. self.video_path = None: This attribute stores the file path of the currently loaded video. It will be assigned a value when a video file is opened using the application.
6. self.paused = False: This attribute indicates whether the video playback is paused (True) or not (False). Initially, it is set to False, indicating that the video playback is not paused.
7. self.zoom_scale = tk.IntVar(value=1): This attribute represents an IntVar variable, which is a Tkinter variable type used to store integer values. It is initialized with a default value of 1. This variable will be used to control the zoom scale of the video frames.
8. self.frame_index = 0: This attribute stores the index of the currently displayed frame in the video. It keeps track of the position of the video playback.
9. self.start_x = None and self.start_y = None: These attributes store the coordinates of the starting point when dragging the video frame on the canvas. They are initially set to None.
10. self.current_x = 0 and self.current_y = 0: These attributes store the current position of the video frame on the canvas. They are initially set to 0.
11. self.photo = None: This attribute stores a reference to the PhotoImage object representing the current frame being displayed. It is initially set to None.
12. self.create_widgets(): This method call initializes the widgets and UI elements for the video player application. It sets up the layout and functionality of the GUI components.

Creating Widgets

The create_widgets() method within the VideoPlayerApp class initializes and configures various GUI elements for the video player application. Let's examine each part in detail:

1. Canvas for Video Display:
    - Creates a canvas (self.canvas) with a specified width and height (800x600).
    - Binds the <MouseWheel>, <ButtonPress-1>, and <B1-Motion> events to corresponding event handler methods (self.on_mousewheel, self.on_press, self.on_drag).
2. Horizontal Scrollbar:
    - Creates a horizontal scrollbar (self.scrollbar) with orientation set to "horizontal".
    - Binds the scrollbar's command to the on_scroll method.
3. Button to Open Video:
    - Creates a button (self.open_button) labeled "Open Video" with a command to call the open_video method.
4. Combobox for Zoom Scale:
    - Creates a combobox (self.zoom_combobox) to select the zoom scale.
    - Populates the combobox with values ranging from 1 to 10.
    - Binds the <<ComboboxSelected>> event to the update_zoom() method.
5. Label and Entry for Specifying Time:
    - Creates a label (self.time_label) labeled "Jump to Time (s)".
    - Creates an entry (self.time_entry) for entering the time in seconds.
    - Binds the <Return> event to call the jump_to_time() method.
6. Button to Jump to Specified Time:
    - Creates a button (self.jump_button) labeled "Jump to Time" with a command to call the jump_to_time() method.
7. Buttons for Playback Control:
    - Creates buttons for play/pause (self.play_button) and stop (self.stop_button) operations.
    - Binds their respective commands to toggle_play_pause and stop_video methods.
8. Button to Extract Frame:
    - Creates a button (self.extract_button) labeled "Extract Frame" with a command to call the extract_frame() method.
9. Label and Entry for Frame Number:
    - Creates a label (self.frame_label) labeled "Frame Number:".
    - Creates an entry (self.frame_entry) for entering the frame number.
    - Binds the <Return> event to call the extract_frame method.
10. Button to Open Another Instance:
    - Creates a button (self.open_another_button) labeled "Open Another Video Player" with a command to call the open_another_player() method.

- This button allows opening another instance of the video player application.

```python
def create_widgets(self):
    # Canvas to display the video
    canvas_width = 800
    canvas_height = 600
    self.canvas = tk.Canvas(self.master, width=canvas_width, height=canvas_height)
    self.canvas.grid(row=0, column=0, padx=10, pady=10, sticky="nsew")
    self.canvas.bind("<MouseWheel>", self.on_mousewheel)
    self.canvas.bind("<ButtonPress-1>", self.on_press)
    self.canvas.bind("<B1-Motion>", self.on_drag)

    # Scrollbar
    self.scrollbar    =    tk.Scrollbar(self.master,    orient="horizontal",
command=self.on_scroll)
    self.scrollbar.grid(row=1, column=0, sticky="ew")

    self.canvas.configure(xscrollcommand=self.scrollbar.set)

    # Button to open a video file
    self.open_button    =    tk.Button(self.master,    text="Open    Video",
command=self.open_video)
    self.open_button.grid(row=2, column=0, padx=10, pady=5)

    # Combobox for selecting zoom scale
    self.zoom_combobox = ttk.Combobox(self.master, textvariable=self.zoom_scale,
values=list(range(1, 11)))
    self.zoom_combobox.grid(row=2, column=1, padx=10, pady=5)
    self.zoom_combobox.bind("<<ComboboxSelected>>", self.update_zoom)

    # Label and entry for specifying time
    self.time_label = tk.Label(self.master, text="Jump to Time (s):")
    self.time_label.grid(row=0, column=1, padx=10, pady=5, sticky="e")
    self.time_entry = ttk.Entry(self.master)
    self.time_entry.grid(row=0, column=2, padx=10, pady=5, sticky="w")
    self.time_entry.bind("<Return>", lambda event: self.jump_to_time())

    # Button to jump to specified time
    self.jump_button    =    tk.Button(self.master,    text="Jump    to    Time",
command=self.jump_to_time)
    self.jump_button.grid(row=0, column=3, padx=10, pady=5)

    # Button to play/pause the video
    self.play_button    =    tk.Button(self.master,    text="Play/Pause",
command=self.toggle_play_pause)
    self.play_button.grid(row=2, column=2, padx=10, pady=5)

    # Button to stop the video
```

```
        self.stop_button           =          tk.Button(self.master,           text="Stop",
command=self.stop_video)
        self.stop_button.grid(row=2, column=3, padx=10, pady=5)

        # Button to extract frame
        self.extract_button    =    tk.Button(self.master,    text="Extract    Frame",
command=self.extract_frame)
        self.extract_button.grid(row=1, column=1, padx=10, pady=5)

        # Label and entry for frame number
        self.frame_label = tk.Label(self.master, text="Frame Number:")
        self.frame_label.grid(row=1, column=0, padx=10, pady=5, sticky="e")
        self.frame_entry = ttk.Entry(self.master)
        self.frame_entry.grid(row=1, column=2, padx=10, pady=5, sticky="w")
        self.frame_entry.bind("<Return>", lambda event: self.extract_frame())

        # Button to open another instance of the application
        self.open_another_button = tk.Button(self.master, text="Open Another Video
Player", command=self.open_another_player)
        self.open_another_button.grid(row=3, column=0, columnspan=4, padx=10, pady=5)
```

Opening Video

```
    def open_video(self):
        self.video_path   =   filedialog.askopenfilename(filetypes=[("Video   files",
"*.mp4;*.avi;*.mkv")])
        if self.video_path:
            self.video = imageio.get_reader(self.video_path)
            self.play_video()
```

The open_video() method is responsible for allowing the user to select a video file from their file system and loading it into the video player application. Let's break down the functionality step by step:
1. File Dialog Prompt:
    - The filedialog.askopenfilename() function from the filedialog module is used to prompt the user to select a file.
    - The filetypes argument specifies the file types that the user can select. In this case, it allows selecting files with extensions .mp4, .avi, or .mkv.
2. Assigning the Video Path:
    - The selected file path is stored in the self.video_path attribute of the VideoPlayerApp instance. This attribute keeps track of the path to the currently opened video file.

3. Loading the Video:
    - If a video file is selected (i.e., self.video_path is not empty), the imageio.get_reader() function is used to create a reader object for the selected video file.
    - The reader object (self.video) allows the application to read frames from the video file.
4. Playing the Video:
    - After successfully loading the video, the play_video method is called to initiate the playback of the video.
    - This method will start displaying the frames of the video on the canvas, effectively playing the video for the user.

Overall, the open_video() method provides a crucial functionality for the video player application by enabling users to load video files of supported formats and initiate playback. It ensures that the selected video file is valid and accessible before attempting to play it, enhancing the robustness and user experience of the application.

Playing Video

```
def play_video(self):
    if self.video:
        self.paused = False
        self.show_frame()
```

The play_video() method is responsible for initiating the playback of the loaded video in the video player application. Let's dissect its functionality:
1. Video Existence Check:
    - The method begins by checking if a video has been loaded into the application. This is done by evaluating the truthiness of the self.video attribute, which holds the reader object for the video file.
    - If self.video is not None, indicating that a video has been successfully loaded, the playback process continues. Otherwise, the method exits without taking any action.
2. Paused State Update:

    - Upon confirming that a video is available for playback, the self.paused attribute is set to False. This indicates that the video playback is ongoing and not paused.

- Setting self.paused to False ensures that the show_frame() method, responsible for displaying frames of the video, will continue to be called without interruption, effectively playing the video.
3. Frame Display:
    - After updating the paused state, the method calls the show_frame() method to display the current frame of the video on the canvas.
    - This action starts the process of continuously displaying subsequent frames of the video, creating the illusion of motion and initiating the playback for the user.

In summary, the play_video() method serves as the entry point for starting the playback of the loaded video in the video player application. It ensures that the video is available for playback, updates the playback state to indicate that it's not paused, and initiates the display of frames to commence the video playback process.

Stopping Video

```
def stop_video(self):
    self.paused = True
    self.frame_index = 0
    self.current_x = 0
    self.current_y = 0  # Reset the current position
    self.show_frame()
```

The stop_video() method is responsible for stopping the playback of the video in the video player application. Let's break down its functionality:
1. Pause State Update:
    - Initially, the method sets the self.paused attribute to True. This action effectively pauses the playback of the video by preventing further frames from being displayed on the canvas.
2. Frame Index and Position Reset:
    - The method resets the self.frame_index attribute to 0. This ensures that the video playback starts from the beginning when it is resumed or played again.
    - Additionally, it resets the self.current_x and self.current_y attributes to 0. These attributes represent the current position of the video frame on the canvas. Resetting them ensures that the video frame is displayed from the top-left corner of the canvas when the video is stopped.
3. Frame Display:
    - After updating the necessary attributes, the method calls the show_frame() method. This action refreshes the canvas and displays the first frame of the video, effectively stopping the video playback.

In summary, the stop_video() method halts the playback of the video in the video player application by pausing the video, resetting the frame index and position attributes, and refreshing the canvas to display the initial frame of the video.

Toggling Video

```
def toggle_play_pause(self):
    self.paused = not self.paused
    if not self.paused:
        self.play_video()
```

The toggle_play_pause() method in the video player application is responsible for toggling between the play and pause states of the video playback. Let's delve into its functionality:
1. Pause State Toggle:
    - The method toggles the self.paused attribute between True and False by using the logical NOT operator (not). If the video is currently paused (self.paused is True), it sets self.paused to False, indicating that the video should play. If the video is currently playing (self.paused is False), it sets self.paused to True, indicating that the video should pause.
2. Play Video:
    - If the video is not paused (i.e., self.paused is False), the method calls the play_video method to resume or initiate video playback. This ensures that when the user toggles from pause to play, the video continues playing from where it was paused or starts playing if it was stopped.

In summary, the toggle_play_pause() method provides a mechanism for switching between playing and pausing the video playback in the video player application. It toggles the pause state of the video and resumes playback if the video is not paused.

Updating The Zoom Level

```
def update_zoom(self, event=None):
    self.show_frame()
```

The update_zoom() method in the video player application is responsible for updating the zoom level of the displayed video frame. Let's break down its functionality:
1. Event Handling:
    - The method accepts an optional event parameter, which allows it to be triggered by an event, such as a combobox selection.

- If no event is provided (event=None), the method can be called directly to update the zoom level without any specific event triggering it.
2. Updating Zoom Level:
    - The method calls the show_frame() method to update the displayed frame with the new zoom level. This ensures that whenever the zoom scale is changed, the frame is redrawn to reflect the new zoom level.

By invoking the show_frame() method, the update_zoom() method ensures that any change in the zoom scale is immediately reflected in the displayed video frame. This allows users to adjust the zoom level dynamically while viewing the video.

Displaying Video Frames

```
def show_frame(self):
    if self.video:
        if not self.paused:
            self.frame_index += 1
            if self.frame_index >= len(self.video):
                self.frame_index = 0
        if self.frame_index < len(self.video):  # Tambahkan pengecekan di sini
            frame = self.video.get_data(self.frame_index)
            frame = Image.fromarray(frame)
            frame = frame.resize((frame.width * self.zoom_scale.get(), frame.height * self.zoom_scale.get()))
            photo = ImageTk.PhotoImage(frame)
            self.photo = photo  # Simpan referensi objek PhotoImage secara global
            self.canvas.delete("video")  # Hapus gambar sebelumnya
            self.canvas.create_image(self.current_x, self.current_y, anchor="nw", image=photo, tags="video")
            if not self.paused:
                self.canvas.after(30, self.show_frame)
```

The show_frame() method is a crucial part of the video player application. It's responsible for displaying video frames on the canvas. Here's a detailed explanation of its functionality:
1. Video Playback:
    - The method first checks if there's a loaded video (if self.video:). If there is, it proceeds to display the frames.
    - It then checks if the video is currently paused (if not self.paused:). If it's not paused, it increments the frame_index to advance to the next frame. This allows for continuous playback if the video is not paused.
2. Looping Behavior:
    - If the frame_index exceeds the total number of frames in the video, it resets the frame_index to 0. This creates a looping behavior, ensuring that the video starts

again from the beginning once it reaches the end (if self.frame_index >= len(self.video): self.frame_index = 0).
3. Displaying Frames:
   - The method retrieves the frame from the video using self.video.get_data(self.frame_index).
   - It converts the frame to a PIL Image object using Image.fromarray(frame).
   - The method resizes the frame based on the current zoom scale (self.zoom_scale.get()) to adjust its dimensions according to the user's preference.
   - It creates a PhotoImage object (photo) from the resized frame.
   - The self.photo attribute is updated to keep a reference to the current PhotoImage object.
   - Any previous frame displayed on the canvas with the tag "video" is deleted (self.canvas.delete("video")) to avoid overlapping frames.
   - The new frame is then drawn on the canvas at the specified coordinates (self.canvas.create_image(self.current_x, self.current_y, anchor="nw", image=photo, tags="video")).
4. Continuous Playback:
   - If the video is not paused, the method schedules itself to be called again after a delay of 30 milliseconds using self.canvas.after(30, self.show_frame()). This creates a continuous playback loop, where frames are displayed one after the other at a regular interval as long as the video is playing.

Handling Mouse Wheel Events

```
def on_mousewheel(self, event):
    direction = event.delta // 120
    current_value = int(self.zoom_scale.get())
    if direction == 1 and current_value < 10:
        current_value += 1
    elif direction == -1 and current_value > 1:
        current_value -= 1
    self.zoom_scale.set(current_value)
    self.update_zoom()
```

The on_mousewheel() method is responsible for handling mouse wheel events, which control the zoom level of the displayed video frames. Here's a breakdown of its functionality:
1. Event Handling:
   - The method takes an event parameter representing the mouse wheel event that triggers the function.
2. Determining Direction:

- It calculates the direction of the mouse wheel rotation based on the event.delta attribute. The event.delta value indicates the amount of rotation, typically in multiples of 120 for a single notch of the mouse wheel.
- By dividing event.delta by 120, the method determines the direction of rotation. A positive result indicates upward rotation (zoom in), while a negative result indicates downward rotation (zoom out).

3. Adjusting Zoom Scale:
   - The current zoom scale is retrieved using self.zoom_scale.get(), converted to an integer, and stored in current_value.
   - If the mouse wheel is rotated upwards (direction == 1) and the current zoom scale is less than 10 (maximum zoom level), the zoom scale is increased by one (current_value += 1).
   - If the mouse wheel is rotated downwards (direction == -1) and the current zoom scale is greater than 1 (minimum zoom level), the zoom scale is decreased by one (current_value -= 1).

4. Updating Zoom Scale:
   - After adjusting the zoom scale, the method sets the updated value back to the zoom_scale variable using self.zoom_scale.set(current_value).

5. Updating Frame Display:
   - Finally, the update_zoom() method is called to reflect the changes in the displayed frame according to the new zoom scale.

Handling Mouse Button Press Events

```
def on_press(self, event):
    self.start_x = event.x
    self.start_y = event.y
```

The on_press() method is triggered when the left mouse button is pressed within the canvas area where the video is displayed. Below is a detailed explanation of its functionality:

1. Event Handling:
   - The method takes an event parameter, which represents the mouse button press event that triggers the function.

2. Storing Mouse Coordinates:

   - It retrieves the x and y coordinates of the mouse pointer when the left mouse button is pressed.

- The event.x and event.y attributes provide the coordinates of the mouse pointer relative to the canvas.
3. Storing Start Position:
    - The x-coordinate of the mouse pointer (event.x) is stored in the self.start_x attribute.
    - Similarly, the y-coordinate of the mouse pointer (event.y) is stored in the self.start_y attribute.
    - These attributes will be used to track the starting position of the mouse pointer for drag operations.

The purpose of this method is to capture the starting position of the mouse pointer when the left mouse button is pressed, which is essential for tracking mouse movements during drag operations within the canvas.

Handling Mouse Drag Events

```
def on_drag(self, event):
    if self.start_x and self.start_y:
        x_offset = event.x - self.start_x
        y_offset = event.y - self.start_y
        self.current_x += x_offset  # Update current position
        self.current_y += y_offset  # Update current position
        self.canvas.move("video", x_offset, y_offset)
        self.start_x = event.x
        self.start_y = event.y
```

The on_drag() method is responsible for handling mouse drag events within the canvas area where the video is displayed. Let's break down its functionality in detail:
1. Event Handling:
    - The method takes an event parameter, representing the mouse drag event that triggers the function.
2. Checking Start Coordinates:
    - It first checks whether the start_x and start_y attributes have been initialized. These attributes store the initial coordinates where the left mouse button was pressed (in the on_press() method).
3. Calculating Offset:
    - It calculates the offset of the mouse pointer from its starting position to the current position.
    - The x_offset is determined by subtracting the starting x-coordinate (self.start_x) from the current x-coordinate (event.x).

- Similarly, the y_offset is calculated by subtracting the starting y-coordinate (self.start_y) from the current y-coordinate (event.y).
4. Updating Current Position:
    - It updates the current position (self.current_x and self.current_y) by adding the respective offset values.
    - These attributes track the current position of the video frame within the canvas.
5. Moving the Video Frame:
    - The canvas.move() method is used to move the video frame (identified by the tag "video") by the calculated offset values.
    - This action effectively drags the video frame within the canvas.
6. Updating Start Coordinates:
    - Finally, it updates the start_x and start_y attributes with the current mouse coordinates (event.x and event.y). This ensures that subsequent drag movements are calculated correctly relative to the new starting position.

Overall, this method facilitates the interactive dragging of the video frame within the canvas area by adjusting its position based on the mouse movements.

Handling Horizontal Scrolling in Scrollbar

```
def on_scroll(self, *args):
    scroll_pos = self.scrollbar.get()
    self.current_x = -scroll_pos * self.canvas.winfo_width()
    self.canvas.xview_moveto(scroll_pos)
    self.frame_index = int(scroll_pos * len(self.video))  # Update frame index
    self.show_frame()
```

The on_scroll() method is triggered when the user interacts with the scrollbar associated with horizontal scrolling. Let's explore its functionality in detail:
1. Parameters:
    - The method takes *args as a parameter, allowing it to accept any number of positional arguments.
2. Scrollbar Position:
    - It retrieves the current position of the scrollbar using the get() method of the scrollbar widget. This position represents the fraction of the scrollbar's span that is currently visible.
3. Calculating Canvas Offset:
    - Based on the scrollbar position, it calculates the horizontal offset (self.current_x) for the canvas.

- The negative of the scrollbar position multiplied by the canvas width (self.canvas.winfo_width()) determines the offset. This ensures that the canvas shifts leftward as the scrollbar moves to the right.
4. Adjusting Canvas View:
    - It updates the canvas view by invoking the xview_moveto() method, which scrolls the canvas horizontally to the specified position.
    - This action updates the visible portion of the canvas to match the scrollbar's position.
5. Updating Frame Index:
    - It recalculates the current frame index (self.frame_index) based on the scrollbar position and the total number of frames in the video.
    - This adjustment ensures that the correct frame is displayed corresponding to the scrollbar's position.
6. Refreshing Display:
    - Finally, it calls the show_frame() method to update the display with the newly adjusted frame index.
    - This ensures that the video frame shown on the canvas reflects the changes made by scrolling.

Overall, the on_scroll() method synchronizes the canvas view with the scrollbar position, allowing users to navigate through the video frames horizontally by scrolling.

Navigating to Specific Time Points

```
def jump_to_time(self):
    time_str = self.time_entry.get()
    try:
        time_seconds = float(time_str)
        if 0 <= time_seconds:
            self.frame_index = int(time_seconds * self.video.get_meta_data()['fps'])
            self.show_frame()
    except ValueError:
        pass
```

The jump_to_time() method allows users to navigate to a specific time in the video. Let's break down its functionality:
1. Getting Time Input:
    - It retrieves the time input from the entry widget self.time_entry where users can enter the desired time in seconds.
2. Converting Time to Seconds:

- The method attempts to convert the input string (time_str) to a floating-point value representing time in seconds using float().
- If the conversion is successful and the time is non-negative (0 or greater), the method proceeds; otherwise, it exits early.

3. Calculating Frame Index:
    - It calculates the frame index corresponding to the specified time by multiplying the time in seconds by the frames per second (FPS) of the video.
    - The FPS value is obtained from the video's metadata using self.video.get_meta_data()['fps'].

4. Updating Frame Display:
    - After obtaining the frame index, it updates self.frame_index to reflect the calculated value.
    - Then, it calls the show_frame() method to display the frame corresponding to the new frame index on the canvas.

5. Exception Handling:
    - The method uses a try-except block to catch any potential ValueError that may occur during the conversion of the input string to a floating-point value.
    - If an exception occurs, it simply passes and does nothing, allowing the program to continue execution without interruption.

In summary, the jump_to_time() method facilitates seamless navigation to specific time points in the video, providing users with a convenient way to locate and view desired segments of the video content.

Extracting and Displaying Specific Frame

```
def extract_frame(self):
    frame_number_str = self.frame_entry.get()
    try:
        frame_number = int(frame_number_str)
        if 0 <= frame_number < len(self.video):
            frame = self.video.get_data(frame_number)
            self.show_extracted_frame(frame, frame_number)
    except ValueError:
        pass
```

The extract_frame() method serves to extract and display a specific frame from the video based on the user's input. Let's delve into its functionality:

1. Input Retrieval:
    - The method retrieves the frame number specified by the user through the frame_entry widget, which provides an entry field for entering the frame number.

2. Frame Extraction:
    - It attempts to convert the input string (frame_number_str) to an integer representing the frame number using int(frame_number_str).
    - If the conversion is successful and the frame number is within the valid range (from 0 to the total number of frames in the video), it proceeds to extract the corresponding frame using self.video.get_data(frame_number).
3. Display of Extracted Frame:
    - Upon successfully extracting the frame, it calls the show_extracted_frame method, passing the extracted frame and its corresponding frame number.
    - This function displays the extracted frame along with additional information such as histograms and MD5 hash values.
4. Exception Handling:
    - The method employs a try-except block to catch any potential errors that may arise during the conversion of the frame number input string to an integer.
    - If an error occurs (e.g., due to non-integer input), it gracefully handles the exception, ensuring that the program does not crash.

Overall, the extract_frame() method facilitates the extraction and display of a specific frame from the video, enhancing user interaction by allowing them to inspect individual frames in detail.

Displaying Extracted Frame and Its Histogram

```python
def show_extracted_frame(self, frame, frame_number):
    extracted_frame_window = tk.Toplevel(self.master)
    extracted_frame_window.title(f"Frame yang Diekstraksi (Frame {frame_number}) --- RISMON HASIHOLAN SIANIPAR")

    extracted_frame_label = tk.Label(extracted_frame_window, text=f"Frame yang Diekstraksi (Frame {frame_number})")
    extracted_frame_label.pack()

    height, width, _ = frame.shape  # Get dimensions of the frame
    extracted_photo = ImageTk.PhotoImage(image=Image.fromarray(frame))

    extracted_frame_canvas = tk.Canvas(extracted_frame_window, width=width, height=height)
    extracted_frame_canvas.pack()
    extracted_frame_canvas.create_image(0, 0, anchor="nw", image=extracted_photo)
    extracted_frame_canvas.image = extracted_photo

    # Plot histogram for each RGB channel
    fig, axs = plt.subplots(1, 3, figsize=(18, 4))
    for i, color in enumerate(['r', 'g', 'b']):
```

```
            axs[i].hist(frame[:,:,i].ravel(), bins=64, range=(0, 255), color=color,
alpha=0.7)
            axs[i].set_title(f"Histogram    Kanal    {color.upper()}    (Frame
{frame_number})")
            axs[i].set_xlabel("Nilai Piksel")
            axs[i].set_ylabel("Frekuensi")
        plt.tight_layout()

        # Calculate MD5 hash value of the frame
        md5_hash = hashlib.md5(frame).hexdigest()

        # Display MD5 hash value
        md5_label  =  tk.Label(extracted_frame_window,  text=f"Nilai  Hash  MD5:
{md5_hash}", font=("Arial", 20))
        md5_label.pack()

        hist_canvas = FigureCanvasTkAgg(fig, master=extracted_frame_window)
        hist_canvas.draw()
        hist_canvas.get_tk_widget().pack()
```

The show_extracted_frame() method is responsible for displaying an extracted frame along with its histogram and MD5 hash value in a separate window. Here's a detailed explanation of each step within this method:

1. Creating a New Window (tk.Toplevel):
    - It creates a new top-level window (extracted_frame_window) using tk.Toplevel.
    - Sets the title of the window to include the frame number being displayed.
2. Displaying Frame Information:
    - Adds a label (extracted_frame_label) to the window to indicate the frame number being displayed.
3. Displaying the Frame:
    - Retrieves the dimensions of the frame using frame.shape to determine its height and width.
    - Converts the frame array (frame) to a PIL Image using Image.fromarray.
    - Converts the PIL Image to a Tkinter-compatible image (ImageTk.PhotoImage) and assigns it to extracted_photo.
    - Creates a canvas (extracted_frame_canvas) within the window and displays the image using create_image.
4. Plotting Histogram:
    - Creates a subplot with three axes to display histograms for the red, green, and blue channels.
    - Iterates over each channel, computes the histogram using plt.hist, and plots it.
    - Sets titles, x-axis labels, and y-axis labels for each histogram.
    - Ensures proper layout using plt.tight_layout().

5. Calculating MD5 Hash:
   - Computes the MD5 hash value of the frame array using hashlib.md5(frame).hexdigest().
6. Displaying MD5 Hash:
   - Adds a label (md5_label) to the window to display the MD5 hash value.
7. Displaying Histogram Canvas:
   - Embeds the histogram plot into the Tkinter window using FigureCanvasTkAgg.
   - Draws the histogram canvas and packs it into the window.

This method provides a comprehensive view of the extracted frame, including visual representation (frame image and histogram) and metadata (MD5 hash value).

Creating Another Instance

```
def open_another_player(self):
    # Open another instance of the application
    root = tk.Toplevel(self.master)
    app = VideoPlayerApp(root)
```

The open_another_player() method within the VideoPlayerApp class is responsible for creating another instance of the video player application when invoked. Here's a breakdown of what this method does:
1. Creating a New Top-Level Window:
   - It creates a new top-level window (Toplevel) associated with the existing Tkinter application (self.master).
   - This new window will serve as the container for the second instance of the video player application.
2. Instantiating Another VideoPlayerApp:
   - Creates an instance of the VideoPlayerApp class within the newly created top-level window.
   - The root window for this instance is set to the newly created top-level window, effectively embedding the new video player application within it.
3. Launching the New Video Player:

   - Upon execution, this method opens a new instance of the video player application within a separate window, allowing users to interact with multiple instances of the application simultaneously.
   - Each instance of the video player operates independently, allowing users to view different videos or analyze different segments of the same video concurrently.

By providing the ability to open multiple instances of the video player application, users can conveniently compare and analyze different videos or segments side by side, enhancing their overall viewing and analysis experience.

Entry Point of Application

```
def main():
    root = tk.Tk()
    app = VideoPlayerApp(root)
    root.mainloop()

if __name__ == "__main__":
    main()
```

The main() function serves as the entry point for the video player application. Here's how it works:
1. Creating the Root Window:
    - It creates the main application window using tk.Tk(), which represents the root window of the Tkinter application.
2. Instantiating the VideoPlayerApp:
    - It creates an instance of the VideoPlayerApp class, passing the root window (root) as its argument.
    - This instance of the VideoPlayerApp becomes the main application within the root window.
3. Starting the Main Event Loop:
    - It starts the Tkinter event loop by calling root.mainloop().
    - This loop continuously listens for user events, such as button clicks and key presses, and responds accordingly.
    - The event loop continues running until the user closes the main application window.
4. Conditional Execution:
    - The if __name__ == "__main__": block ensures that the main() function is only executed if the script is run directly (not imported as a module).
    - This is a common Python idiom that allows the script to be both run as a standalone program and imported as a module into other scripts without executing the main code block.

By encapsulating the creation of the root window, instantiation of the VideoPlayerApp, and starting the event loop within the main() function, the code follows best practices for readability, organization, and reusability. It provides a clear entry point for the application and separates the application logic from the script's main execution context.

Running Program

Run program. The GUI is shown below.

Then, click Open Video button and choose a video file. The GUI is shown below.

Then, type a specific frame number (115, for example). The MD5 hash value and histogram of each channel RGB will be displayed as shown below.

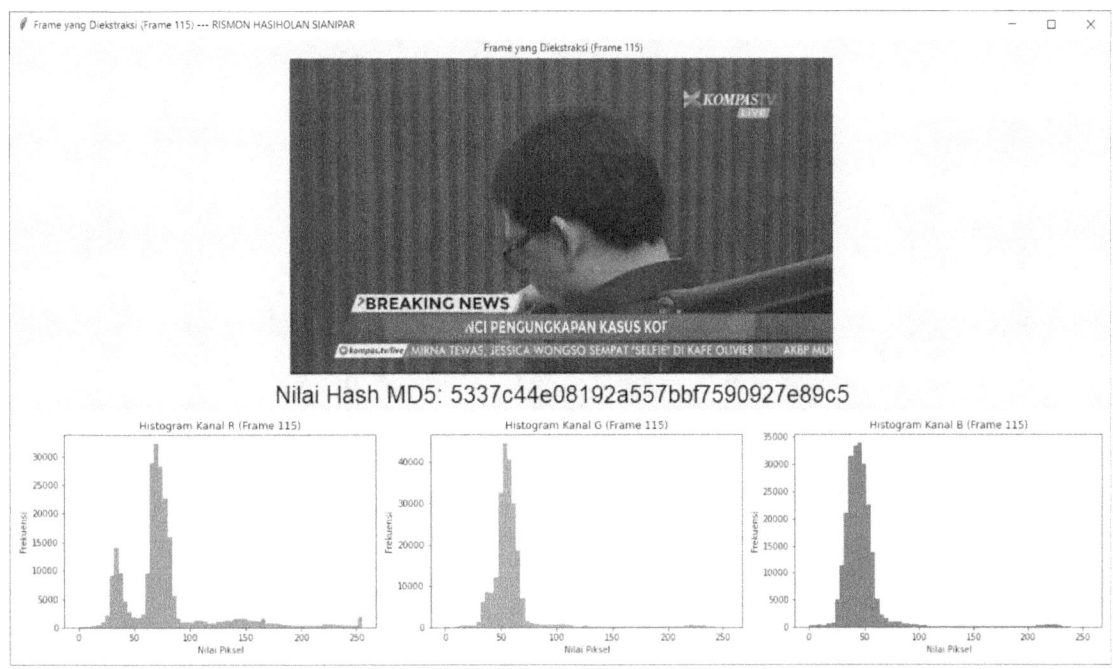

Then, type another specific frame number (233, for example). The MD5 hash value and histogram of each channel RGB will be displayed as shown below.

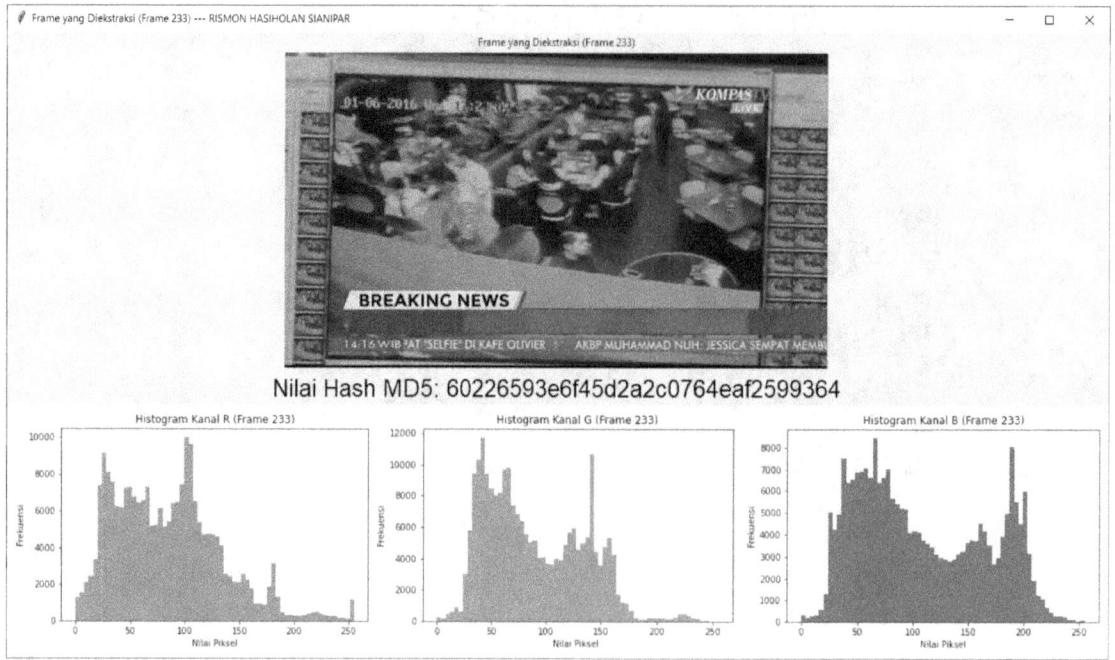

FULL SOURCE CODE

```python
import tkinter as tk
from tkinter import ttk
from tkinter import filedialog
from PIL import Image, ImageTk
import imageio
import matplotlib.pyplot as plt
from matplotlib.backends.backend_tkagg import FigureCanvasTkAgg
import hashlib

class VideoPlayerApp:
    def __init__(self, master):
        self.master = master
        self.master.title("FRAME HASHING AND HISTOGRAM---RISMON HASIHOLAN SIANIPAR")

        self.video = None
        self.video_path = None
        self.paused = False
        self.zoom_scale = tk.IntVar(value=1)
        self.frame_index = 0
        self.start_x = None
        self.start_y = None
        self.current_x = 0
        self.current_y = 0
```

```python
        self.photo = None  # Save object reference to PhotoImage globally

        self.create_widgets()

    def create_widgets(self):
        # Canvas to display the video
        canvas_width = 800
        canvas_height = 600
        self.canvas = tk.Canvas(self.master, width=canvas_width, height=canvas_height)
        self.canvas.grid(row=0, column=0, padx=10, pady=10, sticky="nsew")
        self.canvas.bind("<MouseWheel>", self.on_mousewheel)
        self.canvas.bind("<ButtonPress-1>", self.on_press)
        self.canvas.bind("<B1-Motion>", self.on_drag)

        # Scrollbar
        self.scrollbar = tk.Scrollbar(self.master, orient="horizontal", command=self.on_scroll)
        self.scrollbar.grid(row=1, column=0, sticky="ew")

        self.canvas.configure(xscrollcommand=self.scrollbar.set)

        # Button to open a video file
        self.open_button = tk.Button(self.master, text="Open Video", command=self.open_video)
        self.open_button.grid(row=2, column=0, padx=10, pady=5)

        # Combobox for selecting zoom scale
        self.zoom_combobox = ttk.Combobox(self.master, textvariable=self.zoom_scale, values=list(range(1, 11)))
        self.zoom_combobox.grid(row=2, column=1, padx=10, pady=5)
        self.zoom_combobox.bind("<<ComboboxSelected>>", self.update_zoom)

        # Label and entry for specifying time
        self.time_label = tk.Label(self.master, text="Jump to Time (s):")
        self.time_label.grid(row=0, column=1, padx=10, pady=5, sticky="e")
        self.time_entry = ttk.Entry(self.master)
        self.time_entry.grid(row=0, column=2, padx=10, pady=5, sticky="w")
        self.time_entry.bind("<Return>", lambda event: self.jump_to_time())

        # Button to jump to specified time
        self.jump_button = tk.Button(self.master, text="Jump to Time", command=self.jump_to_time)
        self.jump_button.grid(row=0, column=3, padx=10, pady=5)

        # Button to play/pause the video
        self.play_button = tk.Button(self.master, text="Play/Pause", command=self.toggle_play_pause)
        self.play_button.grid(row=2, column=2, padx=10, pady=5)

        # Button to stop the video
        self.stop_button = tk.Button(self.master, text="Stop", command=self.stop_video)
        self.stop_button.grid(row=2, column=3, padx=10, pady=5)

        # Button to extract frame
        self.extract_button = tk.Button(self.master, text="Extract Frame", command=self.extract_frame)
```

```python
        self.extract_button.grid(row=1, column=1, padx=10, pady=5)

        # Label and entry for frame number
        self.frame_label = tk.Label(self.master, text="Frame Number:")
        self.frame_label.grid(row=1, column=0, padx=10, pady=5, sticky="e")
        self.frame_entry = ttk.Entry(self.master)
        self.frame_entry.grid(row=1, column=2, padx=10, pady=5, sticky="w")
        self.frame_entry.bind("<Return>", lambda event: self.extract_frame())

        # Button to open another instance of the application
        self.open_another_button = tk.Button(self.master, text="Open Another Video Player", command=self.open_another_player)
        self.open_another_button.grid(row=3, column=0, columnspan=4, padx=10, pady=5)

    def open_video(self):
        self.video_path = filedialog.askopenfilename(filetypes=[("Video files", "*.mp4;*.avi;*.mkv")])
        if self.video_path:
            self.video = imageio.get_reader(self.video_path)
            self.play_video()

    def play_video(self):
        if self.video:
            self.paused = False
            self.show_frame()

    def stop_video(self):
        self.paused = True
        self.frame_index = 0
        self.current_x = 0
        self.current_y = 0  # Reset the current position
        self.show_frame()

    def toggle_play_pause(self):
        self.paused = not self.paused
        if not self.paused:
            self.play_video()

    def update_zoom(self, event=None):
        self.show_frame()

    def show_frame(self):
        if self.video:
            if not self.paused:
                self.frame_index += 1
                if self.frame_index >= len(self.video):
                    self.frame_index = 0
            if self.frame_index < len(self.video):  # Tambahkan pengecekan di sini
                frame = self.video.get_data(self.frame_index)
                frame = Image.fromarray(frame)
                frame = frame.resize((frame.width * self.zoom_scale.get(), frame.height * self.zoom_scale.get()))
                photo = ImageTk.PhotoImage(frame)
                self.photo = photo  # Simpan referensi objek PhotoImage secara global
                self.canvas.delete("video")  # Hapus gambar sebelumnya
                self.canvas.create_image(self.current_x, self.current_y, anchor="nw", image=photo, tags="video")
                if not self.paused:
```

```python
            self.canvas.after(30, self.show_frame)

    def on_mousewheel(self, event):
        direction = event.delta // 120
        current_value = int(self.zoom_scale.get())
        if direction == 1 and current_value < 10:
            current_value += 1
        elif direction == -1 and current_value > 1:
            current_value -= 1
        self.zoom_scale.set(current_value)
        self.update_zoom()

    def on_press(self, event):
        self.start_x = event.x
        self.start_y = event.y

    def on_drag(self, event):
        if self.start_x and self.start_y:
            x_offset = event.x - self.start_x
            y_offset = event.y - self.start_y
            self.current_x += x_offset  # Update current position
            self.current_y += y_offset  # Update current position
            self.canvas.move("video", x_offset, y_offset)
            self.start_x = event.x
            self.start_y = event.y

    def on_scroll(self, *args):
        scroll_pos = self.scrollbar.get()
        self.current_x = -scroll_pos * self.canvas.winfo_width()
        self.canvas.xview_moveto(scroll_pos)
        self.frame_index = int(scroll_pos * len(self.video))  # Update frame index
        self.show_frame()

    def jump_to_time(self):
        time_str = self.time_entry.get()
        try:
            time_seconds = float(time_str)
            if 0 <= time_seconds:
                self.frame_index = int(time_seconds *
self.video.get_meta_data()['fps'])
                self.show_frame()
        except ValueError:
            pass

    def extract_frame(self):
        frame_number_str = self.frame_entry.get()
        try:
            frame_number = int(frame_number_str)
            if 0 <= frame_number < len(self.video):
                frame = self.video.get_data(frame_number)
                self.show_extracted_frame(frame, frame_number)
        except ValueError:
            pass

    def show_extracted_frame(self, frame, frame_number):
        extracted_frame_window = tk.Toplevel(self.master)
```

```python
        extracted_frame_window.title(f"Frame yang Diekstraksi (Frame {frame_number}) --- RISMON HASIHOLAN SIANIPAR")

        extracted_frame_label = tk.Label(extracted_frame_window, text=f"Frame yang Diekstraksi (Frame {frame_number})")
        extracted_frame_label.pack()

        height, width, _ = frame.shape  # Get dimensions of the frame
        extracted_photo = ImageTk.PhotoImage(image=Image.fromarray(frame))

        extracted_frame_canvas = tk.Canvas(extracted_frame_window, width=width, height=height)
        extracted_frame_canvas.pack()
        extracted_frame_canvas.create_image(0, 0, anchor="nw", image=extracted_photo)
        extracted_frame_canvas.image = extracted_photo

        # Plot histogram for each RGB channel
        fig, axs = plt.subplots(1, 3, figsize=(18, 4))
        for i, color in enumerate(['r', 'g', 'b']):
            axs[i].hist(frame[:,:,i].ravel(), bins=64, range=(0, 255), color=color, alpha=0.7)
            axs[i].set_title(f"Histogram Kanal {color.upper()} (Frame {frame_number})")
            axs[i].set_xlabel("Nilai Piksel")
            axs[i].set_ylabel("Frekuensi")
        plt.tight_layout()

        # Calculate MD5 hash value of the frame
        md5_hash = hashlib.md5(frame).hexdigest()

        # Display MD5 hash value
        md5_label = tk.Label(extracted_frame_window, text=f"Nilai Hash MD5: {md5_hash}", font=("Arial", 20))
        md5_label.pack()

        hist_canvas = FigureCanvasTkAgg(fig, master=extracted_frame_window)
        hist_canvas.draw()
        hist_canvas.get_tk_widget().pack()

    def open_another_player(self):
        # Open another instance of the application
        root = tk.Toplevel(self.master)
        app = VideoPlayerApp(root)

def main():
    root = tk.Tk()
    app = VideoPlayerApp(root)
    root.mainloop()

if __name__ == "__main__":
    main()
```

COMPUTING HASH VALUE OF A VIDEO FILE

COMPUTING HASH VALUE OF A VIDEO FILE

The code defines a GUI application using the Tkinter library in Python, named "Video Hash GUI," which facilitates the calculation and display of hash values for video files.

Firstly, the GUI application is initialized with Tkinter, creating a window titled "Video Hash GUI." It comprises two main sections: one for displaying the selected video and the other for listing hash values calculated from the video frames. Various buttons are included to interact with the video, such as opening a video file, playing, pausing, and stopping the video playback, calculating hash values, saving hash values to a file, and opening a new instance of the application.

Secondly, upon clicking the "Open Video" button, a file dialog prompts the user to select a video file (supported formats include .mp4 and .avi). Once a file is selected, the application uses OpenCV to capture the video and displays it in the GUI. The video frames are converted from BGR to RGB format using OpenCV and then converted to a format compatible with Tkinter's PhotoImage.

Thirdly, the "Play," "Pause," and "Stop" buttons control the video playback. When the "Play" button is clicked, the application continuously displays the video frames at a rate of 10 milliseconds per frame until paused or stopped. The "Pause" button halts the playback, while the "Stop" button terminates the video capture and clears the video display.

Fourthly, the "Calculate Hash" button triggers the computation of hash values for the video frames. This process iterates through each frame, converts it to RGB format, and computes hash values using various algorithms such as MD5, SHA-1, SHA-256, and others. The resulting hash values are then displayed in the hash listbox.

Lastly, the "Save Hashes" button allows users to save the computed hash values to a text file. Upon clicking this button, a file dialog prompts the user to specify the file path and name for saving. If a valid file path is provided, the hash values are written to the file, with each hash value displayed in the same format as in the hash listbox. A success message dialog confirms the successful saving of hash values.

In summary, the "Video Hash GUI" application provides a user-friendly interface for loading, playing, and analyzing video files by computing hash values for each frame. It offers essential functionalities such as video playback control, hash calculation, and hash value saving, making it a useful tool for various applications involving video analysis and verification.

Importing Libraries

```
import tkinter as tk
from tkinter import filedialog, messagebox
import cv2
import hashlib
import subprocess
from PIL import Image, ImageTk
```

The code snippet imports several libraries in Python. Let's break down each import statement and explain the purpose of each library:
- import tkinter as tk: Tkinter is Python's de-facto standard GUI (Graphical User Interface) toolkit. It provides a set of tools for creating GUI applications. In this import statement, tk is an alias used to refer to the tkinter module, making it more convenient to access its classes and functions.
- from tkinter import filedialog, messagebox: This line imports specific modules from the tkinter library. filedialog provides dialogs for file operations, such as opening and saving files. messagebox provides dialogs for displaying messages to the user, such as warnings, information, or errors.
- import cv2: OpenCV (Open Source Computer Vision Library) is a popular open-source computer vision and machine learning software library. It provides various functions for image and video processing, including reading, writing, and manipulating images and videos.

- import hashlib: The hashlib module provides a secure way to generate various types of cryptographic hash functions. Hash functions take an input (or 'message') and return a fixed-size string of bytes. These functions are commonly used for data integrity verification, password storage, and digital signatures.
- import subprocess: The subprocess module allows you to spawn new processes, connect to their input/output/error pipes, and obtain their return codes. It provides a way to interact with the operating system and execute external commands or programs from within a Python script.
- from PIL import Image, ImageTk: PIL (Python Imaging Library) is a library for image processing tasks in Python. It allows for various image manipulations, such as opening, editing, and saving images. ImageTk is a module within PIL that provides support for displaying images in Tkinter GUI applications.

In summary, the import statements in the code snippet bring in essential libraries for creating a GUI application with Tkinter, processing images and videos with OpenCV and PIL, performing cryptographic operations with hashlib, and executing external processes with subprocess. These libraries collectively provide the necessary tools for building a functional and interactive GUI application for video hashing and processing.

Structure and Behavior of GUI

```
class VideoHashGUI:
    def __init__(self, root):
        self.root = root
        self.root.title("Video Hash GUI")

        self.video_frame = tk.LabelFrame(self.root, text="Video")
        self.video_frame.pack(padx=10, pady=10)

        self.hash_frame = tk.LabelFrame(self.root, text="Hash Values")
        self.hash_frame.pack(padx=10, pady=10)

        self.video_label = tk.Label(self.video_frame)
        self.video_label.pack()

        self.hash_listbox = tk.Listbox(self.hash_frame, width=70, font=('Helvetica', 12))  # Lebar diperbesar menjadi 70
        self.hash_listbox.pack()

        self.open_button = tk.Button(self.root, text="Open Video", command=self.open_video)
        self.open_button.pack(side=tk.LEFT, padx=5)

        self.play_button = tk.Button(self.root, text="Play", command=self.play_video)
        self.play_button.pack(side=tk.LEFT, padx=5)
```

```
        self.pause_button = tk.Button(self.root, text="Pause", 
command=self.pause_video)
        self.pause_button.pack(side=tk.LEFT, padx=5)

        self.stop_button = tk.Button(self.root, text="Stop", command=self.stop_video)
        self.stop_button.pack(side=tk.LEFT, padx=5)

        self.calculate_button = tk.Button(self.root, text="Calculate Hash", 
command=self.calculate_hash)
        self.calculate_button.pack(side=tk.LEFT, padx=5)

        self.save_button = tk.Button(self.root, text="Save Hashes", 
command=self.save_hashes)
        self.save_button.pack(side=tk.LEFT, padx=5)

        self.open_new_instance_button = tk.Button(self.root, text="Open New 
Instance", command=self.open_new_instance)
        self.open_new_instance_button.pack(side=tk.LEFT, padx=5)

        self.video_capture = None
        self.playing = False
```

The code defines a Python class named VideoHashGUI, which serves as the backbone for creating a graphical user interface (GUI) application for video hashing. Let's examine the class and its components in detail:

1. Constructor (__init__):
    - The __init__ method initializes an instance of the VideoHashGUI class.
    - It takes a parameter root, which represents the Tkinter root window.
    - The root window is assigned to the self.root attribute, and its title is set to "Video Hash GUI" using self.root.title("Video Hash GUI").
    - Two label frames (self.video_frame and self.hash_frame) are created within the root window to organize different sections of the GUI. These frames serve as containers for other GUI elements.
    - Inside each label frame, relevant widgets like labels (self.video_label), listboxes (self.hash_listbox), and buttons (self.open_button, self.play_button, etc.) are created and packed with appropriate configurations (e.g., text, commands, padding, etc.).
    - The buttons are associated with specific commands that trigger corresponding actions when clicked (e.g., opening a video file, playing/pausing/stopping video playback, calculating hash values, saving hash values, and opening a new instance of the application).
    - The video_capture attribute is initialized to None, indicating that no video is currently loaded, and the playing attribute is initialized to False, indicating that video playback is not active.
2. Methods:

- open_video(): Prompts the user to select a video file using a file dialog and initializes video capture using OpenCV if a file is selected.
- display_video(): Displays the video frames captured by OpenCV in the GUI. This method is called recursively to continuously display frames while video playback is active.
- play_video(), pause_video(), stop_video(): Control the playback state of the video.
- calculate_hash(): Computes hash values for video frames using various hashing algorithms from the hashlib module and displays the results in the hash listbox.
- save_hashes(): Saves the computed hash values to a text file selected by the user using a file dialog.
- open_new_instance(): Opens a new instance of the application using the subprocess module, allowing multiple instances of the GUI to run simultaneously.

Overall, the VideoHashGUI class encapsulates the structure and behavior of a GUI application for video hashing, providing a user-friendly interface for video manipulation and hash computation.

Opening and Selecting Video File

```
def open_video(self):
    file_path = filedialog.askopenfilename(filetypes=[("Video files", "*.mp4;*.avi")])
    if file_path:
        self.video_capture = cv2.VideoCapture(file_path)
        self.display_video()
```

The open_video() method in the VideoHashGUI class facilitates the process of opening a video file selected by the user. Let's examine this method in detail:

1. Prompting User for Video File:
    - The filedialog.askopenfilename() function from Tkinter's filedialog module is used to display a file dialog, allowing the user to select a video file.
    - The filetypes parameter is specified to filter the file types displayed in the dialog. In this case, it restricts the selection to files with extensions .mp4 and .avi and displays only files with the description "Video files".
2. Opening Selected Video File:
    - If the user selects a video file and clicks the "Open" button in the file dialog, the askopenfilename() function returns the file path as a string.
    - The if file_path: condition checks if a valid file path is returned. If so, it indicates that the user has selected a video file.
3. Initializing Video Capture:

- If a valid file path is obtained, a VideoCapture object is created using OpenCV's cv2.VideoCapture() function, passing the selected file path as an argument.
- The VideoCapture object is assigned to the self.video_capture attribute of the VideoHashGUI instance, allowing access to the video data within other methods of the class.

4. Displaying Video:
    - After opening the video file, the display_video() method is called to start displaying the video frames in the GUI.
    - This method displays the video frames captured by the VideoCapture object and continuously updates the display until the end of the video or until the user interrupts the playback.

In summary, the open_video() method provides functionality for selecting and opening a video file, initializing a VideoCapture object to access the video data, and initiating the display of video frames in the GUI using the display_video() method. This allows users to interactively load and view video files within the application's graphical interface.

Displaying Video

```
def display_video(self):
    if self.video_capture:
        ret, frame = self.video_capture.read()
        if ret:
            frame = cv2.cvtColor(frame, cv2.COLOR_BGR2RGB)
            image = Image.fromarray(frame)
            imgtk = ImageTk.PhotoImage(image=image)
            self.video_label.imgtk = imgtk
            self.video_label.config(image=imgtk)
            if self.playing:
                self.root.after(10, self.display_video)
        else:
            messagebox.showwarning("Warning", "End of video reached.")
```

The display_video() method in the VideoHashGUI class handles the process of displaying video frames within the graphical user interface (GUI). Let's break down this method step by step:

1. Checking Video Capture Object:
    - The method begins with a check to ensure that the self.video_capture attribute, which holds the VideoCapture object, is not None. If there is a valid VideoCapture object, the method proceeds to read and display video frames.
2. Reading Video Frame:

- The self.video_capture.read() function reads the next frame from the video file. It returns two values: ret, which indicates whether a frame was successfully read, and frame, which holds the actual frame data.
3. Displaying Frame:
    - If a frame is successfully read (ret is True), the method converts the frame from the OpenCV's default BGR color space to RGB color space using cv2.cvtColor(). This conversion is necessary because Tkinter requires images in RGB format.
    - The converted frame is then converted to a PIL Image object using Image.fromarray().
    - Next, an ImageTk.PhotoImage object (imgtk) is created from the PIL Image, allowing the image to be displayed in the Tkinter GUI.
    - The imgtk object is assigned to the self.video_label.imgtk attribute, ensuring that the image is retained even after the method finishes execution.
    - Finally, the self.video_label widget's image is configured to display the current frame using self.video_label.config(image=imgtk).
4. Continuously Updating Display:
    - If the video is currently playing (self.playing is True), the method schedules itself to be called again after a short delay (10 milliseconds) using self.root.after(10, self.display_video).
    - This creates a loop where the display_video() method is called repeatedly, effectively playing the video in real-time.
5. Handling End of Video:
    - If the read() function returns False (indicating the end of the video file), a warning message is displayed using messagebox.showwarning().

In summary, the display_video() method continuously reads video frames from the VideoCapture object, converts them to the appropriate format, and displays them in the GUI. This method provides real-time video playback functionality within the application's graphical interface.

Playing, Pausing, and Stopping Video

```
def play_video(self):
    if self.video_capture:
        self.playing = True
        self.display_video()

def pause_video(self):
    self.playing = False

def stop_video(self):
```

```
        self.playing = False
        if self.video_capture:
            self.video_capture.release()
            self.video_label.config(image='')
```

The code snippet contains three methods (play_video(), pause_video(), and stop_video()) within the VideoHashGUI class. Let's examine each method and its functionality:

1. play_video(self):
    - This method is called when the user clicks the "Play" button in the GUI.
    - It first checks if a video capture object (self.video_capture) exists. If not, the method cannot proceed further.
    - If a video capture object is available, it sets the self.playing attribute to True, indicating that video playback is active.
    - Then, it calls the display_video() method to start displaying video frames in the GUI. This method continuously updates the video display until the end of the video or until playback is paused or stopped.
2. pause_video(self):
    - This method is called when the user clicks the "Pause" button in the GUI.
    - It simply sets the self.playing attribute to False, indicating that video playback is paused. This halts the continuous display of video frames initiated by the play_video() method.
3. stop_video(self):
    - This method is called when the user clicks the "Stop" button in the GUI.
    - It sets the self.playing attribute to False, indicating that video playback is stopped.
    - If a video capture object (self.video_capture) exists, it releases the video capture resource using the release() method. This frees up system resources associated with the video capture object.
    - Finally, it clears the video label (self.video_label) by configuring its image to an empty string, effectively removing the displayed video frames from the GUI.

In summary, these methods provide control over video playback within the GUI application. The play_video() method initiates playback, the pause_video() method pauses playback, and the stop_video() method stops playback and releases associated resources. These functionalities allow users to interactively control the video display according to their preferences.

Calculating Hash Values

```
    def calculate_hash(self):
        if self.video_capture:
```

```
            hash_algorithms = ['md5', 'sha1', 'sha256', 'sha224', 'sha384', 'sha512',
'blake2b', 'ripemd160']
            self.hash_listbox.delete(0, tk.END)
            hash_values = {}
            while True:
                ret, frame = self.video_capture.read()
                if not ret:
                    break
                frame = cv2.cvtColor(frame, cv2.COLOR_BGR2RGB)
                for algorithm in hash_algorithms:
                    if algorithm not in hash_values:
                        hash_values[algorithm] = hashlib.new(algorithm)
                    hash_values[algorithm].update(frame.tobytes())
                for algorithm, hash_obj in hash_values.items():
                    hash_value = hash_obj.hexdigest()
                    self.hash_listbox.insert(tk.END, f"{algorithm}--> {hash_value}")
```

The calculate_hash() method within the VideoHashGUI class is responsible for computing hash values for each frame of the video using specified hashing algorithms and displaying the results in the hash listbox widget. Let's break down the functionality of this method:

1. Checking Video Capture Object:
   - The method begins with a check to ensure that the self.video_capture attribute is not None, indicating that a video capture object has been initialized. If there's no video capture object, the method cannot proceed further.
2. Defining Hashing Algorithms:
   - An array hash_algorithms is defined, containing the names of various hashing algorithms such as MD5, SHA-1, SHA-256, etc. These algorithms will be used to compute hash values for each frame.
3. Clearing Hash Listbox:
   - The delete() method of the hash_listbox widget is called to clear any existing items in the hash listbox before displaying new hash values.
4. Computing Hash Values:
   - The method enters a loop to read each frame from the video using self.video_capture.read().
   - Inside the loop, the ret variable indicates whether a frame was successfully read. If no frame is read (i.e., ret is False), the loop is terminated.
   - Each frame is converted from the BGR color space (the default color format used by OpenCV) to RGB color space using cv2.cvtColor().
   - For each frame, the method iterates through the defined hash_algorithms array and computes the hash value using the hashlib.new() and update() methods. If the hash algorithm has not been initialized yet, a new hash object is created.

- The hash value is then inserted into the hash_listbox widget, along with the corresponding algorithm name, using the insert() method.
5. Displaying Hash Values:
    - After computing hash values for all frames, the method iterates through the hash_values dictionary and inserts each hash value into the hash_listbox, along with the name of the hashing algorithm.

In summary, the calculate_hash() method provides functionality to compute hash values for each frame of the video using specified hashing algorithms and displays the results in the GUI. This allows users to analyze the content of the video and verify its integrity through hash comparison.

Saving Hash Values

```
def save_hashes(self):
    if self.hash_listbox.size() > 0:
        file_path = filedialog.asksaveasfilename(defaultextension=".txt",
filetypes=[("Text files", "*.txt")])
        if file_path:
            with open(file_path, "w") as file:
                for index in range(self.hash_listbox.size()):
                    file.write(self.hash_listbox.get(index) + "\n")
            messagebox.showinfo("Success", "Hashes saved successfully.")
```

The save_hashes() method within the VideoHashGUI class facilitates the process of saving the computed hash values to a text file. Let's examine the functionality of this method:
1. Checking Hash Listbox Size:
    - The method begins by checking if the hash listbox (self.hash_listbox) contains any hash values. If the size of the listbox is greater than zero, it indicates that there are hash values to be saved.
2. Prompting User for File Path:
    - If the hash listbox is not empty, the method prompts the user to specify the file path and name for saving the hash values using the filedialog.asksaveasfilename() function. This function displays a file dialog allowing the user to select or specify a file for saving.
3. Saving Hash Values to File:
    - If a valid file path is provided by the user, the method opens the specified file in write mode ("w") using a with statement and writes each hash value from the hash listbox to the file.
    - The self.hash_listbox.get(index) function retrieves the hash value at the specified index in the listbox.

- Each hash value is written to the file followed by a newline character ("\n"), ensuring that each hash value is written on a separate line.
4. Displaying Success Message:
    - After successfully saving the hash values to the file, a message dialog box is displayed using messagebox.showinfo() to inform the user that the operation was successful.
    - The dialog box displays the message "Hashes saved successfully."

In summary, the save_hashes() method provides functionality for saving the computed hash values from the hash listbox to a text file. This allows users to preserve the hash values for later reference or analysis, enhancing the utility of the application for video hashing and verification purposes.

Opening Another Instance of Application

```
def open_new_instance(self):
    subprocess.Popen(["python", __file__])
```

The open_new_instance() method within the VideoHashGUI class allows users to open a new instance of the application. Let's examine its functionality:
1. Using subprocess.Popen():
    - This method utilizes the subprocess.Popen() function to open a new process.
    - The Popen() function takes a list containing the command and arguments to be executed. In this case, it takes ["python", __file__] as arguments.
    - python is the command to execute, which launches another Python interpreter.
    - __file__ is a special Python variable that represents the current script's file name. In this context, it refers to the current Python script containing the VideoHashGUI class.
2. Opening Another Instance of the Application:
    - By executing subprocess.Popen(["python", __file__]), a new instance of the Python interpreter is launched, executing the same script that contains the VideoHashGUI class.
    - This effectively opens another instance of the application, allowing multiple instances of the GUI to run simultaneously.

In summary, the open_new_instance() method provides functionality for spawning a new process, opening another instance of the application. This feature enables users to run multiple instances of the video hashing GUI concurrently, facilitating multitasking and enhancing usability.

Entry Point For Running Program

```
if __name__ == "__main__":
    root = tk.Tk()
    app = VideoHashGUI(root)
    root.mainloop()
```

The if __name__ == "__main__": block at the end of the script serves as the entry point for running the video hashing GUI application when the script is executed as the main program. Let's break down this block:
1. Creating Tkinter Root Window:
    - tk.Tk() creates the main window (root window) for the Tkinter application.
2. Initializing VideoHashGUI Instance:
    - app = VideoHashGUI(root) initializes an instance of the VideoHashGUI class, passing the root window (root) as an argument. This sets up the graphical user interface for the video hashing application.
3. Starting Tkinter Main Loop:
    - root.mainloop() starts the Tkinter event loop, which listens for user events (e.g., mouse clicks, keyboard inputs) and updates the GUI accordingly.
    - This loop continues running until the user closes the application window, at which point the program exits.

In summary, the if __name__ == "__main__": block orchestrates the execution of the video hashing GUI application by creating the necessary Tkinter components, initializing the VideoHashGUI instance, and starting the main event loop to handle user interactions and maintain the GUI's responsiveness.

Running Program

Run program and the GUI is displayed as shown below.

Click on Open Video. The video now is displayed in the GUI as shown below.

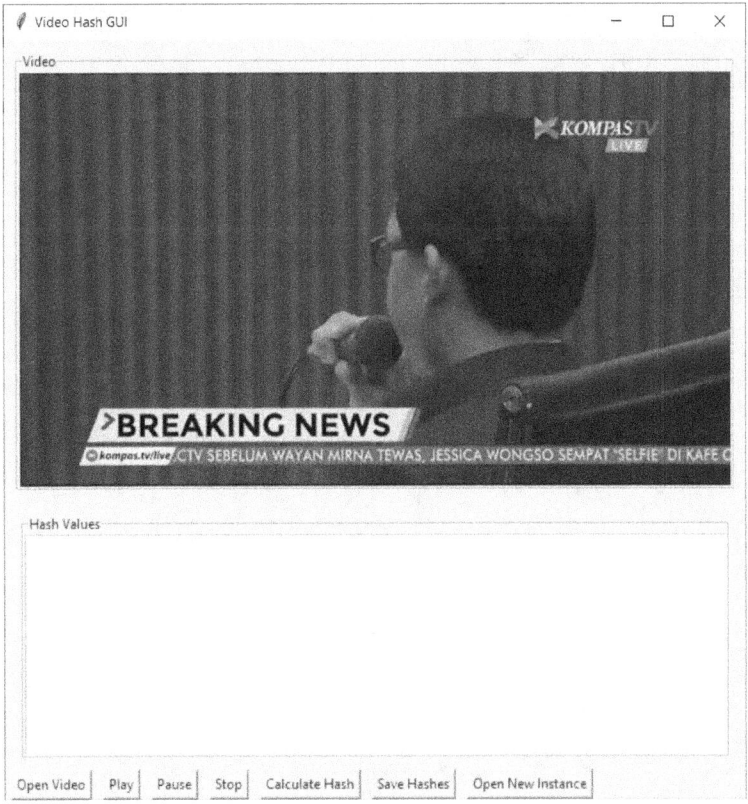

Then, click on Calculate Hash button. Then, the hash value of each hash function is displayed below.

FULL SOURCE CODE

```python
import tkinter as tk
from tkinter import filedialog, messagebox
import cv2
import hashlib
import subprocess
from PIL import Image, ImageTk

class VideoHashGUI:
    def __init__(self, root):
        self.root = root
        self.root.title("Video Hash GUI")

        self.video_frame = tk.LabelFrame(self.root, text="Video")
        self.video_frame.pack(padx=10, pady=10)

        self.hash_frame = tk.LabelFrame(self.root, text="Hash Values")
        self.hash_frame.pack(padx=10, pady=10)
```

```python
        self.video_label = tk.Label(self.video_frame)
        self.video_label.pack()

        self.hash_listbox = tk.Listbox(self.hash_frame, width=70, font=('Helvetica',
12))  # Lebar diperbesar menjadi 70
        self.hash_listbox.pack()

        self.open_button = tk.Button(self.root, text="Open Video",
command=self.open_video)
        self.open_button.pack(side=tk.LEFT, padx=5)

        self.play_button = tk.Button(self.root, text="Play", command=self.play_video)
        self.play_button.pack(side=tk.LEFT, padx=5)

        self.pause_button = tk.Button(self.root, text="Pause",
command=self.pause_video)
        self.pause_button.pack(side=tk.LEFT, padx=5)

        self.stop_button = tk.Button(self.root, text="Stop", command=self.stop_video)
        self.stop_button.pack(side=tk.LEFT, padx=5)

        self.calculate_button = tk.Button(self.root, text="Calculate Hash",
command=self.calculate_hash)
        self.calculate_button.pack(side=tk.LEFT, padx=5)

        self.save_button = tk.Button(self.root, text="Save Hashes",
command=self.save_hashes)
        self.save_button.pack(side=tk.LEFT, padx=5)

        self.open_new_instance_button = tk.Button(self.root, text="Open New
Instance", command=self.open_new_instance)
        self.open_new_instance_button.pack(side=tk.LEFT, padx=5)

        self.video_capture = None
        self.playing = False

    def open_video(self):
        file_path = filedialog.askopenfilename(filetypes=[("Video files",
"*.mp4;*.avi")])
        if file_path:
            self.video_capture = cv2.VideoCapture(file_path)
            self.display_video()

    def display_video(self):
        if self.video_capture:
            ret, frame = self.video_capture.read()
            if ret:
                frame = cv2.cvtColor(frame, cv2.COLOR_BGR2RGB)
                image = Image.fromarray(frame)
                imgtk = ImageTk.PhotoImage(image=image)
                self.video_label.imgtk = imgtk
                self.video_label.config(image=imgtk)
                if self.playing:
                    self.root.after(10, self.display_video)
            else:
                messagebox.showwarning("Warning", "End of video reached.")

    def play_video(self):
```

```python
            if self.video_capture:
                self.playing = True
                self.display_video()

    def pause_video(self):
        self.playing = False

    def stop_video(self):
        self.playing = False
        if self.video_capture:
            self.video_capture.release()
            self.video_label.config(image='')

    def calculate_hash(self):
        if self.video_capture:
            hash_algorithms = ['md5', 'sha1', 'sha256', 'sha224', 'sha384', 'sha512', 'blake2b', 'ripemd160']
            self.hash_listbox.delete(0, tk.END)
            hash_values = {}
            while True:
                ret, frame = self.video_capture.read()
                if not ret:
                    break
                frame = cv2.cvtColor(frame, cv2.COLOR_BGR2RGB)
                for algorithm in hash_algorithms:
                    if algorithm not in hash_values:
                        hash_values[algorithm] = hashlib.new(algorithm)
                    hash_values[algorithm].update(frame.tobytes())
            for algorithm, hash_obj in hash_values.items():
                hash_value = hash_obj.hexdigest()
                self.hash_listbox.insert(tk.END, f"{algorithm}--> {hash_value}")

    def save_hashes(self):
        if self.hash_listbox.size() > 0:
            file_path = filedialog.asksaveasfilename(defaultextension=".txt", filetypes=[("Text files", "*.txt")])
            if file_path:
                with open(file_path, "w") as file:
                    for index in range(self.hash_listbox.size()):
                        file.write(self.hash_listbox.get(index) + "\n")
                    messagebox.showinfo("Success", "Hashes saved successfully.")

    def open_new_instance(self):
        subprocess.Popen(["python", __file__])

if __name__ == "__main__":
    root = tk.Tk()
    app = VideoHashGUI(root)
    root.mainloop()
```

COMPUTING HASH VALUE OF EIGHT DIFFERENT HASH FUNCTIONS ON EACH FRAME IN VIDEO AND DISPLAYING ITS RGB HISTORGAM

COMPUTING HASH VALUE OF EIGHT DIFFERENT HASH FUNCTION ON EACH FRAME IN VIDEO AND DISPLAYING ITS RGB HISTORGAM

The code below defines a graphical user interface (GUI) application for playing videos, extracting frames, and displaying histograms of the video frames. Let's summarize its key components and functionalities:

1. GUI Layout:
    - The GUI consists of two main panels: one for displaying the video and another for control buttons.
    - The video panel contains a canvas for displaying video frames, along with a horizontal scrollbar for navigating through the video frames.
    - The control panel includes buttons and widgets for opening a video file, selecting zoom scale, specifying time, playing/pausing the video, stopping the video, extracting frames, and opening another instance of the application.
2. Video Playback:

- Users can open video files (in formats such as MP4, AVI, and MKV) using the "Open Video" button. The imageio library is used to read video frames.
- The "Play/Pause" button toggles video playback, allowing users to play or pause the video stream.
- The "Stop" button halts video playback and resets the frame index to the beginning of the video.

3. Frame Extraction:
   - Users can extract frames from the video by specifying the frame number using the entry widget and clicking the "Extract Frame" button.
   - Extracted frames are displayed in a separate window along with histograms showing the distribution of pixel values in the RGB channels.

4. Interactivity:
   - Users can interact with the video display canvas by dragging the mouse to pan the video frame and using the mouse wheel to zoom in/out.
   - The GUI provides functionality for jumping to a specific time in the video by entering a time value and clicking the "Jump to Time" button.

5. Multiple Instances:
   - The application supports opening multiple instances, allowing users to work with multiple videos simultaneously. The "Open Another Video Player" button opens a new instance of the application in a separate window.

Overall, the application offers a user-friendly interface for video playback, frame extraction, and histogram visualization, enhancing the user's ability to analyze and manipulate video content effectively. Through its intuitive layout and interactive features, the application provides a versatile tool for video processing tasks.

Importing Libraries

```
import tkinter as tk
from tkinter import ttk
from tkinter import filedialog
from PIL import Image, ImageTk
import imageio
import matplotlib.pyplot as plt
from matplotlib.backends.backend_tkagg import FigureCanvasTkAgg
import hashlib
import numpy as np
```

The code imports several libraries and modules commonly used for developing graphical user interface (GUI) applications, image processing, and data visualization. Let's examine each import statement:

1. import tkinter as tk:
   - This imports the Tkinter library, which is a standard GUI toolkit for Python. It provides various widgets and methods for creating graphical interfaces.
2. from tkinter import ttk:
   - This imports the ttk module from Tkinter. ttk (Themed Tkinter) provides enhanced versions of standard Tkinter widgets with a more modern and consistent look.
3. from tkinter import filedialog:
   - This imports the filedialog module from Tkinter, which provides dialogs for opening and saving files. It allows users to browse files and select file paths interactively.
4. from PIL import Image, ImageTk:
   - This imports the Image and ImageTk modules from the Python Imaging Library (PIL), now known as Pillow. PIL/Pillow is a powerful library for opening, manipulating, and saving many different image file formats.
5. import imageio:
   - This imports the imageio library, which is used for reading and writing a wide range of image and video formats. It provides an easy-to-use interface for working with multimedia data.
6. import matplotlib.pyplot as plt:
   - This imports the pyplot module from the Matplotlib library. Matplotlib is a popular plotting library for creating static, animated, and interactive visualizations in Python.
7. from matplotlib.backends.backend_tkagg import FigureCanvasTkAgg:
   - This imports the FigureCanvasTkAgg class from the Matplotlib backend for embedding Matplotlib figures into Tkinter applications. It allows Matplotlib plots to be displayed within Tkinter GUIs.
8. import hashlib:
   - This imports the hashlib module, which provides cryptographic hash functions. It allows developers to generate hash values (checksums) for data integrity verification and security purposes.
9. import numpy as np:
   - This imports the NumPy library, which is a fundamental package for numerical computing with Python. NumPy provides support for large, multi-dimensional arrays and matrices, along with a collection of mathematical functions to operate on these arrays efficiently.

In summary, the imported libraries and modules provide a comprehensive toolkit for developing GUI applications with advanced image processing, data visualization, and cryptographic capabilities in Python. These libraries enable developers to create sophisticated applications for a wide range of tasks, from simple image viewing utilities to complex scientific analysis tools.

Class and Its Constructor

```
class VideoPlayerApp:
    def __init__(self, master):
        self.master = master
        self.master.title("FRAME HASHING AND HISTOGRAM---RISMON HASIHOLAN SIANIPAR")

        self.video = None
        self.video_path = None
        self.paused = False
        self.zoom_scale = tk.IntVar(value=1)
        self.frame_index = 0
        self.start_x = None
        self.start_y = None
        self.current_x = 0
        self.current_y = 0
        self.photo = None  # Save object reference to PhotoImage globally

        self.create_widgets()
```

This code defines a class named VideoPlayerApp, which serves as the backbone for a video player application with features such as frame hashing and histogram visualization. Let's break down the attributes and methods defined within this class:
1. Attributes:
    - master: Represents the master (parent) widget or window where the video player GUI will be placed.
    - video: Represents the video content loaded into the player.
    - video_path: Stores the file path of the loaded video.
    - paused: Boolean flag indicating whether the video playback is paused (True) or active (False).
    - zoom_scale: Tkinter IntVar variable storing the current zoom scale of the video display.
    - frame_index: Integer value representing the index of the currently displayed frame in the video.
    - start_x, start_y: Stores the starting coordinates of mouse events for panning.

- current_x, current_y: Represents the current coordinates of the video display canvas for panning.
- photo: Stores the reference to the PhotoImage object representing the current video frame.
2. Initialization Method (__init__):
    - Initializes the attributes of the VideoPlayerApp class.
    - Sets the title of the master window to "FRAME HASHING AND HISTOGRAM---RISMON HASIHOLAN SIANIPAR".
    - Calls the create_widgets() method to create the GUI components.
3. Method: create_widgets():
    - Creates the graphical widgets and components for the video player GUI.
    - Sets up the video display canvas, horizontal scrollbar, and control buttons (such as open video, zoom scale combobox, jump to time entry, play/pause button, stop button, extract frame button, and open another video player button).
4. Additional Functionality:
    - The class is expected to have additional methods for handling user interactions, such as loading video files, playing/pausing the video, stopping video playback, updating zoom scale, displaying frames, handling mouse events for panning, scrolling through frames, jumping to specific times, extracting frames, and opening another instance of the video player.

Overall, the VideoPlayerApp class lays the foundation for building a video player application with advanced functionalities like frame hashing and histogram visualization. It provides a structured approach to handling video content and user interactions within a Tkinter-based graphical interface.

Creating Widgets

```python
def create_widgets(self):
    # Panel for video display
    video_panel = tk.Frame(self.master)
    video_panel.grid(row=0, column=0, padx=10, pady=10, sticky="nsew")

    # Canvas to display the video
    canvas_width = 800
    canvas_height = 600
    self.canvas = tk.Canvas(video_panel, width=canvas_width, height=canvas_height)
    self.canvas.pack(side="top", fill="both", expand=True)
    self.canvas.bind("<MouseWheel>", self.on_mousewheel)
    self.canvas.bind("<ButtonPress-1>", self.on_press)
```

```python
        self.canvas.bind("<B1-Motion>", self.on_drag)

        # Scrollbar
        self.scrollbar = tk.Scrollbar(video_panel, orient="horizontal", command=self.on_scroll)
        self.scrollbar.pack(side="bottom", fill="x")

        self.canvas.configure(xscrollcommand=self.scrollbar.set)

        # Panel for control buttons
        control_panel = tk.Frame(self.master)
        control_panel.grid(row=1, column=0, padx=10, pady=(0, 10), sticky="ew")

        # Button to open a video file
        self.open_button = tk.Button(control_panel, text="Open Video", command=self.open_video)
        self.open_button.grid(row=0, column=0, padx=10, pady=5)

        # Combobox for selecting zoom scale
        self.zoom_combobox = ttk.Combobox(control_panel, textvariable=self.zoom_scale, values=list(range(1, 11)))
        self.zoom_combobox.grid(row=0, column=1, padx=10, pady=5)
        self.zoom_combobox.bind("<<ComboboxSelected>>", self.update_zoom)

        # Label and entry for specifying time
        self.time_label = tk.Label(control_panel, text="Jump to Time (s):")
        self.time_label.grid(row=0, column=2, padx=10, pady=5, sticky="e")
        self.time_entry = ttk.Entry(control_panel)
        self.time_entry.grid(row=0, column=3, padx=10, pady=5, sticky="w")
        self.time_entry.bind("<Return>", lambda event: self.jump_to_time())

        # Button to jump to specified time
        self.jump_button = tk.Button(control_panel, text="Jump to Time", command=self.jump_to_time)
        self.jump_button.grid(row=0, column=4, padx=10, pady=5)

        # Button to play/pause the video
        self.play_button = tk.Button(control_panel, text="Play/Pause", command=self.toggle_play_pause)
        self.play_button.grid(row=0, column=5, padx=10, pady=5)

        # Button to stop the video
        self.stop_button = tk.Button(control_panel, text="Stop", command=self.stop_video)
        self.stop_button.grid(row=0, column=6, padx=10, pady=5)

        # Button to extract frame
```

```
        self.extract_button = tk.Button(control_panel, text="Extract Frame", 
command=self.extract_frame)
        self.extract_button.grid(row=1, column=0, padx=10, pady=5)

        # Label and entry for frame number
        self.frame_label = tk.Label(control_panel, text="Frame Number:")
        self.frame_label.grid(row=1, column=1, padx=10, pady=5, sticky="e")
        self.frame_entry = ttk.Entry(control_panel)
        self.frame_entry.grid(row=1, column=2, padx=10, pady=5, sticky="w")
        self.frame_entry.bind("<Return>", lambda event: self.extract_frame())

        # Button to open another instance of the application
        self.open_another_button = tk.Button(control_panel, text="Open Another Video 
Player", command=self.open_another_player)
        self.open_another_button.grid(row=2, column=0, columnspan=7, padx=10, pady=5)
```

The create_widgets() method is responsible for setting up the graphical user interface (GUI) components of the video player application. Here's a breakdown of each widget and its functionality:

1. Video Panel:
   - A Frame widget named video_panel is created to hold the video display canvas and scrollbar.
   - The frame is placed at row 0, column 0 of the master widget (self.master) with a padding of 10 pixels on all sides.
   - The sticky parameter is set to "nsew" to allow the frame to expand in all directions if the master widget is resized.
2. Canvas for Video Display:
   - A Canvas widget named self.canvas is created within the video_panel frame to display the video frames.
   - It is configured to have a fixed width of 800 pixels and a height of 600 pixels.
   - The canvas is packed at the top of the video_panel frame, and it fills both horizontally and vertically to adapt to resizing.
   - Event bindings are set up for mouse wheel scrolling ("<MouseWheel>"), left mouse button press ("<ButtonPress-1>"), and mouse drag ("<B1-Motion>").
3. Scrollbar:
   - A horizontal Scrollbar widget named self.scrollbar is created within the video_panel frame.
   - It is placed at the bottom of the frame and configured to fill the horizontal space.
   - The scrollbar's orientation is set to "horizontal", and it is linked to the on_scroll method for handling scrolling events.
4. Control Panel:

- Another Frame widget named control_panel is created to hold control buttons for the video player.
- This frame is placed at row 1, column 0 of the master widget with padding on the x-axis and y-axis.
- The sticky parameter is set to "ew" to allow the frame to expand horizontally if the master widget is resized.

5. Control Buttons:
    - Several control buttons are added to the control_panel frame:
    - "Open Video": Opens a dialog to select and load a video file.
    - Zoom Scale Combobox: Allows the user to select the zoom scale for video display.
    - Jump to Time Entry: Allows the user to input a specific time in seconds to jump to within the video.
    - "Jump to Time" Button: Initiates the jump to the specified time.
    - "Play/Pause" Button: Toggles between playing and pausing the video.
    - "Stop" Button: Stops the video playback.
    - "Extract Frame" Button: Extracts and displays the frame corresponding to the specified frame number.
    - Frame Number Label and Entry: Allows the user to input a specific frame number to extract.
    - "Open Another Video Player" Button: Opens another instance of the video player application.

These widgets and buttons collectively provide the user interface for interacting with the video player application, allowing users to control video playback, adjust display settings, and navigate through the video content.

Opening, Playing, Stopping, and Toggling Video

```
    def open_video(self):
        self.video_path = filedialog.askopenfilename(filetypes=[("Video files",
"*.mp4;*.avi;*.mkv")])
        if self.video_path:
            self.video = imageio.get_reader(self.video_path)
            self.play_video()

    def play_video(self):
        if self.video:
            self.paused = False
            self.show_frame()
```

```python
def stop_video(self):
    self.paused = True
    self.frame_index = 0
    self.current_x = 0
    self.current_y = 0  # Reset the current position
    self.show_frame()

def toggle_play_pause(self):
    self.paused = not self.paused
    if not self.paused:
        self.play_video()
```

The following methods handle video loading, playback, and control functionalities:
1. open_video(self):
    - This method is invoked when the user clicks the "Open Video" button.
    - It opens a file dialog using filedialog.askopenfilename() to allow the user to select a video file (with extensions .mp4, .avi, or .mkv).
    - If a valid video file is selected, its path is stored in self.video_path.
    - The selected video file is then loaded using imageio.get_reader() to create a video reader object (self.video).
    - Once the video is loaded, the play_video() method is called to initiate playback.
2. play_video(self):
    - This method is responsible for playing the video.
    - It sets the self.paused flag to False to indicate that the video is playing.
    - It then calls the show_frame() method to display the current frame.
3. stop_video(self):
    - This method stops the video playback.
    - It sets the self.paused flag to True to pause the video.
    - Additionally, it resets the self.frame_index, self.current_x, and self.current_y attributes to reset the video to the beginning and the canvas position to the top-left corner.
    - Finally, it calls show_frame() to display the initial frame after stopping the video.
4. toggle_play_pause(self):
    - This method toggles between playing and pausing the video.
    - It flips the value of the self.paused flag.
    - If the video is not paused (i.e., playing), it calls the play_video() method to continue playback.

These methods collectively enable users to load video files, play/pause the video, and stop video playback as per their interaction with the video player application. Additionally, they ensure proper handling of video states and synchronization with the graphical user interface.

Updating Zoom Level

```
def update_zoom(self, event=None):
    self.show_frame()
```

The update_zoom() method is responsible for updating the zoom level of the video display canvas. Here's a breakdown of its functionality:
1. Method Signature:
   The method signature indicates that update_zoom() takes an optional event parameter. This parameter allows the method to be bound to an event, such as a combobox selection change.
2. Functionality:
   - When called, the method simply invokes the show_frame() method.
   - The purpose of calling show_frame() here is to update the display with the current frame while considering the new zoom level.
   - By calling show_frame(), the video player application ensures that any changes in the zoom scale are immediately reflected in the displayed video frames.
3. Optional Event Parameter:
   - The method is designed to accept an optional event parameter, which allows it to be used as a callback function for events triggered by GUI elements like combobox selection changes.
   - If bound to an event, such as a combobox selection change event, the method can respond dynamically to user interactions, updating the zoom level based on the selected value.

Overall, the update_zoom() method serves as a convenient way to refresh the video display with the current frame while taking into account any changes in the zoom scale. It ensures that the video player application maintains visual consistency and responsiveness when users adjust the zoom level through GUI interactions.

Showing Frame

```
def show_frame(self):
    if self.video:
        if not self.paused:
            self.frame_index += 1
            if self.frame_index >= len(self.video):
                self.frame_index = 0  # Reset frame index if it exceeds the maximum index
        if 0 <= self.frame_index < len(self.video):  # Check if frame index is within range
            try:
                frame = self.video.get_data(self.frame_index)
```

```
                    frame = Image.fromarray(frame)
                    frame = frame.resize((frame.width * self.zoom_scale.get(),
frame.height * self.zoom_scale.get()))
                    photo = ImageTk.PhotoImage(frame)
                    self.photo = photo  # Save object reference to PhotoImage
globally
                    self.canvas.delete("video")  # Delete previous image
                    self.canvas.create_image(self.current_x, self.current_y,
anchor="nw", image=photo, tags="video")
                    if not self.paused:
                        self.canvas.after(30, self.show_frame)
            except Exception as e:
                print("Error:", e)
```

The show_frame() method is responsible for displaying video frames on the canvas. Here's a detailed explanation of its functionality:

1. Video Playback Control:
   - The method first checks if a video is loaded (if self.video) and whether the playback is paused (if not self.paused).
   - If the video is not paused, the frame index is incremented to proceed to the next frame. If the frame index exceeds the maximum index (len(self.video)), it is reset to 0 to loop back to the beginning of the video.

2. Frame Display:
   - Once the appropriate frame index is determined, the method retrieves the corresponding frame data using self.video.get_data(self.frame_index).
   - The frame data is converted to an Image object using Image.fromarray(frame).
   - The Image object is then resized based on the current zoom scale (self.zoom_scale.get()) to adjust the displayed frame size.
   - Finally, the resized frame is converted to a PhotoImage object (photo), and its reference is stored in self.photo to prevent it from being garbage collected.
   - The canvas is cleared of any previous images tagged as "video" (self.canvas.delete("video")), and the new frame is displayed using self.canvas.create_image().

3. Continued Playback:
   - If the video is not paused, the method schedules the next frame to be displayed after a delay of 30 milliseconds using self.canvas.after(30, self.show_frame).
   - This scheduling allows for smooth and continuous video playback by updating the canvas with successive frames at regular intervals.

4. Error Handling:
   - The method includes exception handling to catch any errors that may occur during frame retrieval or processing. If an error occurs, it prints the error message to the console for debugging purposes.

Overall, the show_frame() method ensures the continuous display of video frames on the canvas while taking into account the current playback state and zoom scale. It forms the core functionality of the video player application by providing smooth and responsive video playback capabilities.

Enhancing User Interaction

```
def on_mousewheel(self, event):
    direction = event.delta // 120
    current_value = int(self.zoom_scale.get())
    if direction == 1 and current_value < 10:
        current_value += 1
    elif direction == -1 and current_value > 1:
        current_value -= 1
    self.zoom_scale.set(current_value)
    self.update_zoom()

def on_press(self, event):
    self.start_x = event.x
    self.start_y = event.y

def on_drag(self, event):
    if self.start_x and self.start_y:
        x_offset = event.x - self.start_x
        y_offset = event.y - self.start_y
        self.current_x += x_offset  # Update current position
        self.current_y += y_offset  # Update current position
        self.canvas.move("video", x_offset, y_offset)
        self.start_x = event.x
        self.start_y = event.y

def on_scroll(self, *args):
    scroll_pos = self.scrollbar.get()
    self.current_x = -scroll_pos * self.canvas.winfo_width()
    self.canvas.xview_moveto(scroll_pos)
    self.frame_index = int(scroll_pos * len(self.video))  # Update frame index
    self.show_frame()
```

The additional methods on_mousewheel(), on_press(), on_drag(), and on_scroll() provide interactivity to the video player application. Here's an explanation of each method:
1. on_mousewheel(self, event):
    - This method handles mouse wheel events, which are used to control the zoom level of the displayed video frames.
    - It calculates the direction of the mouse wheel movement (direction) and adjusts the current zoom scale (current_value) accordingly.
    - The zoom scale is limited to a range between 1 and 10 to prevent excessive zooming.
    - Finally, it updates the zoom scale and calls the update_zoom method to reflect the changes in frame size.

2. on_press(self, event):
   - This method is triggered when the user presses the left mouse button on the canvas.
   - It records the coordinates (event.x, event.y) of the mouse cursor when the press event occurs, indicating the starting position for dragging.
3. on_drag(self, event):
   - This method allows the user to drag the displayed video frame within the canvas.
   - It calculates the offset between the current mouse position (event.x, event.y) and the starting position (self.start_x, self.start_y).
   - The current position (self.current_x, self.current_y) is updated based on the offset, and the video frame is moved accordingly using the canvas.move method.
4. on_scroll(self, *args):
   - This method is called when the horizontal scrollbar is manipulated.
   - It retrieves the current scrollbar position (scroll_pos) and calculates the corresponding frame index based on the position relative to the video length.
   - The canvas is scrolled horizontally to align with the selected frame, and the show_frame() method is called to display the updated frame.

These methods enhance user interaction with the video player application by providing functionalities such as zooming, panning, and frame navigation, thus improving the overall user experience.

Jumping to a Specific Time in Video

```
def jump_to_time(self):
    time_str = self.time_entry.get()
    try:
        time_seconds = float(time_str)
        if 0 <= time_seconds:
            self.frame_index = int(time_seconds * self.video.get_meta_data()['fps'])
            self.show_frame()
    except ValueError:
        pass
```

The jump_to_time() method allows users to jump to a specific time in the video. Here's a breakdown of how it works:
1. Retrieving Input:
   - It retrieves the time input from the time_entry widget, which is an entry field where users can input the time they want to jump to.
2. Converting to Seconds:

- The input time is converted to seconds by parsing it as a float value. This ensures flexibility in accepting time input in various formats (e.g., seconds, milliseconds).
- If the input cannot be converted to a float (e.g., if the input contains non-numeric characters), a ValueError is raised, and the method gracefully handles this exception by doing nothing (pass statement).

3. Calculating Frame Index:
    - Once the time in seconds is obtained, it's multiplied by the frames per second (FPS) of the video, which is retrieved from the video metadata using self.video.get_meta_data()['fps'].
    - This calculation yields the frame index corresponding to the specified time in the video.
4. Updating Display:
    - The frame_index attribute is updated with the calculated frame index.
    - Finally, the show_frame() method is called to display the frame corresponding to the new frame index.

By providing this functionality, users can easily navigate to specific moments in the video by entering the desired time, enhancing the usability and efficiency of the application.

Extracting Frame

```
def extract_frame(self):
    frame_number_str = self.frame_entry.get()
    try:
        frame_number = int(frame_number_str)
        if 0 <= frame_number < len(self.video):
            frame = self.video.get_data(frame_number)
            self.show_extracted_frame(frame, frame_number)
    except ValueError:
        pass
```

The extract_frame() method enables users to extract and display a specific frame from the video. Here's how it operates:

1. Retrieving Frame Number Input:
    - It retrieves the frame number input from the frame_entry widget, which is an entry field where users can input the frame number they want to extract.
2. Converting to Integer:
    - The input frame number is converted to an integer. This ensures that the application can handle only valid numerical inputs for frame numbers.

- If the input cannot be converted to an integer (e.g., if the input contains non-numeric characters), a ValueError is raised, and the method gracefully handles this exception by doing nothing (pass statement).
3. Checking Validity:
    - If the converted frame number falls within the valid range of frame indices (i.e., between 0 and the total number of frames in the video), the method proceeds with frame extraction.
    - Otherwise, if the frame number is out of range, no action is taken.
4. Extracting and Displaying Frame:
    - If the frame number is valid, the method extracts the corresponding frame from the video using self.video.get_data(frame_number).
    - The extracted frame, along with its frame number, is passed to the show_extracted_frame() method for display.

By implementing this functionality, users can easily select specific frames of interest for further analysis or examination, enhancing the utility and versatility of the application.

Showing Extracted Frame

```
def show_extracted_frame(self, frame, frame_number):
    extracted_frame_window = tk.Toplevel(self.master)
    extracted_frame_window.title(f"Frame yang Diekstraksi (Frame {frame_number}) --- RISMON HASIHOLAN SIANIPAR")

    extracted_frame_label = tk.Label(extracted_frame_window, text=f"Frame yang Diekstraksi (Frame {frame_number})")
    extracted_frame_label.pack()

    height, width, _ = frame.shape  # Get dimensions of the frame
    extracted_photo = ImageTk.PhotoImage(image=Image.fromarray(frame))

    extracted_frame_canvas = tk.Canvas(extracted_frame_window, width=width, height=height)
    extracted_frame_canvas.pack()
    extracted_frame_canvas.create_image(0, 0, anchor="nw", image=extracted_photo)
    extracted_frame_canvas.image = extracted_photo

    # Plot histogram for each RGB channel
    fig, axs = plt.subplots(1, 3, figsize=(20, 3))
    colors = ['red', 'green', 'blue']
    for i, color in enumerate(['R', 'G', 'B']):
        hist, bins, _ = axs[i].hist(frame[:,:,i].ravel(), bins=64, range=(0, 255), color=colors[i], alpha=0.7)
```

```python
        axs[i].set_title(f"Histogram of {color} Channel (Frame {frame_number})",
fontsize=14, fontweight='bold', color='blue')
        axs[i].set_xlabel("Pixel Value", fontsize=12)
        axs[i].set_ylabel("Frequency", fontsize=12)
        axs[i].grid(True, linestyle='--', linewidth=0.5, color='gray', alpha=0.5)
        axs[i].tick_params(axis='both', which='major', labelsize=10)

        # Add frequency values above each bar
        for bar, frequency in zip(hist, bins[1:]):
            if bar > 0:
                axs[i].annotate(f'{frequency:.0f}', xy=(bins[np.where(hist == bar)[0][0]] + (bins[1] - bins[0]) / 2, bar),
                                xytext=(0, 3), textcoords='offset points',
ha='center', va='bottom', fontsize=6)
        plt.tight_layout()

        # Calculate multiple hash values of the frame
        hash_algorithms = ['md5', 'sha1', 'sha256', 'sha224', 'sha384', 'sha512',
'blake2b', 'ripemd160']
        hash_values = {}
        for algorithm in hash_algorithms:
            hash_obj = hashlib.new(algorithm)
            hash_obj.update(frame.tobytes())
            hash_value = hash_obj.hexdigest()
            hash_values[algorithm] = hash_value

        # Display hash values
        hash_listbox = tk.Listbox(extracted_frame_window, height=8, width=40,
font=("Arial", 13), bg="gray25", fg="white")
        hash_listbox.pack(fill=tk.BOTH, expand=True)

        # Add horizontal scrollbar if needed
        scrollbar = tk.Scrollbar(extracted_frame_window, orient=tk.HORIZONTAL,
command=hash_listbox.xview)
        scrollbar.pack(side=tk.BOTTOM, fill=tk.X)
        hash_listbox.config(xscrollcommand=scrollbar.set)

        for algorithm, value in hash_values.items():
            hash_listbox.insert(tk.END, f"{algorithm}: {value}")


        hist_canvas = FigureCanvasTkAgg(fig, master=extracted_frame_window)
        hist_canvas.draw()
        hist_canvas.get_tk_widget().pack()
```

The show_extracted_frame() method is responsible for displaying a window containing information about the extracted frame. Here's how it works:

1. Creating a New Window:
    - It creates a new Toplevel window (extracted_frame_window) to display the extracted frame along with its details.
2. Setting Window Title:
    - The window title is set to include the frame number, providing context for the user.
3. Displaying Frame:
    - The extracted frame is displayed in a Canvas widget (extracted_frame_canvas) within the window.
    - The frame is converted to a PhotoImage object (extracted_photo) using ImageTk.PhotoImage, which allows for display in the Canvas.
4. Plotting Histogram:
    - Histograms for each RGB channel of the frame are plotted using matplotlib.
    - Three subplots (axs) are created for the red, green, and blue channels, respectively.
    - Histograms are plotted using axs.hist, and frequency values are annotated above each bar.
5. Calculating Hash Values:
    - Hash values for the frame are calculated using various algorithms (e.g., MD5, SHA-1) from the hashlib module.
    - Each hash value is inserted into a Listbox widget (hash_listbox) for display.
6. Displaying Hash Values:
    - Hash values are displayed in the hash_listbox, allowing users to view the hashes calculated for the frame.
    - If the content exceeds the width of the Listbox, a horizontal scrollbar is added for navigation.
7. Displaying Histogram Plot:
    - The histogram plot is displayed using FigureCanvasTkAgg, allowing users to visualize the distribution of pixel values in the frame.

By providing detailed information about the extracted frame, including its visual representation and associated histogram and hash values, users can analyze and inspect specific frames of interest more effectively within the application's interface.

Opening Another Instance of Application

```
def open_another_player(self):
    # Open another instance of the application
    root = tk.Toplevel(self.master)
    app = VideoPlayerApp(root)
```

The open_another_player() method serves to open another instance of the video player application within a new window. Here's a breakdown of its functionality:
1. Creating a New Window:
    - It creates a new Toplevel window (root) to host the additional instance of the video player application.
2. Initializing a New Instance:
    - Within this new window, a new instance of the VideoPlayerApp class (app) is instantiated. This effectively creates a separate instance of the video player application with its own set of widgets and functionalities.
3. Independent Application:
    - The new instance of the video player application operates independently of the original instance. Any actions performed in one instance do not affect the other, allowing users to interact with multiple video players simultaneously.

By enabling the opening of multiple instances of the application, users have the flexibility to work with multiple videos or analyze different sections of the same video concurrently, enhancing their overall user experience and workflow efficiency.

Entry Point of Application

```
def main():
    root = tk.Tk()
    app = VideoPlayerApp(root)
    root.mainloop()

if __name__ == "__main__":
    main()
```

The main function serves as the entry point of the video player application. Here's how it works:
1. Root Window Initialization:
    - It creates the main application window using tk.Tk() and assigns it to the variable root.
2. Video Player Application Instance:
    - It instantiates the VideoPlayerApp class, passing the root window as its master, which initializes the video player application within the main window.
3. Event Loop:
    - It starts the event loop by calling root.mainloop(), which continuously listens for events (such as user interactions) and updates the GUI accordingly.
4. Conditional Execution:

- The if __name__ == "__main__": block ensures that main is executed only if the script is run directly (not imported as a module). This is a common Python idiom to prevent code from running when a module is imported as part of another script.

By encapsulating the instantiation of the VideoPlayerApp class and the event loop within the main function, the script maintains modularity and can be easily integrated into larger projects or executed standalone as a video player application.

Running Program
Run Program. The GUI is displayed below.

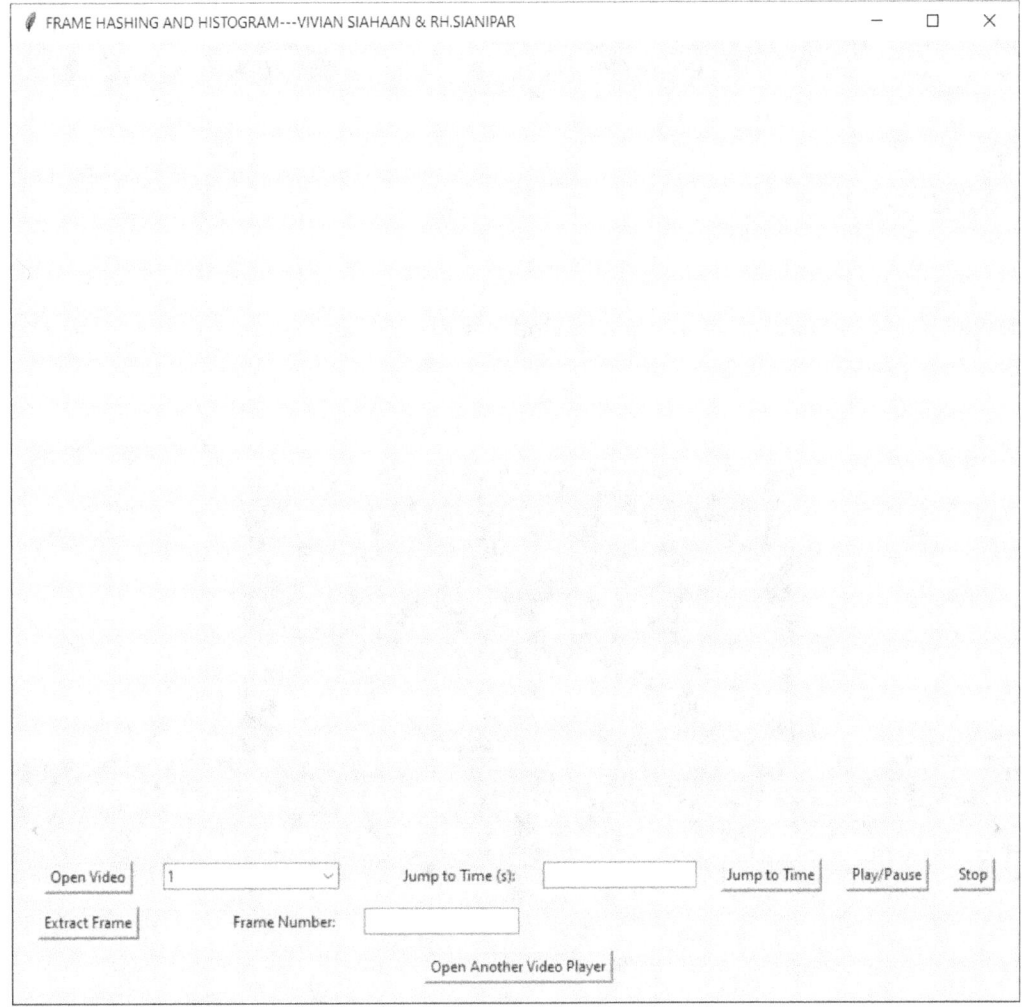

Then, click on Open Video button, choose a video file and type a specific frame number (115):

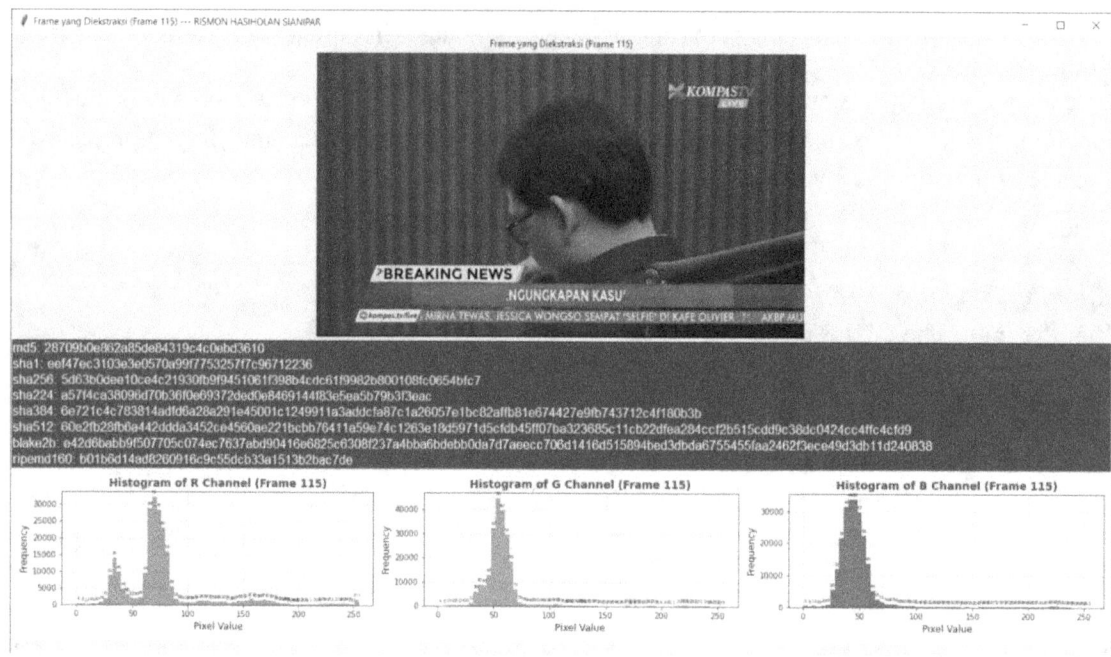

Then, click on Open Video button, choose another video file and type a specific frame number (221):

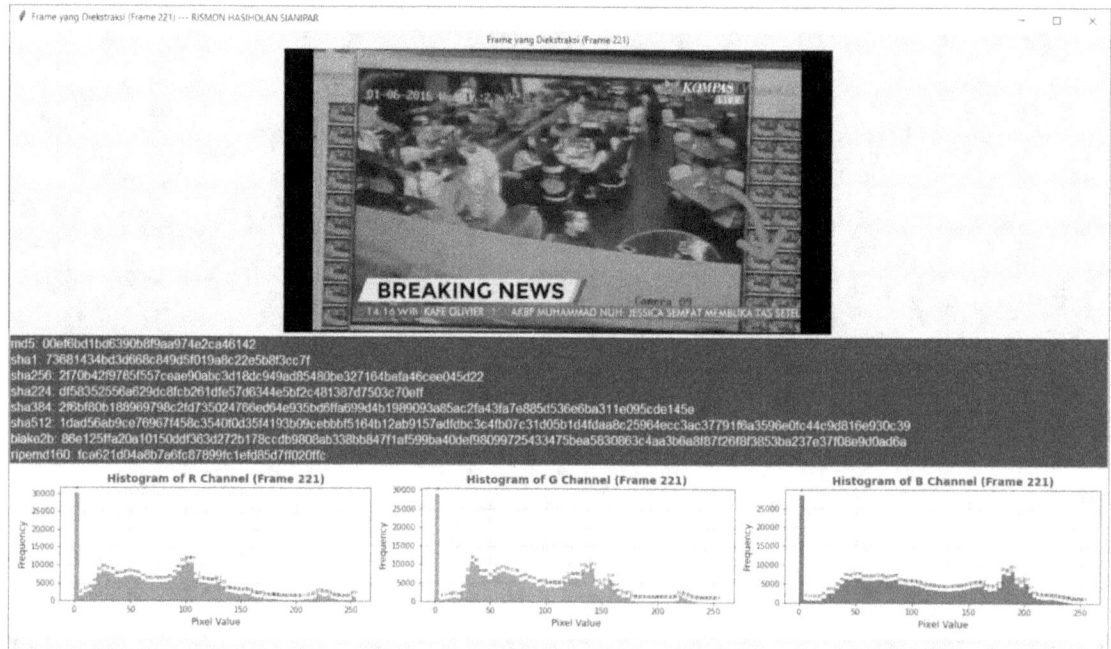

Then, type another specific frame number (315):

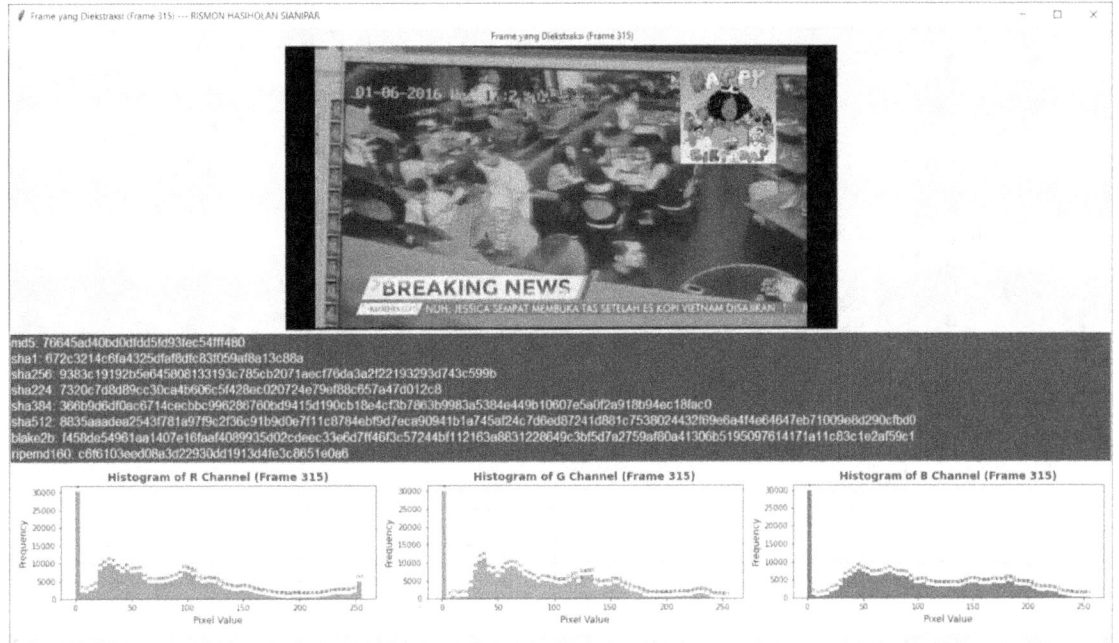

Full Source Code

```python
import tkinter as tk
from tkinter import ttk
from tkinter import filedialog
from PIL import Image, ImageTk
import imageio
import matplotlib.pyplot as plt
from matplotlib.backends.backend_tkagg import FigureCanvasTkAgg
import hashlib
import numpy as np


class VideoPlayerApp:
    def __init__(self, master):
        self.master = master
        self.master.title("FRAME HASHING AND HISTOGRAM---VIVIAN SIAHAAN - RH.SIANIPAR")

        self.video = None
        self.video_path = None
        self.paused = False
        self.zoom_scale = tk.IntVar(value=1)
        self.frame_index = 0
        self.start_x = None
        self.start_y = None
        self.current_x = 0
```

```python
        self.current_y = 0
        self.photo = None  # Save object reference to PhotoImage globally

        self.create_widgets()

    def create_widgets(self):
        # Panel for video display
        video_panel = tk.Frame(self.master)
        video_panel.grid(row=0, column=0, padx=10, pady=10, sticky="nsew")

        # Canvas to display the video
        canvas_width = 800
        canvas_height = 600
        self.canvas = tk.Canvas(video_panel, width=canvas_width, height=canvas_height)
        self.canvas.pack(side="top", fill="both", expand=True)
        self.canvas.bind("<MouseWheel>", self.on_mousewheel)
        self.canvas.bind("<ButtonPress-1>", self.on_press)
        self.canvas.bind("<B1-Motion>", self.on_drag)

        # Scrollbar
        self.scrollbar = tk.Scrollbar(video_panel, orient="horizontal", command=self.on_scroll)
        self.scrollbar.pack(side="bottom", fill="x")

        self.canvas.configure(xscrollcommand=self.scrollbar.set)

        # Panel for control buttons
        control_panel = tk.Frame(self.master)
        control_panel.grid(row=1, column=0, padx=10, pady=(0, 10), sticky="ew")

        # Button to open a video file
        self.open_button = tk.Button(control_panel, text="Open Video", command=self.open_video)
        self.open_button.grid(row=0, column=0, padx=10, pady=5)

        # Combobox for selecting zoom scale
        self.zoom_combobox = ttk.Combobox(control_panel, textvariable=self.zoom_scale, values=list(range(1, 11)))
        self.zoom_combobox.grid(row=0, column=1, padx=10, pady=5)
        self.zoom_combobox.bind("<<ComboboxSelected>>", self.update_zoom)

        # Label and entry for specifying time
        self.time_label = tk.Label(control_panel, text="Jump to Time (s):")
        self.time_label.grid(row=0, column=2, padx=10, pady=5, sticky="e")
        self.time_entry = ttk.Entry(control_panel)
        self.time_entry.grid(row=0, column=3, padx=10, pady=5, sticky="w")
        self.time_entry.bind("<Return>", lambda event: self.jump_to_time())

        # Button to jump to specified time
        self.jump_button = tk.Button(control_panel, text="Jump to Time", command=self.jump_to_time)
        self.jump_button.grid(row=0, column=4, padx=10, pady=5)

        # Button to play/pause the video
        self.play_button = tk.Button(control_panel, text="Play/Pause", command=self.toggle_play_pause)
        self.play_button.grid(row=0, column=5, padx=10, pady=5)
```

```python
        # Button to stop the video
        self.stop_button = tk.Button(control_panel, text="Stop", 
command=self.stop_video)
        self.stop_button.grid(row=0, column=6, padx=10, pady=5)

        # Button to extract frame
        self.extract_button = tk.Button(control_panel, text="Extract Frame", 
command=self.extract_frame)
        self.extract_button.grid(row=1, column=0, padx=10, pady=5)

        # Label and entry for frame number
        self.frame_label = tk.Label(control_panel, text="Frame Number:")
        self.frame_label.grid(row=1, column=1, padx=10, pady=5, sticky="e")
        self.frame_entry = ttk.Entry(control_panel)
        self.frame_entry.grid(row=1, column=2, padx=10, pady=5, sticky="w")
        self.frame_entry.bind("<Return>", lambda event: self.extract_frame())

        # Button to open another instance of the application
        self.open_another_button = tk.Button(control_panel, text="Open Another Video 
Player", command=self.open_another_player)
        self.open_another_button.grid(row=2, column=0, columnspan=7, padx=10, pady=5)

    def open_video(self):
        self.video_path = filedialog.askopenfilename(filetypes=[("Video files", 
"*.mp4;*.avi;*.mkv")])
        if self.video_path:
            self.video = imageio.get_reader(self.video_path)
            self.play_video()

    def play_video(self):
        if self.video:
            self.paused = False
            self.show_frame()

    def stop_video(self):
        self.paused = True
        self.frame_index = 0
        self.current_x = 0
        self.current_y = 0  # Reset the current position
        self.show_frame()

    def toggle_play_pause(self):
        self.paused = not self.paused
        if not self.paused:
            self.play_video()

    def update_zoom(self, event=None):
        self.show_frame()

    def show_frame(self):
        if self.video:
            if not self.paused:
                self.frame_index += 1
                if self.frame_index >= len(self.video):
                    self.frame_index = 0  # Reset frame index if it exceeds the 
maximum index
```

```python
            if 0 <= self.frame_index < len(self.video):  # Check if frame index is within range
                try:
                    frame = self.video.get_data(self.frame_index)
                    frame = Image.fromarray(frame)
                    frame = frame.resize((frame.width * self.zoom_scale.get(), frame.height * self.zoom_scale.get()))
                    photo = ImageTk.PhotoImage(frame)
                    self.photo = photo  # Save object reference to PhotoImage globally
                    self.canvas.delete("video")  # Delete previous image
                    self.canvas.create_image(self.current_x, self.current_y, anchor="nw", image=photo, tags="video")
                    if not self.paused:
                        self.canvas.after(30, self.show_frame)
                except Exception as e:
                    print("Error:", e)

    def on_mousewheel(self, event):
        direction = event.delta // 120
        current_value = int(self.zoom_scale.get())
        if direction == 1 and current_value < 10:
            current_value += 1
        elif direction == -1 and current_value > 1:
            current_value -= 1
        self.zoom_scale.set(current_value)
        self.update_zoom()

    def on_press(self, event):
        self.start_x = event.x
        self.start_y = event.y

    def on_drag(self, event):
        if self.start_x and self.start_y:
            x_offset = event.x - self.start_x
            y_offset = event.y - self.start_y
            self.current_x += x_offset  # Update current position
            self.current_y += y_offset  # Update current position
            self.canvas.move("video", x_offset, y_offset)
            self.start_x = event.x
            self.start_y = event.y

    def on_scroll(self, *args):
        scroll_pos = self.scrollbar.get()
        self.current_x = -scroll_pos * self.canvas.winfo_width()
        self.canvas.xview_moveto(scroll_pos)
        self.frame_index = int(scroll_pos * len(self.video))  # Update frame index
        self.show_frame()

    def jump_to_time(self):
        time_str = self.time_entry.get()
        try:
            time_seconds = float(time_str)
            if 0 <= time_seconds:
                self.frame_index = int(time_seconds * self.video.get_meta_data()['fps'])
                self.show_frame()
        except ValueError:
```

```python
            pass

    def extract_frame(self):
        frame_number_str = self.frame_entry.get()
        try:
            frame_number = int(frame_number_str)
            if 0 <= frame_number < len(self.video):
                frame = self.video.get_data(frame_number)
                self.show_extracted_frame(frame, frame_number)
        except ValueError:
            pass

    def show_extracted_frame(self, frame, frame_number):
        extracted_frame_window = tk.Toplevel(self.master)
        extracted_frame_window.title(f"Frame yang Diekstraksi (Frame {frame_number}) --- RISMON HASIHOLAN SIANIPAR")

        extracted_frame_label = tk.Label(extracted_frame_window, text=f"Frame yang Diekstraksi (Frame {frame_number})")
        extracted_frame_label.pack()

        height, width, _ = frame.shape  # Get dimensions of the frame
        extracted_photo = ImageTk.PhotoImage(image=Image.fromarray(frame))

        extracted_frame_canvas = tk.Canvas(extracted_frame_window, width=width, height=height)
        extracted_frame_canvas.pack()
        extracted_frame_canvas.create_image(0, 0, anchor="nw", image=extracted_photo)
        extracted_frame_canvas.image = extracted_photo

        # Plot histogram for each RGB channel
        fig, axs = plt.subplots(1, 3, figsize=(20, 3))
        colors = ['red', 'green', 'blue']
        for i, color in enumerate(['R', 'G', 'B']):
            hist, bins, _ = axs[i].hist(frame[:,:,i].ravel(), bins=64, range=(0, 255), color=colors[i], alpha=0.7)
            axs[i].set_title(f"Histogram of {color} Channel (Frame {frame_number})", fontsize=14, fontweight='bold', color='blue')
            axs[i].set_xlabel("Pixel Value", fontsize=12)
            axs[i].set_ylabel("Frequency", fontsize=12)
            axs[i].grid(True, linestyle='--', linewidth=0.5, color='gray', alpha=0.5)
            axs[i].tick_params(axis='both', which='major', labelsize=10)

            # Add frequency values above each bar
            for bar, frequency in zip(hist, bins[1:]):
                if bar > 0:
                    axs[i].annotate(f'{frequency:.0f}', xy=(bins[np.where(hist == bar)[0][0]] + (bins[1] - bins[0]) / 2, bar),
                                    xytext=(0, 3), textcoords='offset points',
                                    ha='center', va='bottom', fontsize=6)
        plt.tight_layout()

        # Calculate multiple hash values of the frame
        hash_algorithms = ['md5', 'sha1', 'sha256', 'sha224', 'sha384', 'sha512', 'blake2b', 'ripemd160']
        hash_values = {}
        for algorithm in hash_algorithms:
            hash_obj = hashlib.new(algorithm)
```

```python
            hash_obj.update(frame.tobytes())
            hash_value = hash_obj.hexdigest()
            hash_values[algorithm] = hash_value

        # Display hash values
        hash_listbox = tk.Listbox(extracted_frame_window, height=8, width=40, 
font=("Arial", 13), bg="gray25", fg="white")
        hash_listbox.pack(fill=tk.BOTH, expand=True)

        # Add horizontal scrollbar if needed
        scrollbar = tk.Scrollbar(extracted_frame_window, orient=tk.HORIZONTAL, 
command=hash_listbox.xview)
        scrollbar.pack(side=tk.BOTTOM, fill=tk.X)
        hash_listbox.config(xscrollcommand=scrollbar.set)

        for algorithm, value in hash_values.items():
            hash_listbox.insert(tk.END, f"{algorithm}: {value}")


        hist_canvas = FigureCanvasTkAgg(fig, master=extracted_frame_window)
        hist_canvas.draw()
        hist_canvas.get_tk_widget().pack()

    def open_another_player(self):
        # Open another instance of the application
        root = tk.Toplevel(self.master)
        app = VideoPlayerApp(root)

def main():
    root = tk.Tk()
    app = VideoPlayerApp(root)
    root.mainloop()

if __name__ == "__main__":
    main()
```

DETECTING EDGES ON EACH FRAME IN VIDEO

DETECTING EDGES ON EACH FRAME IN VIDEO

This project implemens a Python application using the tkinter library to create a video player with edge detection capabilities. The purpose of the code is to allow users to open video files, play, pause, stop, and extract frames from the video. Additionally, the application provides functionality for edge detection using various algorithms and displays the detected edges in a separate window along with histograms and hash values.

The VideoPlayerEdge class encapsulates the functionality of the application. Upon initialization, it sets up the main window with widgets for displaying the video, control buttons, and panels for histograms and hash values. Users can interact with the application by opening video files, controlling playback, jumping to specific times, and extracting frames.

The open_video method allows users to select a video file from their system, which is then loaded into the application using the imageio library. The play_video(), stop_video(), and toggle_play_pause() methods control the playback of the video, while the jump_to_time method enables users to jump to a specific time in the video.

The extract_frame() method allows users to extract frames from the video and display them in a separate window. This window includes the extracted frame, edge detection canvas, histograms for each RGB channel, and hash values computed for the frame. The apply_edge_detection()

method applies various edge detection algorithms to the extracted frame and displays the results in the edge detection canvas.

The code also provides implementations for several edge detection algorithms, including Canny, Sobel, Prewitt, Laplacian, Scharr, Roberts, FreiChen, Kirsch, Robinson, and Gaussian. These algorithms are applied to each RGB channel of the extracted frame, and the resulting edge-detected images are displayed in the edge detection canvas.

Finally, the open_another_player() method allows users to open another instance of the application in a separate window, enabling simultaneous playback and analysis of multiple videos. The main function initializes the main application window and starts the event loop. Overall, the code provides a comprehensive video player with edge detection functionality for users to analyze video content visually.

Importing Libraries

```
import tkinter as tk
from tkinter import ttk
from tkinter import filedialog
from PIL import Image, ImageTk
import imageio
import matplotlib.pyplot as plt
from matplotlib.backends.backend_tkagg import FigureCanvasTkAgg
import hashlib
import numpy as np
import cv2
import re
```

This code imports several libraries that are commonly used for developing graphical user interfaces (GUIs), image processing, and data visualization applications in Python:
- tkinter: This library provides the Tk GUI toolkit for creating graphical user interfaces in Python. It is the standard GUI toolkit for Python and provides various widgets and tools for building interactive applications.
- ttk: This submodule of tkinter provides access to the Tk themed widget set, which includes more modern and visually appealing widgets compared to the standard Tkinter widgets.
- filedialog: This submodule of tkinter provides dialog boxes for file selection, allowing users to choose files from their system.
- PIL (Python Imaging Library) / Pillow: This library provides image processing capabilities in Python. It is used for opening, manipulating, and saving many different image file formats.
- imageio: This library provides an easy interface to read and write a wide range of image data, including animated images, video files, and volumetric data.

- matplotlib.pyplot: This library is widely used for creating static, animated, and interactive visualizations in Python. It provides a MATLAB-like plotting interface for generating plots and charts.
- matplotlib.backends.backend_tkagg: This module provides the backend for embedding matplotlib figures into Tkinter applications. It allows matplotlib plots to be displayed within Tkinter GUI windows.
- hashlib: This library provides cryptographic hash functions in Python. It is used for generating hash values of data, which can be used for various purposes such as data integrity verification and secure storage.
- numpy: This library is a fundamental package for scientific computing with Python. It provides support for large, multi-dimensional arrays and matrices, along with a collection of mathematical functions to operate on these arrays efficiently.
- cv2 (OpenCV): This library is a popular computer vision library with a wide range of functions for image and video analysis, including object detection, image processing, and machine learning.
- re (Regular Expressions): This module provides support for regular expressions in Python. It is used for pattern matching and string manipulation tasks.

These libraries provide the necessary tools and functionalities for building applications that involve GUIs, image processing, data visualization, and cryptographic operations.

Class and Its Constructor

```python
class VideoPlayerEdge:
    def __init__(self, master):
        self.master = master
        self.master.title("FRAME EDGE DETECTION---VIVIAN SIAHAAN & RH.SIANIPAR")

        self.video = None
        self.video_path = None
        self.paused = False
        self.zoom_scale = tk.IntVar(value=1)
        self.frame_index = 0
        self.start_x = None
        self.start_y = None
        self.current_x = 0
        self.current_y = 0
        self.photo = None  # Save object reference to PhotoImage globally

        self.create_widgets()
```

This VideoPlayerEdge class serves as the core component of a video player application with edge detection capabilities. Let's break down the purpose of its attributes and methods:

1. __init__(self, master): This method serves as the constructor of the VideoPlayerEdge class. It initializes various attributes of the video player instance.
    - self.master: This attribute stores the reference to the master (parent) widget, typically a Tkinter window, where the video player will be placed.
    - self.master.title("FRAME EDGE DETECTION---VIVIAN SIAHAAN & RH.SIANIPAR"): This line sets the title of the Tkinter window to "FRAME EDGE DETECTION---VIVIAN SIAHAAN & RH.SIANIPAR".
    - self.video: This attribute stores the video object, which represents the currently loaded video file.
    - self.video_path: This attribute stores the path of the video file currently being played.
    - self.paused: This attribute is a boolean flag indicating whether the video playback is paused (True) or active (False).
    - self.zoom_scale: This attribute stores an IntVar object representing the zoom scale of the video display.
    - self.frame_index: This attribute stores the index of the current frame being displayed.
    - self.start_x, self.start_y: These attributes store the starting coordinates of a mouse drag event used for panning the video display.
    - self.current_x, self.current_y: These attributes store the current coordinates of the video display after panning.
    - self.photo: This attribute stores a reference to the PhotoImage object representing the current frame displayed in the video player.
2. create_widgets(self): This method is responsible for creating and configuring the GUI widgets for the video player.
    - It creates a canvas widget to display the video frames.
    - It creates a scrollbar widget for horizontal scrolling.
    - It creates buttons for controlling video playback (open, play/pause, stop, jump to time, extract frame).
    - It creates an entry and a combobox for specifying and selecting the zoom scale.
    - It binds event handlers for mouse wheel scrolling, mouse button press, and mouse button drag events.

Overall, the __init__() method initializes the attributes needed for video playback and edge detection, while the create_widgets method sets up the graphical user interface for the video player application.

Creating Widgets

```python
    def create_widgets(self):
        # Panel for video display
        video_panel = tk.Frame(self.master)
        video_panel.grid(row=0, column=0, padx=10, pady=10, sticky="nsew")

        # Canvas to display the video
        canvas_width = 800
        canvas_height = 600
        self.canvas = tk.Canvas(video_panel, width=canvas_width, height=canvas_height)
        self.canvas.pack(side="top", fill="both", expand=True)
        self.canvas.bind("<MouseWheel>", self.on_mousewheel)
        self.canvas.bind("<ButtonPress-1>", self.on_press)
        self.canvas.bind("<B1-Motion>", self.on_drag)

        # Scrollbar
        self.scrollbar = tk.Scrollbar(video_panel, orient="horizontal", command=self.on_scroll)
        self.scrollbar.pack(side="bottom", fill="x")

        self.canvas.configure(xscrollcommand=self.scrollbar.set)

        # Panel for control buttons
        control_panel = tk.Frame(self.master)
        control_panel.grid(row=1, column=0, padx=10, pady=(0, 10), sticky="ew")

        # Button to open a video file
        self.open_button = tk.Button(control_panel, text="Open Video", command=self.open_video)
        self.open_button.grid(row=0, column=0, padx=10, pady=5)

        # Combobox for selecting zoom scale
        self.zoom_combobox = ttk.Combobox(control_panel, textvariable=self.zoom_scale, values=list(range(1, 11)))
        self.zoom_combobox.grid(row=0, column=1, padx=10, pady=5)
        self.zoom_combobox.bind("<<ComboboxSelected>>", self.update_zoom)

        # Label and entry for specifying time
        self.time_label = tk.Label(control_panel, text="Jump to Time (s):")
        self.time_label.grid(row=0, column=2, padx=10, pady=5, sticky="e")
        self.time_entry = ttk.Entry(control_panel)
        self.time_entry.grid(row=0, column=3, padx=10, pady=5, sticky="w")
        self.time_entry.bind("<Return>", lambda event: self.jump_to_time())

        # Button to jump to specified time
```

```
        self.jump_button = tk.Button(control_panel, text="Jump to Time", 
command=self.jump_to_time)
        self.jump_button.grid(row=0, column=4, padx=10, pady=5)

        # Button to play/pause the video
        self.play_button = tk.Button(control_panel, text="Play/Pause", 
command=self.toggle_play_pause)
        self.play_button.grid(row=0, column=5, padx=10, pady=5)

        # Button to stop the video
        self.stop_button = tk.Button(control_panel, text="Stop", 
command=self.stop_video)
        self.stop_button.grid(row=0, column=6, padx=10, pady=5)

        # Button to extract frame
        self.extract_button = tk.Button(control_panel, text="Extract Frame", 
command=self.extract_frame)
        self.extract_button.grid(row=1, column=0, padx=10, pady=5)

        # Label and entry for frame number
        self.frame_label = tk.Label(control_panel, text="Frame Number:")
        self.frame_label.grid(row=1, column=1, padx=10, pady=5, sticky="e")
        self.frame_entry = ttk.Entry(control_panel)
        self.frame_entry.grid(row=1, column=2, padx=10, pady=5, sticky="w")
        self.frame_entry.bind("<Return>", lambda event: self.extract_frame())

        # Button to open another instance of the application
        self.open_another_button = tk.Button(control_panel, text="Open Another Video 
Player", command=self.open_another_player)
        self.open_another_button.grid(row=2, column=0, columnspan=7, padx=10, pady=5)
```

The create_widgets() method is responsible for creating the graphical user interface (GUI) elements of the video player application. Let's examine each widget created:

1. Video Panel and Canvas:
   - video_panel: A frame widget used to contain the video canvas.
   - self.canvas: A canvas widget where video frames will be displayed. It's configured to fill its parent widget (video_panel) and expand to fill available space. Mouse wheel scrolling ("<MouseWheel>"), mouse button press ("<ButtonPress-1>"), and mouse button drag ("<B1-Motion>") events are bound to this canvas.
2. Scrollbar:
   - self.scrollbar: A horizontal scrollbar widget attached to the video canvas. It allows users to scroll horizontally when the video width exceeds the canvas width.
3. Control Panel and Buttons:
   - control_panel: Another frame widget used to contain control buttons.

- self.open_button: Button to open a video file. When clicked, it triggers the open_video method.
- self.zoom_combobox: Combobox for selecting the zoom scale. It's bound to the update_zoom method.
- self.time_label, self.time_entry, self.jump_button: Widgets for specifying and jumping to a specific time in the video.
- self.play_button: Button to play/pause the video. Clicking toggles between play and pause states.
- self.stop_button: Button to stop the video playback.
- self.extract_button: Button to extract a frame from the video. Clicking triggers the extract_frame method.
- self.frame_label, self.frame_entry: Label and entry widgets for specifying the frame number to extract.
- self.open_another_button: Button to open another instance of the video player application. Clicking triggers the open_another_player method.

These widgets collectively provide the user interface elements necessary for controlling video playback, adjusting settings like zoom scale, jumping to specific times, and extracting frames, thereby enhancing the user experience of the video player application.

Opening, Playing, Stopping, and Toggling Video

```python
def open_video(self):
    self.video_path = filedialog.askopenfilename(filetypes=[("Video files", "*.mp4;*.avi;*.mkv")])
    if self.video_path:
        self.video = imageio.get_reader(self.video_path)
        self.play_video()

def play_video(self):
    if self.video:
        self.paused = False
        self.show_frame()

def stop_video(self):
    self.paused = True
    self.frame_index = 0
    self.current_x = 0
    self.current_y = 0   # Reset the current position
    self.show_frame()

def toggle_play_pause(self):
    self.paused = not self.paused
    if not self.paused:
        self.play_video()
```

These methods are responsible for handling video playback within the application:
1. open_video():
    - This method opens a file dialog window to prompt the user to select a video file.
    - If a file is selected (self.video_path is not None), it uses imageio.get_reader to open the selected video file for reading.
    - After successfully opening the video file, it calls the play_video() method to start playing the video.
2. play_video():
    - This method starts playing the video if one is loaded (self.video is not None).
    - It sets self.paused to False, indicating that the video is playing, and then calls the show_frame() method to display the video frames.
3. stop_video():
    - This method stops the video playback.
    - It sets self.paused to True, indicating that the video is paused.
    - Additionally, it resets self.frame_index, self.current_x, and self.current_y to their initial values, effectively resetting the video playback to the beginning.
4. toggle_play_pause():
    - This method toggles the play/pause state of the video.
    - If the video is currently paused (self.paused is True), it sets self.paused to False and resumes playback by calling self.play_video().
    - If the video is currently playing (self.paused is False), it sets self.paused to True, effectively pausing the video playback.

These methods collectively allow users to open, play, pause, and stop video playback within the application, providing essential functionality for interacting with the loaded video file.

Showing Frame

```
def update_zoom(self, event=None):
    self.show_frame()

def show_frame(self):
    if self.video:
        if not self.paused:
            self.frame_index += 1
            if self.frame_index >= len(self.video):
                self.frame_index = 0  # Reset frame index if it exceeds the maximum index
        if 0 <= self.frame_index < len(self.video):  # Check if frame index is within range
            try:
                frame = self.video.get_data(self.frame_index)
                frame = Image.fromarray(frame)
```

```
                    frame = frame.resize((frame.width * self.zoom_scale.get(),
frame.height * self.zoom_scale.get()))
                    photo = ImageTk.PhotoImage(frame)
                    self.photo = photo  # Save object reference to PhotoImage
globally
                    self.canvas.delete("video")  # Delete previous image
                    self.canvas.create_image(self.current_x, self.current_y,
anchor="nw", image=photo, tags="video")
                    if not self.paused:
                        self.canvas.after(30, self.show_frame)
                except Exception as e:
                    print("Error:", e)
```

The update_zoom() and show_frame() methods are crucial for displaying video frames with optional zoom functionality. Here's a breakdown of each:

1. update_zoom():
    - This method is triggered whenever the zoom scale is updated, either by manually selecting a value from the combobox or programmatically changing the zoom scale variable.
    - It simply calls the show_frame() method, refreshing the displayed frame with the updated zoom scale.
2. show_frame():
    - This method is responsible for displaying the current frame of the video on the canvas.
    - If a video is loaded (self.video is not None), it proceeds to retrieve the next frame.
    - If the video is playing (not paused), it increments the frame_index to move to the next frame. If the end of the video is reached, it resets the index to 0 to loop the video.
    - It checks if the current frame_index is within the range of available frames in the video.
    - Inside the try block, it attempts to retrieve the frame using self.video.get_data and converts it to a PIL Image object.
    - It then resizes the frame based on the current zoom scale (self.zoom_scale.get()), creating a zoomed-in or zoomed-out effect.
    - The resized frame is converted to a PhotoImage object using ImageTk.PhotoImage.
    - The new PhotoImage object is assigned to self.photo to maintain a reference and prevent it from being garbage collected.
    - Previous images on the canvas are deleted, and the new frame is drawn using self.canvas.create_image.
    - If the video is not paused, it schedules the show_frame method to be called again after a delay of 30 milliseconds (giving the appearance of continuous playback).

- Any exceptions that occur during this process are caught and printed to the console.

These methods work together to ensure that the video frames are displayed correctly on the canvas, taking into account the zoom scale and handling of frame index for continuous playback.

Handling Mouse Events

```python
def on_mousewheel(self, event):
    direction = event.delta // 120
    current_value = int(self.zoom_scale.get())
    if direction == 1 and current_value < 10:
        current_value += 1
    elif direction == -1 and current_value > 1:
        current_value -= 1
    self.zoom_scale.set(current_value)
    self.update_zoom()

def on_press(self, event):
    self.start_x = event.x
    self.start_y = event.y

def on_drag(self, event):
    if self.start_x and self.start_y:
        x_offset = event.x - self.start_x
        y_offset = event.y - self.start_y
        self.current_x += x_offset  # Update current position
        self.current_y += y_offset  # Update current position
        self.canvas.move("video", x_offset, y_offset)
        self.start_x = event.x
        self.start_y = event.y

def on_scroll(self, *args):
    scroll_pos = self.scrollbar.get()
    self.current_x = -scroll_pos * self.canvas.winfo_width()
    self.canvas.xview_moveto(scroll_pos)
    self.frame_index = int(scroll_pos * len(self.video))  # Update frame index
    self.show_frame()
```

These three methods, on_mousewheel(), on_press(), and on_drag(), handle user interactions with the canvas, such as zooming and panning, while on_scroll() manages horizontal scrolling:
1. on_mousewheel():
    - This method is triggered when the user scrolls the mouse wheel while the canvas has focus.
    - It calculates the direction of the mouse wheel movement (event.delta) and adjusts the zoom scale accordingly, within the range of 1 to 10.
    - After updating the zoom scale, it calls self.update_zoom() to refresh the displayed frame with the new zoom level.

2. on_press():
   - This method is called when the user presses the left mouse button on the canvas (<ButtonPress-1> event).
   - It records the coordinates (event.x and event.y) where the mouse click occurred, which will be used for panning.
3. on_drag():
   - This method is triggered when the user drags the mouse after clicking on the canvas (<B1-Motion> event).
   - It calculates the offset of the mouse movement relative to the initial click position (self.start_x and self.start_y).
   - It updates the current position (self.current_x and self.current_y) based on the offset and moves the video frame accordingly using self.canvas.move.
4. on_scroll():
   - This method is called when the horizontal scrollbar value changes.
   - It retrieves the current scrollbar position (scroll_pos) and calculates the corresponding x-coordinate for panning the video frame.
   - The canvas view is adjusted horizontally using self.canvas.xview_moveto, and the frame index is updated based on the scrollbar position to synchronize the frame displayed with the scrollbar position.
   - Finally, it calls self.show_frame() to display the updated frame.

These methods collectively enable the user to interact with the video player interface, zooming in/out, panning the video frame, and scrolling through the video timeline horizontally.

Jumping to a Specific Time

```python
def jump_to_time(self):
    time_str = self.time_entry.get()
    try:
        time_seconds = float(time_str)
        if 0 <= time_seconds:
            self.frame_index = int(time_seconds * self.video.get_meta_data()['fps'])
            self.show_frame()
    except ValueError:
        pass
```

The jump_to_time() method allows the user to jump to a specific time in the video based on the input provided in the entry widget (self.time_entry). Here's a breakdown of how it works:
1. It retrieves the time string entered by the user from the entry widget using self.time_entry.get().

2. It attempts to convert the time string to a floating-point number representing seconds using float(time_str).
3. If the conversion is successful and the resulting time value is non-negative, it calculates the corresponding frame index based on the frame rate (fps) of the video obtained from its metadata. The frame index is computed as int(time_seconds * self.video.get_meta_data()['fps']).
4. It calls self.show_frame() to display the frame corresponding to the calculated frame index, effectively jumping to the specified time in the video.
5. If the time string cannot be converted to a valid floating-point number (e.g., due to invalid input), or if the time value is negative, it catches the ValueError exception and does nothing, allowing the user to retry entering a valid time value.

This method provides a convenient way for users to navigate to a specific time point in the video by inputting the desired time in seconds.

Showing Extracted Frame

```python
def extract_frame(self):
    frame_number_str = self.frame_entry.get()
    try:
        frame_number = int(frame_number_str)
        if 0 <= frame_number < len(self.video):
            frame = self.video.get_data(frame_number)
            self.show_extracted_frame(frame, frame_number)
    except ValueError:
        pass

def show_extracted_frame(self, frame, frame_number):
    self.extracted_frame_window = tk.Toplevel(self.master)
    self.extracted_frame_window.title(f"EXTRACTED FRAME (Frame {frame_number}) --- VIVIAN SIAHAAN & RH.SIANIPAR")

    extracted_frame_label = tk.Label(self.extracted_frame_window, text=f"Frame yang Diekstraksi (Frame {frame_number})")
    extracted_frame_label.pack()

    height, width, _ = frame.shape  # Get dimensions of the frame
    extracted_photo = ImageTk.PhotoImage(image=Image.fromarray(frame))

    # Create a panel for the frame and edge detection canvas
    frame_panel = tk.Frame(self.extracted_frame_window)
    frame_panel.pack(side="top")

    extracted_frame_canvas = tk.Canvas(frame_panel, width=width, height=height)
    extracted_frame_canvas.pack(side="left")
    extracted_frame_canvas.create_image(0, 0, anchor="nw", image=extracted_photo)
    extracted_frame_canvas.image = extracted_photo

    # Canvas for edge detection result
```

```python
        self.edge_canvas = tk.Canvas(frame_panel, width=width, height=height)
        self.edge_canvas.pack(side="right")

        # Create a panel for histogram plots and hash values
        hist_hash_panel = tk.Frame(self.extracted_frame_window)
        hist_hash_panel.pack(side="bottom", fill="both", expand=True)

        # Plot histogram for each RGB channel
        fig, axs = plt.subplots(1, 3, figsize=(20, 3))
        colors = ['red', 'green', 'blue']
        for i, color in enumerate(['R', 'G', 'B']):
            hist, bins, _ = axs[i].hist(frame[:,:,i].ravel(), bins=64, range=(0, 255), color=colors[i], alpha=0.7)
            axs[i].set_title(f"Histogram of {color} Channel (Frame {frame_number})", fontsize=14, fontweight='bold', color='blue')
            axs[i].set_xlabel("Pixel Value", fontsize=12)
            axs[i].set_ylabel("Frequency", fontsize=12)
            axs[i].grid(True, linestyle='--', linewidth=0.5, color='gray', alpha=0.5)
            axs[i].tick_params(axis='both', which='major', labelsize=10)

            # Add frequency values above each bar
            for bar, frequency in zip(hist, bins[1:]):
                if bar > 0:
                    axs[i].annotate(f'{frequency:.0f}', xy=(bins[np.where(hist == bar)[0][0]] + (bins[1] - bins[0]) / 2, bar),
                                    xytext=(0, 3), textcoords='offset points', ha='center', va='bottom', fontsize=8)

        # Ensure the canvas is updated to display the histogram plots
        plt.tight_layout()
        fig.canvas.draw()

        # Display the histogram plots on a Tkinter canvas
        self.histogram_canvas = FigureCanvasTkAgg(fig, master=hist_hash_panel)
        self.histogram_canvas.get_tk_widget().pack(side=tk.TOP, fill=tk.BOTH, expand=True)
        self.histogram_canvas.draw()

        # Calculate multiple hash values of the frame
        hash_algorithms = ['md5', 'sha1', 'sha256', 'sha224', 'sha384', 'sha512', 'blake2b', 'ripemd160']
        hash_values = {}
        for algorithm in hash_algorithms:
            hash_obj = hashlib.new(algorithm)
            hash_obj.update(frame.tobytes())
            hash_value = hash_obj.hexdigest()
            hash_values[algorithm] = hash_value

        # Edge detection combobox
        edge_detection_label = tk.Label(hist_hash_panel, text="Edge Detection Method:")
        edge_detection_label.pack()

        self.edge_detection_method = ttk.Combobox(hist_hash_panel, values=["None", "Canny", "Sobel", "Prewitt", "Laplacian", "Scharr", "Roberts", "FreiChen", "Kirsch", "Robinson", "Gaussian"])
        self.edge_detection_method.pack()
        self.edge_detection_method.current(0)  # Set default method
```

```
        self.edge_detection_method.bind("<<ComboboxSelected>>", 
self.apply_edge_detection)

        # Display hash values
        self.hash_listbox = tk.Listbox(hist_hash_panel, height=8, width=40, 
font=("Arial", 13), bg="blue", fg="white")
        self.hash_listbox.pack(fill=tk.BOTH, expand=True)
        
        # Add horizontal scrollbar if needed
        scrollbar = tk.Scrollbar(hist_hash_panel, orient=tk.HORIZONTAL, 
command=self.hash_listbox.xview)
        scrollbar.pack(side=tk.BOTTOM, fill=tk.X)
        self.hash_listbox.config(xscrollcommand=scrollbar.set)

        for algorithm, value in hash_values.items():
            self.hash_listbox.insert(tk.END, f"{algorithm}: {value}")
```

The show_extracted_frame() method is responsible for displaying detailed information about the extracted frame, including its visual representation, histograms for each RGB channel, hash values computed using various algorithms, and options for edge detection methods. Here's a breakdown of its functionality:

1. It creates a new window (Toplevel) to display the extracted frame, with a title indicating the frame number.
2. It creates a label to indicate the extracted frame number.
3. It computes the height and width of the frame using the shape attribute of the frame obtained from frame.shape.
4. It converts the frame to a PhotoImage object using ImageTk.PhotoImage(image=Image.fromarray(frame)).
5. It creates a panel (frame_panel) to contain the visual representation of the extracted frame and the canvas for edge detection.
6. It creates a canvas (extracted_frame_canvas) to display the visual representation of the extracted frame and adds the image to it using create_image.
7. It creates another canvas (self.edge_canvas) for displaying edge detection results (this will be updated later).
8. It creates another panel (hist_hash_panel) to contain histogram plots, hash values, and options for edge detection methods.
9. It plots histograms for each RGB channel of the extracted frame using Matplotlib.
10. It creates a Tkinter canvas (self.histogram_canvas) to display the histogram plots.
11. It calculates multiple hash values of the extracted frame using different hashing algorithms and displays them in a listbox (self.hash_listbox).
12. It creates a combobox (self.edge_detection_method) for selecting different edge detection methods and binds it to the apply_edge_detection() method.
13. Finally, it populates the listbox with the hash values calculated using various algorithms.

This method provides a comprehensive view of the extracted frame, including its visual representation, histograms, hash values, and options for edge detection methods.

Applying Canny, Sobel, Prewitt, and Laplacian Edge Detectors

```
# Define functions for edge detection methods
    def apply_canny(self, frame):
        return [cv2.Canny(frame[:,:,i], 5, 50) for i in range(3)]

    def apply_sobel(self, frame):
        return [cv2.Sobel(frame[:,:,i], cv2.CV_64F, 1, 1, ksize=3) for i in range(3)]

    def apply_prewitt(self, frame):
        kernelx = np.array([[1, 1, 1], [0, 0, 0], [-1, -1, -1]])
        kernely = np.array([[-1, 0, 1], [-1, 0, 1], [-1, 0, 1]])
        return [cv2.bitwise_or(cv2.filter2D(frame[:,:,i], -1, kernelx),
                        cv2.filter2D(frame[:,:,i], -1, kernely)) for i in range(3)]

    def apply_laplacian(self, frame):
        return [cv2.Laplacian(frame[:,:,i], cv2.CV_64F) for i in range(3)]
```

Let's break down each edge detection method in detail:
1. Canny Edge Detection:
    - Description: The Canny edge detection algorithm is a multi-stage process that detects edges in images. It's known for its accuracy and robustness.
    - Function (apply_canny):
        - Takes a frame (an image) as input.
        - Applies the Canny edge detection algorithm separately to each color channel (R, G, B) of the frame.
        - Parameters for cv2.Canny function:
            - frame[:,:,i]: Selects the ith color channel of the frame.
            - 5 and 50: Threshold parameters for edge detection.
        - Returns a list containing the edge-detected frames for each color channel.
2. Sobel Edge Detection:
    - Description: The Sobel edge detection algorithm computes the gradient of the image intensity function, highlighting regions of high spatial intensity change.
    - Function (apply_sobel):
        - Takes a frame as input.
        - Applies the Sobel edge detection separately to each color channel of the frame.
        - Parameters for cv2.Sobel function:

- frame[:,:,i]: Selects the ith color channel of the frame.
- cv2.CV_64F: Output data type (64-bit float).
- 1 and 1: Order of the derivative in x and y directions.
- ksize=3: Size of the extended Sobel kernel.
- Returns a list containing the edge-detected frames for each color channel.
3. Prewitt Edge Detection:
    - Description: The Prewitt edge detection algorithm is similar to Sobel but uses a different convolution kernel.
    - Function (apply_prewitt):
        - Takes a frame as input.
        - Defines Prewitt kernels for horizontal and vertical edge detection.
        - Applies these kernels separately to each color channel of the frame using cv2.filter2D.
        - Combines the horizontal and vertical edge-detected results using cv2.bitwise_or.
        - Returns a list containing the edge-detected frames for each color channel.
4. Laplacian Edge Detection:
    - Description: The Laplacian edge detection algorithm computes the second derivative of the image, which emphasizes regions of rapid intensity change.
    - Function (apply_laplacian):
        - Takes a frame as input.
        - Applies the Laplacian edge detection separately to each color channel of the frame.
        - Parameters for cv2.Laplacian function:
            - frame[:,:,i]: Selects the ith color channel of the frame.
            - cv2.CV_64F: Output data type (64-bit float).
        - Returns a list containing the edge-detected frames for each color channel.

These functions process each color channel independently and return edge-detected results, which can be visualized or further processed as needed. They provide different approaches to detecting edges in images, each with its own characteristics and applications.

Applying Scharr Edge Detector

```
def apply_scharr(self, frame):
    edges = []
    for i in range(3):
        # Pre-process the image with Gaussian blur for noise reduction
        smoothed_frame = cv2.GaussianBlur(frame[:,:,i], (3, 3), 0)
        # Apply the Scharr operator
```

```
            gradient_x = cv2.Scharr(smoothed_frame, cv2.CV_64F, 1, 0)
            gradient_y = cv2.Scharr(smoothed_frame, cv2.CV_64F, 0, 1)
            # Compute the gradient magnitude
            gradient_magnitude = cv2.magnitude(gradient_x, gradient_y)
            # Apply thresholding to the gradient magnitude
            _, thresholded_edge = cv2.threshold(gradient_magnitude, 50, 255,
cv2.THRESH_BINARY)
            edges.append(thresholded_edge)
        return edges
```

Now, let's break down each step:
1. Loop Over Color Channels:
    - The method loops over each color channel (Red, Green, Blue) of the input frame. This loop ensures that edge detection is performed separately for each color channel.
2. Gaussian Blur:
    - Before applying the Scharr operator, the image is pre-processed with Gaussian blur (cv2.GaussianBlur) to reduce noise. This step helps in producing smoother gradient images and enhances the quality of edge detection.
3. Scharr Operator:
    - The Scharr operator (cv2.Scharr) is applied to the pre-processed image to compute the gradients in both horizontal (x) and vertical (y) directions separately.
    - The operator provides a more isotropic response compared to the Sobel operator, making it suitable for detecting edges in all directions.
4. Gradient Magnitude:
    - After computing the gradients in both directions, the gradient magnitude is calculated using the cv2.magnitude function. This represents the strength of edges at each pixel location.
5. Thresholding:
    - Thresholding (cv2.threshold) is applied to the gradient magnitude to obtain binary edge images. Pixels with gradient magnitudes above a certain threshold (50 in this case) are considered as edges and set to white (255), while others are set to black (0).
6. Storage and Return:
    - The resulting binary edge images for each color channel are stored in a list named edges.
    - Finally, the list of edge-detected images is returned as the output of the method.

Overall, the apply_scharr() method applies the Scharr edge detection algorithm to each color channel of the input frame, producing separate edge images for each channel, which can be further used for visualization or analysis.

Applying Roberts Edge Detector

```
def apply_roberts(self, frame):
    edges = []
    for i in range(3):
        # Define Roberts kernels for diagonal gradients
        kernel1 = np.array([[1, 0], [0, -1]])
        kernel2 = np.array([[0, 1], [-1, 0]])
        # Apply Roberts kernels to compute gradients in both diagonal directions
        gradient1 = cv2.filter2D(frame[:,:,i], -1, kernel1)
        gradient2 = cv2.filter2D(frame[:,:,i], -1, kernel2)
        # Compute gradient magnitude
        gradient_magnitude = np.sqrt(gradient1**2 + gradient2**2)
        # Convert gradient magnitude to unsigned 8-bit integer
        gradient_magnitude = gradient_magnitude.astype(np.uint8)
        # Apply thresholding to the gradient magnitude
        _, thresholded_edge = cv2.threshold(gradient_magnitude, 5, 255, cv2.THRESH_BINARY)
        edges.append(thresholded_edge)
    return edges
```

Let's delve deeper into each step of the apply_roberts() method:
1. Loop Over Color Channels:
   - In this method, the input frame is assumed to be a 3-channel image (commonly in the RGB format). The method iterates over each color channel individually to perform edge detection separately for each channel. This ensures that edge detection is applied to each color component independently, preserving the color information in the resulting edge images.
2. Define Roberts Kernels:
   - The Roberts edge detection method utilizes two simple 2x2 kernels to detect edges in diagonal directions. These kernels are designed to respond strongly to changes in pixel intensity along diagonals. The first kernel detects edges with a positive slope, while the second detects edges with a negative slope.
3. Apply Roberts Kernels:
   - The cv2.filter2D function from the OpenCV library is employed to convolve the Roberts kernels with the respective color channel of the input frame. Convolution involves sliding the kernel over the image and computing the sum of element-wise products at each position. This process effectively computes the gradient in the diagonal direction for each pixel.
4. Compute Gradient Magnitude:
   - The gradient magnitude represents the strength of the edge at each pixel location. It is computed using the Euclidean distance formula, which combines the gradients obtained from the two Roberts kernels. This step calculates the magnitude of the gradient vector for each pixel, indicating how rapidly pixel intensity changes in the image.

5. Convert to Unsigned 8-bit Integer:
    - The gradient magnitude values are converted to unsigned 8-bit integers using the astype method of NumPy arrays. This conversion ensures that the gradient magnitude values are within the range [0, 255], which is suitable for representing image pixel intensities.
6. Thresholding:
    - Thresholding is applied to the gradient magnitude image to obtain a binary edge image. In this step, pixels with gradient magnitudes above a certain threshold value are considered as edges and set to white (255), while pixels with lower magnitudes are set to black (0). This binary image highlights regions of significant intensity changes, which typically correspond to edges in the original image.
7. Storage and Return:
    - The resulting binary edge images for each color channel are stored in a list named edges. By storing the edge-detected images separately for each channel, it allows for further analysis and processing while preserving color information. Finally, the list of edge images is returned as the output of the method.

By following these steps, the apply_roberts() method effectively detects edges in the input frame using the Roberts edge detection algorithm, providing detailed information about diagonal edge structures present in the image.

Applying FreiChen Edge Detector

```python
def apply_freichen(self, frame):
    edges = []
    for i in range(3):
        # Define FreiChen kernels for gradient computation
        kernelx = np.array([[-1, -np.sqrt(2), -1], [0, 0, 0], [1, np.sqrt(2), 1]])
        kernely = np.array([[-1, 0, 1], [-np.sqrt(2), 0, np.sqrt(2)], [-1, 0, 1]])
        # Compute gradients in both x and y directions
        gradientx = cv2.filter2D(frame[:,:,i], -1, kernelx)
        gradienty = cv2.filter2D(frame[:,:,i], -1, kernely)
        # Compute gradient magnitude
        gradient_magnitude = np.sqrt(gradientx**2 + gradienty**2)
        # Apply thresholding to the original image
        _, thresholded_edge = cv2.threshold(frame[:,:,i], 75, 255, cv2.THRESH_BINARY)
        edges.append(thresholded_edge)
    return edges
```

Let's break down the apply_freichen() method step by step:
1. Loop Over Color Channels:

- Similar to previous methods, this function iterates over each color channel of the input frame (assumed to be in RGB format) to perform edge detection separately for each channel.
2. Define FreiChen Kernels:
    - FreiChen edge detection method utilizes two convolution kernels, kernelx and kernely, for computing gradients in both the horizontal and vertical directions. These kernels are specifically designed to emphasize edges and suppress noise.
3. Compute Gradients:
    - The cv2.filter2D function is applied to convolve each color channel of the input frame with the defined FreiChen kernels. This process computes the gradient in both the horizontal (x) and vertical (y) directions.
4. Compute Gradient Magnitude:
    - The gradient magnitude is calculated from the horizontal and vertical gradients obtained in the previous step. It represents the strength of the edge at each pixel location and is computed using the Euclidean distance formula.
5. Thresholding:
    - Instead of applying thresholding directly to the gradient magnitude, this method applies thresholding to the original intensity values of the color channel. It thresholds each color channel separately based on its pixel intensity values. Pixels with intensities above a certain threshold are considered as edges and set to white (255), while others are set to black (0).
6. Storage and Return:
    - The resulting thresholded edge images for each color channel are stored in a list named edges. By storing the thresholded images separately for each channel, it allows for further analysis and processing while preserving color information. Finally, the list of thresholded edge images is returned as the output of the method.

Overall, the apply_freichen() method applies the FreiChen edge detection algorithm to each color channel of the input frame, highlighting edges based on pixel intensities and providing detailed edge information for further analysis.

Applying Kirsch Edge Detector

```
def apply_kirsch(self, frame):
    edges = []
    for i in range(3):
        # Apply Kirsch edge detection filter
        kirsch_kernel = np.array([[-3, -3, 5], [-3, 0, 5], [-3, -3, 5]])
        edge = cv2.filter2D(frame[:,:,i], -1, kirsch_kernel)
        # Apply threshold to enhance the edge effect
        _, thresholded_edge = cv2.threshold(edge, 40, 255, cv2.THRESH_BINARY)
        edges.append(thresholded_edge)
```

```
return edges
```

Let's delve deeper into each step of the apply_kirsch() method:
1. Loop Over Color Channels:
    - The method starts by iterating over each color channel of the input frame. In typical color images represented in RGB format, there are three color channels: Red, Green, and Blue. By processing each channel separately, the algorithm can detect edges in each color component individually.
2. Kirsch Edge Detection Filter:
    - The core of the Kirsch edge detection method lies in its convolution kernel. The kernel used here is a 3x3 matrix designed to detect edges by emphasizing intensity changes in different directions. Each element of the kernel represents a weight assigned to the corresponding pixel in the image. The specific kernel used in this implementation is:

```
[[-3, -3,  5],
 [-3,  0,  5],
 [-3, -3,  5]]
```

    When convolved with an image, this kernel enhances the differences in pixel intensities along edges. Positive values in the kernel emphasize intensity increases, while negative values emphasize decreases. By summing the weighted pixel values in a neighborhood around each pixel, the convolution operation effectively highlights edges in the image.
3. Thresholding:
    - After applying the Kirsch filter, the resulting image contains enhanced edges. However, these edges are represented as a range of pixel intensities. To extract clear edges from the filtered image, thresholding is applied. Thresholding is a simple image segmentation technique that divides the image into two regions: one representing the edges and the other representing the background.
    - In this implementation, a threshold value of 40 is chosen. Pixels with intensities above this threshold are considered part of an edge and set to white (255 in grayscale representation), while pixels below the threshold are considered background and set to black (0). This binary image effectively highlights the edges detected by the Kirsch filter.
4. Storage and Return:
    - The thresholded edge images for each color channel are stored in a list named edges. By storing the thresholded images separately for each channel, the method preserves color information while providing edge detection results. This allows for further analysis or processing of the individual color channels if needed.

- Finally, the list of thresholded edge images is returned as the output of the method, providing a comprehensive edge detection result for the input frame.

Applying Robinson Edge Detector

```
def apply_robinson(self, frame):
    edges = []
    for i in range(3):
        # Apply Robinson edge detection filter
        robinson_kernel = np.array([[-1, 0, 1], [-2, 0, 2], [-1, 0, 1]])
        edge = cv2.filter2D(frame[:,:,i], -1, robinson_kernel)
        # Apply threshold to enhance the edge effect
        _, thresholded_edge = cv2.threshold(edge, 15, 255, cv2.THRESH_BINARY)
        edges.append(thresholded_edge)
    return edges
```

Let's break down the apply_robinson() method into individual steps:
1. Initialize an empty list to store edge images:
    - Create an empty list named edges. This list will store the thresholded edge images obtained after applying the Robinson edge detection filter to each color channel of the input frame.
2. Loop over color channels:
    - Iterate over each color channel of the input frame. In a typical RGB image, there are three color channels: Red, Green, and Blue.
3. Define the Robinson edge detection filter:
    - Define the Robinson edge detection kernel as a 3x3 numpy array:

    ```
    robinson_kernel = np.array([[-1, 0, 1], [-2, 0, 2], [-1, 0, 1]])
    ```

    - This kernel emphasizes intensity changes in different directions, including horizontal, vertical, and diagonal changes. It is designed to detect edges by convolving it with an image.
4. Apply the Robinson filter to the current color channel:
    - Use the cv2.filter2D function to convolve the Robinson kernel with the current color channel of the input frame:

    ```
    edge = cv2.filter2D(frame[:,:,i], -1, robinson_kernel)
    ```

    - This operation enhances intensity changes in the image, highlighting potential edges.

5. Threshold the edge image:
    - Apply thresholding to the filtered image to obtain a binary image where pixels above a certain intensity threshold are considered part of an edge, while pixels below the threshold are considered background:

      `_, thresholded_edge = cv2.threshold(edge, 15, 255, cv2.THRESH_BINARY)`

    - Pixels with intensities greater than or equal to 15 are set to 255 (white), indicating edges, while pixels below this threshold are set to 0 (black), indicating background.
6. Store the thresholded edge image:
    - Append the thresholded edge image obtained from the current color channel to the edges list:
      `edges.append(thresholded_edge)`

7. Return the list of thresholded edge images:
    - After processing all color channels, the edges list contains the thresholded edge images for each channel.
    - Return the list of thresholded edge images as the output of the method. This provides a comprehensive edge detection result for the input frame, preserving color information.

Applying Gaussian Edge Detector

```
def apply_gaussian(self, frame):
    # Apply Gaussian blur to each channel before edge detection
    blurred_frame = [cv2.GaussianBlur(frame[:,:,i], (5, 5), 0) for i in range(3)]
    # Detect edges using Canny edge detection algorithm
    return [cv2.Canny(blurred_frame[i], 10, 50) for i in range(3)]
```

Let's break down the apply_gaussian() method into individual steps:
1. Apply Gaussian blur to each channel:
    - Gaussian blur is applied to each color channel of the input frame to reduce noise and smooth out the image. This helps in improving the performance of edge detection algorithms by reducing the impact of noise and minor fluctuations in pixel intensity.
    - Gaussian blur is a widely used image processing technique for noise reduction and image smoothing.
    - The cv2.GaussianBlur function is used to apply Gaussian blur. It takes the following parameters:
    - frame[:,:,i]: This selects the i-th color channel of the input frame.

- (5, 5): This specifies the size of the Gaussian kernel used for blurring. Here, a 5x5 kernel is used, which determines the extent of blurring.
- 0: This parameter represents the standard deviation of the Gaussian kernel along the x and y directions. A value of 0 indicates that the standard deviation is calculated based on the kernel size.
- The result of applying Gaussian blur to each color channel is stored in the list blurred_frame.

2. Detect edges using Canny edge detection algorithm:
    - After applying Gaussian blur to each color channel, the Canny edge detection algorithm is used to detect edges in each smoothed channel.
    - The Canny edge detector is a multi-step algorithm that includes gradient calculation, non-maximum suppression, and edge tracking by hysteresis.
    - The cv2.Canny function is employed for edge detection. It takes the following parameters:
    - blurred_frame[i]: This represents the i-th channel after Gaussian blur.
        - 10: This parameter specifies the lower threshold for edge detection. Any gradient value below this threshold is considered as not an edge.
        - 50: This parameter indicates the upper threshold for edge detection. Any gradient value above this threshold is considered as a strong edge.
    - The result of applying Canny edge detection to each channel is stored in the list comprehension, and the list of edge-detected images for each channel is returned as the output of the method.

Applying Various Edge Detection Algorithms

```python
def apply_edge_detection(self, event=None):
    # Get selected method from combobox
    method = self.edge_detection_method.get()

    # Get the current frame number from the title of the tkinter window
    title = self.extracted_frame_window.title()
    frame_numbers = re.findall(r'\d+', title)
    if frame_numbers:
        self.frame_number = int(frame_numbers[-1])  # Extract the last numerical value
    else:
        self.frame_number = 0  # Default frame number if no numerical value is found

    frame = self.video.get_data(self.frame_number)

    # Initialize edges to None
    edges = None

    # Apply edge detection method based on selected method
```

```python
        if method == "Canny":
            edges = self.apply_canny(frame)
        elif method == "Sobel":
            edges = self.apply_sobel(frame)
        elif method == "Prewitt":
            edges = self.apply_prewitt(frame)
        elif method == "None":
            edges = [frame[:,:,i].copy() for i in range(3)]
        elif method == "Laplacian":
            edges = self.apply_laplacian(frame)
        elif method == "Scharr":
            edges = self.apply_scharr(frame)
        elif method == "Roberts":
            edges = self.apply_roberts(frame)
        elif method == "FreiChen":
            edges = self.apply_freichen(frame)
        elif method == "Kirsch":
            edges = self.apply_kirsch(frame)
        elif method == "Robinson":
            edges = self.apply_robinson(frame)
        elif method == "Gaussian":
            edges = self.apply_gaussian(frame)

        # Display edge detection result
        if edges is not None:
            # Combine channels into a single image
            combined_image = self.combine_channels_to_image(edges)

            # Convert the combined image to a PIL Image
            pil_image = Image.fromarray(np.uint8(combined_image))

            # Convert PIL Image to Tkinter PhotoImage
            edge_photo = ImageTk.PhotoImage(image=pil_image)

            # Display the image in the canvas
            self.edge_canvas.create_image(0, 0, anchor="nw", image=edge_photo)
            self.edge_canvas.image = edge_photo

            # Update histogram and hash values
            self.update_histogram_and_hashes(frame, edges)


    def combine_channels_to_image(self, edges):
        # Combine the different color channels into one image
        combined_image = np.stack((edges[0], edges[1], edges[2]), axis=-1)
        return combined_image
```

This code defines a method called apply_edge_detection(). Here's a step-by-step explanation of what it does:
1. Get Selected Edge Detection Method:

- It retrieves the selected edge detection method from a Tkinter combobox widget (self.edge_detection_method.get()). This method would likely be called when the user selects an edge detection method from a dropdown list in the GUI.
2. Extract Frame Number:
    - It extracts the current frame number from the title of a Tkinter window. This frame number is assumed to be present in the window title as a numerical value. Regular expressions (re.findall()) are used to extract this number.
3. Retrieve Frame from Video:
    - It retrieves the frame corresponding to the extracted frame number from a video source (self.video.get_data(self.frame_number)).
4. Initialize edges to None:
    - It initializes a variable named edges to None. This variable will store the edge-detected images.
5. Apply Edge Detection Method:
    - Depending on the selected method, it applies the corresponding edge detection algorithm to the frame. The methods apply_canny(), apply_sobel(), apply_prewitt(), etc.
6. Display Edge Detection Result:
    - If the edges variable is not None (i.e., if edge detection was successful), it combines the channels into a single image and displays the resulting edge-detected image on a Tkinter canvas.
7. Update Histogram and Hash Values:
    - Finally, it updates histogram and hash values based on the original frame and the edge-detected image. The details of this updating process are not provided in the code snippet.

This method effectively serves as a central hub for applying various edge detection algorithms based on user selection and updating the GUI accordingly with the results.

The combine_channels_to_image() takes the detected edges from different color channels and combines them into a single image. Here's a breakdown of what it does:
1. Input Parameters:
    - self: This method belongs to a class, so it receives the instance of the class as the first parameter, conventionally named self.
    - edges: This parameter is a list containing the edge-detected images from different color channels. Each element of the list represents the edges detected in a single color channel.
2. Combining Channels:

- The method uses NumPy's stack function to combine the edge-detected images from different channels into a single image.
- It takes the three elements of the edges list (presumably representing edges detected in the red, green, and blue channels) and stacks them along the last axis (axis=-1), effectively merging them into a single image.
3. Return Value:
    - The method returns the combined image, where the edge-detected images from different channels are stacked together into a single image.

In summary, this method facilitates the combination of edge-detected images from different color channels into a unified image, allowing for the visualization of all detected edges in a single view.

Updating Histogram Plots and Hash Values

```python
def update_histogram_and_hashes(self, frame, edges):
    # Update histogram
    for i, ax in enumerate(self.histogram_canvas.figure.get_axes()):
        ax.clear()
        colors = ['red', 'green', 'blue']
        channel = edges[i]  # Memilih saluran warna yang sesuai dengan indeks
        hist, bins = np.histogram(channel.ravel(), bins=32, range=(0, 255))
        ax.bar(bins[:-1], hist, color=colors[i], alpha=0.7, width=6)  # Menyesuaikan lebar batang histogram
        ax.set_title(f"Histogram of {colors[i]} Channel (Frame {self.frame_number})", fontsize=14, fontweight='bold', color='blue')
        ax.set_xlabel("Pixel Value", fontsize=12)
        ax.set_ylabel("Frequency", fontsize=12)
        ax.grid(True, linestyle='--', linewidth=0.5, color='gray', alpha=0.5)
        ax.tick_params(axis='both', which='major', labelsize=10)
        # Add frequency values above each bar
        for bar, frequency in zip(hist, bins[1:]):
            if bar > 0:
                ax.annotate(f'{frequency:.0f}', xy=(bins[np.where(hist == bar)[0][0]] + (bins[1] - bins[0]) / 2, bar),
                            xytext=(0, 3), textcoords='offset points',
                            ha='center', va='bottom', fontsize=8)
    self.histogram_canvas.draw()

    # Update hash values
    hash_algorithms = ['md5', 'sha1', 'sha256', 'sha224', 'sha384', 'sha512', 'blake2b', 'ripemd160']
    hash_values = {}
    for algorithm in hash_algorithms:
        hash_obj = hashlib.new(algorithm)
        for channel in edges:
            hash_obj.update(channel.tobytes())  # Update hash values based on edge-detected image
        hash_value = hash_obj.hexdigest()
        hash_values[algorithm] = hash_value
```

```
        self.hash_listbox.delete(0, tk.END)  # Clear existing hash values
        for algorithm, value in hash_values.items():
            self.hash_listbox.insert(tk.END, f"{algorithm}: {value}")
```

This method update_histogram_and_hashes() serves to update the histogram plots and hash values based on the edge-detected images. Let's break down its functionality:

1. Input Parameters:
   - self: This parameter refers to the instance of the class.
   - frame: This is the original frame from which edges were detected.
   - edges: This is a list containing the edge-detected images from different color channels.
2. Updating Histogram:
   - The method iterates over each axis of the histogram canvas (self.histogram_canvas.figure.get_axes()).
   - For each axis, it clears any existing plot (ax.clear()).
   - It then computes the histogram for the corresponding edge-detected channel (channel) using NumPy's histogram function.
   - A bar plot of the histogram is created, with appropriate formatting for title, labels, grid, and tick marks.
   - Frequency values are annotated above each bar.
   - This process is repeated for each color channel.
3. Updating Hash Values:
   - Hash values are calculated using various algorithms (hash_algorithms).
   - For each algorithm, a hash object is created using hashlib.new(algorithm).
   - The hash object is updated with the byte representation of each edge-detected channel (channel.tobytes()).
   - The resulting hash value is stored in the hash_values dictionary.
4. Updating GUI:
   - Existing hash values in the hash_listbox are cleared (self.hash_listbox.delete(0, tk.END)).
   - The updated hash values are inserted into the hash_listbox for display.

Overall, this method ensures that both the histogram plots and hash values are updated dynamically based on the latest edge detection results, providing users with up-to-date visualizations and information.

Displaying Edge Detection Result

```
def show_edge_detection_result(self, edges):
    # Combine channels into a single image
    combined_image = self.combine_channels_to_image(edges)

    # Convert the combined image to a PIL Image
    pil_image = Image.fromarray(np.uint8(combined_image))

    # Convert PIL Image to Tkinter PhotoImage
    edge_photo = ImageTk.PhotoImage(image=pil_image)

    # Display the image in the canvas
    self.edge_canvas.create_image(0, 0, anchor="nw", image=edge_photo)
    self.edge_canvas.image = edge_photo
```

This method, show_edge_detection_result(), is responsible for displaying the edge detection result on the canvas. Let's go through its steps:

1. Input Parameter:
    - edges: This is a list containing the edge-detected images from different color channels.
2. Combining Channels to Image:
    - The method first combines the different color channels into a single image using the combine_channels_to_image() method. This results in a combined image where each color channel's edges contribute to the final visualization.
3. Conversion to PIL Image and PhotoImage:
    - The combined image, represented as a NumPy array, is converted to a PIL Image using Image.fromarray(np.uint8(combined_image)). This allows for easier manipulation and display of the image.
    - The PIL Image is then converted to a Tkinter PhotoImage object using ImageTk.PhotoImage(image=pil_image). This is necessary for displaying the image on the Tkinter canvas.
4. Displaying the Image on Canvas:
    - The Tkinter canvas (self.edge_canvas) is used to display the edge detection result.
    - The create_image method is called to create an image item on the canvas. The image is positioned at coordinates (0, 0) with the anchor set to "nw" (northwest).
    - The created image item is associated with the PhotoImage object (edge_photo) to ensure it remains in memory and is not garbage collected.

Overall, this method takes the edge detection results, converts them into a format suitable for display in a Tkinter canvas, and then presents them to the user for visualization.

Open Another Instance of The Application

```
def open_another_player(self):
    # Open another instance of the application
    root = tk.Toplevel(self.master)
    app = VideoPlayerEdge(root)
```

This method, open_another_player(), is designed to open another instance of the application in a new window. Here's what it does:
1. Creating a New Window (Toplevel):
    - It creates a new Tkinter Toplevel window, which is essentially a child window that floats above the main window (self.master) of the application.
2. Instantiating a New Video Player:
    - Within this new window (root), it instantiates another instance of the VideoPlayerEdge class (assuming VideoPlayerEdge is the class name for the video player application). This effectively creates a new instance of the video player within the new window.

By calling this method, users can open multiple instances of the video player application, each running independently in its own window. This can be useful for various purposes, such as comparing videos or analyzing multiple videos simultaneously.

Entry Point for Application

```
def main():
    root = tk.Tk()
    app = VideoPlayerEdge(root)
    root.mainloop()

if __name__ == "__main__":
    main()
```

This main() function is a typical structure for starting a Tkinter application. Here's what it does:
1. Create the Tkinter Root Window:
    - It creates the main application window using tk.Tk() and assigns it to the variable root.
2. Instantiate the Video Player Application:
    - It creates an instance of the VideoPlayerEdge class, passing the root window as its master.
3. Start the Tkinter Event Loop:

- It starts the Tkinter event loop by calling root.mainloop(). This method listens for events such as user inputs and redraws the GUI as necessary.
4. if __name__ == "__main__": Block:
    - This block ensures that the main() function is only executed if the script is run directly, not if it is imported as a module into another script. This is a common Python idiom to prevent code from being executed when imported as a module.

By executing this script directly, the main() function is called, which initializes the Tkinter application and starts the event loop, allowing users to interact with the video player GUI.

Running Program

Run the program. The GUI is shown below:

Then, click on Open Video button. Type a specific frame number, then ENTER.

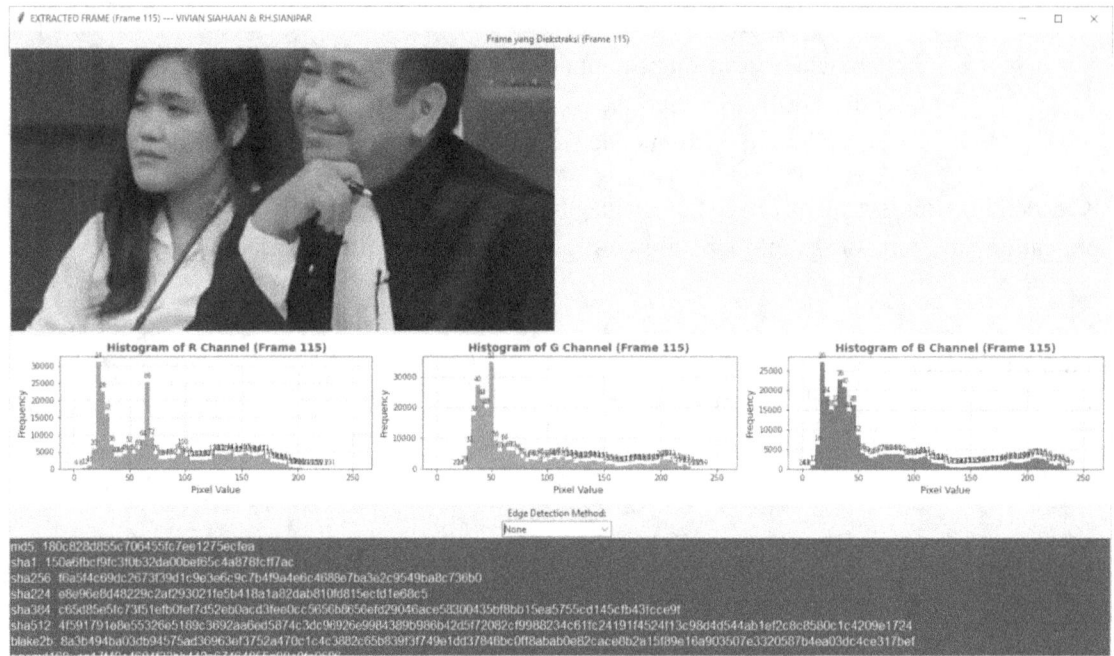

Then, choose one of edge detectors from available combobox:

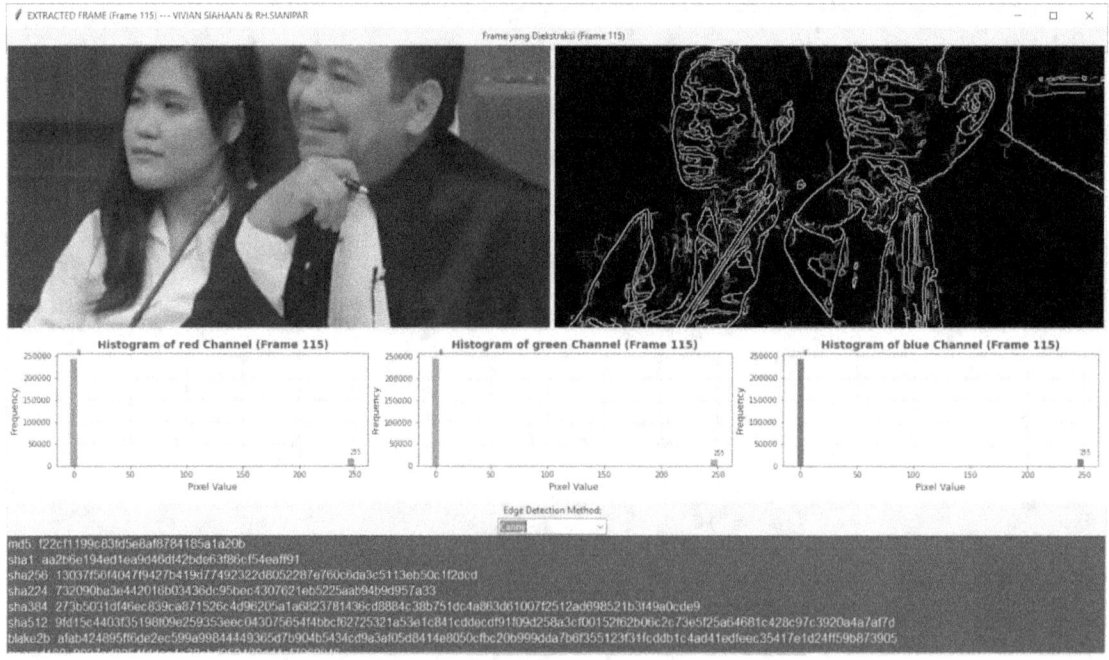

Full Source Code

```
import tkinter as tk
from tkinter import ttk
from tkinter import filedialog
from PIL import Image, ImageTk
import imageio
import matplotlib.pyplot as plt
from matplotlib.backends.backend_tkagg import FigureCanvasTkAgg
import hashlib
import numpy as np
import cv2
import re

class VideoPlayerEdge:
    def __init__(self, master):
        self.master = master
        self.master.title("FRAME EDGE DETECTION---VIVIAN SIAHAAN & RH.SIANIPAR")

        self.video = None
        self.video_path = None
        self.paused = False
        self.zoom_scale = tk.IntVar(value=1)
        self.frame_index = 0
        self.start_x = None
        self.start_y = None
        self.current_x = 0
        self.current_y = 0
        self.photo = None  # Save object reference to PhotoImage globally

        self.create_widgets()

    def create_widgets(self):
        # Panel for video display
        video_panel = tk.Frame(self.master)
        video_panel.grid(row=0, column=0, padx=10, pady=10, sticky="nsew")

        # Canvas to display the video
        canvas_width = 800
        canvas_height = 600
        self.canvas = tk.Canvas(video_panel, width=canvas_width, height=canvas_height)
        self.canvas.pack(side="top", fill="both", expand=True)
        self.canvas.bind("<MouseWheel>", self.on_mousewheel)
        self.canvas.bind("<ButtonPress-1>", self.on_press)
        self.canvas.bind("<B1-Motion>", self.on_drag)

        # Scrollbar
        self.scrollbar = tk.Scrollbar(video_panel, orient="horizontal", command=self.on_scroll)
        self.scrollbar.pack(side="bottom", fill="x")

        self.canvas.configure(xscrollcommand=self.scrollbar.set)

        # Panel for control buttons
        control_panel = tk.Frame(self.master)
        control_panel.grid(row=1, column=0, padx=10, pady=(0, 10), sticky="ew")
```

```python
        # Button to open a video file
        self.open_button = tk.Button(control_panel, text="Open Video", command=self.open_video)
        self.open_button.grid(row=0, column=0, padx=10, pady=5)

        # Combobox for selecting zoom scale
        self.zoom_combobox = ttk.Combobox(control_panel, textvariable=self.zoom_scale, values=list(range(1, 11)))
        self.zoom_combobox.grid(row=0, column=1, padx=10, pady=5)
        self.zoom_combobox.bind("<<ComboboxSelected>>", self.update_zoom)

        # Label and entry for specifying time
        self.time_label = tk.Label(control_panel, text="Jump to Time (s):")
        self.time_label.grid(row=0, column=2, padx=10, pady=5, sticky="e")
        self.time_entry = ttk.Entry(control_panel)
        self.time_entry.grid(row=0, column=3, padx=10, pady=5, sticky="w")
        self.time_entry.bind("<Return>", lambda event: self.jump_to_time())

        # Button to jump to specified time
        self.jump_button = tk.Button(control_panel, text="Jump to Time", command=self.jump_to_time)
        self.jump_button.grid(row=0, column=4, padx=10, pady=5)

        # Button to play/pause the video
        self.play_button = tk.Button(control_panel, text="Play/Pause", command=self.toggle_play_pause)
        self.play_button.grid(row=0, column=5, padx=10, pady=5)

        # Button to stop the video
        self.stop_button = tk.Button(control_panel, text="Stop", command=self.stop_video)
        self.stop_button.grid(row=0, column=6, padx=10, pady=5)

        # Button to extract frame
        self.extract_button = tk.Button(control_panel, text="Extract Frame", command=self.extract_frame)
        self.extract_button.grid(row=1, column=0, padx=10, pady=5)

        # Label and entry for frame number
        self.frame_label = tk.Label(control_panel, text="Frame Number:")
        self.frame_label.grid(row=1, column=1, padx=10, pady=5, sticky="e")
        self.frame_entry = ttk.Entry(control_panel)
        self.frame_entry.grid(row=1, column=2, padx=10, pady=5, sticky="w")
        self.frame_entry.bind("<Return>", lambda event: self.extract_frame())

        # Button to open another instance of the application
        self.open_another_button = tk.Button(control_panel, text="Open Another Video Player", command=self.open_another_player)
        self.open_another_button.grid(row=2, column=0, columnspan=7, padx=10, pady=5)

    def open_video(self):
        self.video_path = filedialog.askopenfilename(filetypes=[("Video files", "*.mp4;*.avi;*.mkv")])
        if self.video_path:
            self.video = imageio.get_reader(self.video_path)
            self.play_video()
```

```python
    def play_video(self):
        if self.video:
            self.paused = False
            self.show_frame()

    def stop_video(self):
        self.paused = True
        self.frame_index = 0
        self.current_x = 0
        self.current_y = 0  # Reset the current position
        self.show_frame()

    def toggle_play_pause(self):
        self.paused = not self.paused
        if not self.paused:
            self.play_video()

    def update_zoom(self, event=None):
        self.show_frame()

    def show_frame(self):
        if self.video:
            if not self.paused:
                self.frame_index += 1
                if self.frame_index >= len(self.video):
                    self.frame_index = 0  # Reset frame index if it exceeds the maximum index
            if 0 <= self.frame_index < len(self.video):  # Check if frame index is within range
                try:
                    frame = self.video.get_data(self.frame_index)
                    frame = Image.fromarray(frame)
                    frame = frame.resize((frame.width * self.zoom_scale.get(), frame.height * self.zoom_scale.get()))
                    photo = ImageTk.PhotoImage(frame)
                    self.photo = photo  # Save object reference to PhotoImage globally
                    self.canvas.delete("video")  # Delete previous image
                    self.canvas.create_image(self.current_x, self.current_y, anchor="nw", image=photo, tags="video")
                    if not self.paused:
                        self.canvas.after(30, self.show_frame)
                except Exception as e:
                    print("Error:", e)

    def on_mousewheel(self, event):
        direction = event.delta // 120
        current_value = int(self.zoom_scale.get())
        if direction == 1 and current_value < 10:
            current_value += 1
        elif direction == -1 and current_value > 1:
            current_value -= 1
        self.zoom_scale.set(current_value)
        self.update_zoom()

    def on_press(self, event):
        self.start_x = event.x
        self.start_y = event.y
```

```python
    def on_drag(self, event):
        if self.start_x and self.start_y:
            x_offset = event.x - self.start_x
            y_offset = event.y - self.start_y
            self.current_x += x_offset  # Update current position
            self.current_y += y_offset  # Update current position
            self.canvas.move("video", x_offset, y_offset)
            self.start_x = event.x
            self.start_y = event.y

    def on_scroll(self, *args):
        scroll_pos = self.scrollbar.get()
        self.current_x = -scroll_pos * self.canvas.winfo_width()
        self.canvas.xview_moveto(scroll_pos)
        self.frame_index = int(scroll_pos * len(self.video))  # Update frame index
        self.show_frame()

    def jump_to_time(self):
        time_str = self.time_entry.get()
        try:
            time_seconds = float(time_str)
            if 0 <= time_seconds:
                self.frame_index = int(time_seconds * self.video.get_meta_data()['fps'])
                self.show_frame()
        except ValueError:
            pass

    def extract_frame(self):
        frame_number_str = self.frame_entry.get()
        try:
            frame_number = int(frame_number_str)
            if 0 <= frame_number < len(self.video):
                frame = self.video.get_data(frame_number)
                self.show_extracted_frame(frame, frame_number)
        except ValueError:
            pass

    def show_extracted_frame(self, frame, frame_number):
        self.extracted_frame_window = tk.Toplevel(self.master)
        self.extracted_frame_window.title(f"EXTRACTED FRAME (Frame {frame_number}) --- VIVIAN SIAHAAN & RH.SIANIPAR")

        extracted_frame_label = tk.Label(self.extracted_frame_window, text=f"Frame yang Diekstraksi (Frame {frame_number})")
        extracted_frame_label.pack()

        height, width, _ = frame.shape  # Get dimensions of the frame
        extracted_photo = ImageTk.PhotoImage(image=Image.fromarray(frame))

        # Create a panel for the frame and edge detection canvas
        frame_panel = tk.Frame(self.extracted_frame_window)
        frame_panel.pack(side="top")

        extracted_frame_canvas = tk.Canvas(frame_panel, width=width, height=height)
        extracted_frame_canvas.pack(side="left")
        extracted_frame_canvas.create_image(0, 0, anchor="nw", image=extracted_photo)
```

```python
            extracted_frame_canvas.image = extracted_photo

            # Canvas for edge detection result
            self.edge_canvas = tk.Canvas(frame_panel, width=width, height=height)
            self.edge_canvas.pack(side="right")

            # Create a panel for histogram plots and hash values
            hist_hash_panel = tk.Frame(self.extracted_frame_window)
            hist_hash_panel.pack(side="bottom", fill="both", expand=True)

            # Plot histogram for each RGB channel
            fig, axs = plt.subplots(1, 3, figsize=(20, 3))
            colors = ['red', 'green', 'blue']
            for i, color in enumerate(['R', 'G', 'B']):
                hist, bins, _ = axs[i].hist(frame[:,:,i].ravel(), bins=64, range=(0, 255), color=colors[i], alpha=0.7)
                axs[i].set_title(f"Histogram of {color} Channel (Frame {frame_number})", fontsize=14, fontweight='bold', color='blue')
                axs[i].set_xlabel("Pixel Value", fontsize=12)
                axs[i].set_ylabel("Frequency", fontsize=12)
                axs[i].grid(True, linestyle='--', linewidth=0.5, color='gray', alpha=0.5)
                axs[i].tick_params(axis='both', which='major', labelsize=10)

                # Add frequency values above each bar
                for bar, frequency in zip(hist, bins[1:]):
                    if bar > 0:
                        axs[i].annotate(f'{frequency:.0f}', xy=(bins[np.where(hist == bar)[0][0]] + (bins[1] - bins[0]) / 2, bar),
                                        xytext=(0, 3), textcoords='offset points', ha='center', va='bottom', fontsize=8)

            # Ensure the canvas is updated to display the histogram plots
            plt.tight_layout()
            fig.canvas.draw()

            # Display the histogram plots on a Tkinter canvas
            self.histogram_canvas = FigureCanvasTkAgg(fig, master=hist_hash_panel)
            self.histogram_canvas.get_tk_widget().pack(side=tk.TOP, fill=tk.BOTH, expand=True)
            self.histogram_canvas.draw()

            # Calculate multiple hash values of the frame
            hash_algorithms = ['md5', 'sha1', 'sha256', 'sha224', 'sha384', 'sha512', 'blake2b', 'ripemd160']
            hash_values = {}
            for algorithm in hash_algorithms:
                hash_obj = hashlib.new(algorithm)
                hash_obj.update(frame.tobytes())
                hash_value = hash_obj.hexdigest()
                hash_values[algorithm] = hash_value

            # Edge detection combobox
            edge_detection_label = tk.Label(hist_hash_panel, text="Edge Detection Method:")
            edge_detection_label.pack()
```

```python
        self.edge_detection_method = ttk.Combobox(hist_hash_panel, values=["None",
"Canny", "Sobel", "Prewitt", "Laplacian", "Scharr", "Roberts", "FreiChen", "Kirsch",
"Robinson", "Gaussian"])
        self.edge_detection_method.pack()
        self.edge_detection_method.current(0)  # Set default method
        self.edge_detection_method.bind("<<ComboboxSelected>>",
self.apply_edge_detection)

        # Display hash values
        self.hash_listbox = tk.Listbox(hist_hash_panel, height=8, width=40,
font=("Arial", 13), bg="blue", fg="white")
        self.hash_listbox.pack(fill=tk.BOTH, expand=True)

        # Add horizontal scrollbar if needed
        scrollbar = tk.Scrollbar(hist_hash_panel, orient=tk.HORIZONTAL,
command=self.hash_listbox.xview)
        scrollbar.pack(side=tk.BOTTOM, fill=tk.X)
        self.hash_listbox.config(xscrollcommand=scrollbar.set)

        for algorithm, value in hash_values.items():
            self.hash_listbox.insert(tk.END, f"{algorithm}: {value}")

    # Define functions for edge detection methods
    def apply_canny(self, frame):
        return [cv2.Canny(frame[:,:,i], 5, 50) for i in range(3)]

    def apply_sobel(self, frame):
        return [cv2.Sobel(frame[:,:,i], cv2.CV_64F, 1, 1, ksize=3) for i in
range(3)]

    def apply_prewitt(self, frame):
        kernelx = np.array([[1, 1, 1], [0, 0, 0], [-1, -1, -1]])
        kernely = np.array([[-1, 0, 1], [-1, 0, 1], [-1, 0, 1]])
        return [cv2.bitwise_or(cv2.filter2D(frame[:,:,i], -1, kernelx),
                     cv2.filter2D(frame[:,:,i], -1, kernely)) for i in
range(3)]

    def apply_laplacian(self, frame):
        return [cv2.Laplacian(frame[:,:,i], cv2.CV_64F) for i in range(3)]

    def apply_scharr(self, frame):
        edges = []
        for i in range(3):
            # Pre-process the image with Gaussian blur for noise reduction
            smoothed_frame = cv2.GaussianBlur(frame[:,:,i], (3, 3), 0)
            # Apply the Scharr operator
            gradient_x = cv2.Scharr(smoothed_frame, cv2.CV_64F, 1, 0)
            gradient_y = cv2.Scharr(smoothed_frame, cv2.CV_64F, 0, 1)
            # Compute the gradient magnitude
            gradient_magnitude = cv2.magnitude(gradient_x, gradient_y)
            # Apply thresholding to the gradient magnitude
            _, thresholded_edge = cv2.threshold(gradient_magnitude, 50, 255,
cv2.THRESH_BINARY)
            edges.append(thresholded_edge)
        return edges

    def apply_roberts(self, frame):
        edges = []
```

```python
        for i in range(3):
            # Define Roberts kernels for diagonal gradients
            kernel1 = np.array([[1, 0], [0, -1]])
            kernel2 = np.array([[0, 1], [-1, 0]])
            # Apply Roberts kernels to compute gradients in both diagonal directions
            gradient1 = cv2.filter2D(frame[:,:,i], -1, kernel1)
            gradient2 = cv2.filter2D(frame[:,:,i], -1, kernel2)
            # Compute gradient magnitude
            gradient_magnitude = np.sqrt(gradient1**2 + gradient2**2)
            # Convert gradient magnitude to unsigned 8-bit integer
            gradient_magnitude = gradient_magnitude.astype(np.uint8)
            # Apply thresholding to the gradient magnitude
            _, thresholded_edge = cv2.threshold(gradient_magnitude, 5, 255, cv2.THRESH_BINARY)
            edges.append(thresholded_edge)
        return edges

    def apply_freichen(self, frame):
        edges = []
        for i in range(3):
            # Define FreiChen kernels for gradient computation
            kernelx = np.array([[-1, -np.sqrt(2), -1], [0, 0, 0], [1, np.sqrt(2), 1]])
            kernely = np.array([[-1, 0, 1], [-np.sqrt(2), 0, np.sqrt(2)], [-1, 0, 1]])
            # Compute gradients in both x and y directions
            gradientx = cv2.filter2D(frame[:,:,i], -1, kernelx)
            gradienty = cv2.filter2D(frame[:,:,i], -1, kernely)
            # Compute gradient magnitude
            gradient_magnitude = np.sqrt(gradientx**2 + gradienty**2)
            # Apply thresholding to the original image
            _, thresholded_edge = cv2.threshold(frame[:,:,i], 75, 255, cv2.THRESH_BINARY)
            edges.append(thresholded_edge)
        return edges

    def apply_kirsch(self, frame):
        edges = []
        for i in range(3):
            # Apply Kirsch edge detection filter
            kirsch_kernel = np.array([[-3, -3, 5], [-3, 0, 5], [-3, -3, 5]])
            edge = cv2.filter2D(frame[:,:,i], -1, kirsch_kernel)
            # Apply threshold to enhance the edge effect
            _, thresholded_edge = cv2.threshold(edge, 40, 255, cv2.THRESH_BINARY)
            edges.append(thresholded_edge)
        return edges

    def apply_robinson(self, frame):
        edges = []
        for i in range(3):
            # Apply Robinson edge detection filter
            robinson_kernel = np.array([[-1, 0, 1], [-2, 0, 2], [-1, 0, 1]])
            edge = cv2.filter2D(frame[:,:,i], -1, robinson_kernel)
            # Apply threshold to enhance the edge effect
            _, thresholded_edge = cv2.threshold(edge, 15, 255, cv2.THRESH_BINARY)
            edges.append(thresholded_edge)
        return edges
```

```python
    def apply_gaussian(self, frame):
        # Apply Gaussian blur to each channel before edge detection
        blurred_frame = [cv2.GaussianBlur(frame[:,:,i], (5, 5), 0) for i in range(3)]
        # Detect edges using Canny edge detection algorithm
        return [cv2.Canny(blurred_frame[i], 10, 50) for i in range(3)]

    def apply_edge_detection(self, event=None):
        # Get selected method from combobox
        method = self.edge_detection_method.get()

        # Get the current frame number from the title of the tkinter window
        title = self.extracted_frame_window.title()
        frame_numbers = re.findall(r'\d+', title)
        if frame_numbers:
            self.frame_number = int(frame_numbers[-1])  # Extract the last numerical value
        else:
            self.frame_number = 0  # Default frame number if no numerical value is found

        frame = self.video.get_data(self.frame_number)

        # Initialize edges to None
        edges = None

        # Apply edge detection method based on selected method
        if method == "Canny":
            edges = self.apply_canny(frame)
        elif method == "Sobel":
            edges = self.apply_sobel(frame)
        elif method == "Prewitt":
            edges = self.apply_prewitt(frame)
        elif method == "None":
            edges = [frame[:,:,i].copy() for i in range(3)]
        elif method == "Laplacian":
            edges = self.apply_laplacian(frame)
        elif method == "Scharr":
            edges = self.apply_scharr(frame)
        elif method == "Roberts":
            edges = self.apply_roberts(frame)
        elif method == "FreiChen":
            edges = self.apply_freichen(frame)
        elif method == "Kirsch":
            edges = self.apply_kirsch(frame)
        elif method == "Robinson":
            edges = self.apply_robinson(frame)
        elif method == "Gaussian":
            edges = self.apply_gaussian(frame)

        # Display edge detection result
        if edges is not None:
            # Combine channels into a single image
            combined_image = self.combine_channels_to_image(edges)

            # Convert the combined image to a PIL Image
            pil_image = Image.fromarray(np.uint8(combined_image))

            # Convert PIL Image to Tkinter PhotoImage
```

```python
            edge_photo = ImageTk.PhotoImage(image=pil_image)

            # Display the image in the canvas
            self.edge_canvas.create_image(0, 0, anchor="nw", image=edge_photo)
            self.edge_canvas.image = edge_photo

        # Update histogram and hash values
        self.update_histogram_and_hashes(frame, edges)

    def combine_channels_to_image(self, edges):
        # Combine the different color channels into one image
        combined_image = np.stack((edges[0], edges[1], edges[2]), axis=-1)
        return combined_image

    def update_histogram_and_hashes(self, frame, edges):
        # Update histogram
        for i, ax in enumerate(self.histogram_canvas.figure.get_axes()):
            ax.clear()
            colors = ['red', 'green', 'blue']
            channel = edges[i]  # Memilih saluran warna yang sesuai dengan indeks
            hist, bins = np.histogram(channel.ravel(), bins=32, range=(0, 255))
            ax.bar(bins[:-1], hist, color=colors[i], alpha=0.7, width=6)  # Menyesuaikan lebar batang histogram
            ax.set_title(f"Histogram of {colors[i]} Channel (Frame {self.frame_number})", fontsize=14, fontweight='bold', color='blue')
            ax.set_xlabel("Pixel Value", fontsize=12)
            ax.set_ylabel("Frequency", fontsize=12)
            ax.grid(True, linestyle='--', linewidth=0.5, color='gray', alpha=0.5)
            ax.tick_params(axis='both', which='major', labelsize=10)
            # Add frequency values above each bar
            for bar, frequency in zip(hist, bins[1:]):
                if bar > 0:
                    ax.annotate(f'{frequency:.0f}', xy=(bins[np.where(hist == bar)[0][0]] + (bins[1] - bins[0]) / 2, bar),
                                xytext=(0, 3), textcoords='offset points',
                                ha='center', va='bottom', fontsize=8)
        self.histogram_canvas.draw()

        # Update hash values
        hash_algorithms = ['md5', 'sha1', 'sha256', 'sha224', 'sha384', 'sha512', 'blake2b', 'ripemd160']
        hash_values = {}
        for algorithm in hash_algorithms:
            hash_obj = hashlib.new(algorithm)
            for channel in edges:
                hash_obj.update(channel.tobytes())  # Update hash values based on edge-detected image
            hash_value = hash_obj.hexdigest()
            hash_values[algorithm] = hash_value

        self.hash_listbox.delete(0, tk.END)  # Clear existing hash values
        for algorithm, value in hash_values.items():
            self.hash_listbox.insert(tk.END, f"{algorithm}: {value}")

    def show_edge_detection_result(self, edges):
        # Combine channels into a single image
        combined_image = self.combine_channels_to_image(edges)
```

```python
        # Convert the combined image to a PIL Image
        pil_image = Image.fromarray(np.uint8(combined_image))

        # Convert PIL Image to Tkinter PhotoImage
        edge_photo = ImageTk.PhotoImage(image=pil_image)

        # Display the image in the canvas
        self.edge_canvas.create_image(0, 0, anchor="nw", image=edge_photo)
        self.edge_canvas.image = edge_photo

    def open_another_player(self):
        # Open another instance of the application
        root = tk.Toplevel(self.master)
        app = VideoPlayerEdge(root)

def main():
    root = tk.Tk()
    app = VideoPlayerEdge(root)
    root.mainloop()

if __name__ == "__main__":
    main()
```

FILTERING EACH FRAME IN VIDEO

FILTERING EACH FRAME IN VIDEO

The project defines a Python class named VideoPlayerFiltering, which implements a graphical user interface (GUI) for playing and processing video files. The class utilizes the Tkinter library for creating the GUI elements, including buttons, labels, and canvases.

Upon initialization, the class sets up various attributes such as the video path, canvas for displaying the video frames, and control buttons for playing, pausing, and stopping the video playback. It also provides functionality for extracting frames from the video and opening another instance of the video player.

The open_video() method allows users to select a video file using a file dialog, and once a video is loaded, the play_video() method initiates the video playback loop. The stop_video() method halts the video playback and resets the frame index to zero.

The class implements event handlers for mouse wheel scrolling, mouse button presses, and dragging events, allowing users to zoom in/out and pan across the video frames displayed on the canvas.

The show_frame method retrieves video frames from the loaded video file, resizes them based on the selected zoom scale, and displays them on the canvas. It also ensures continuous playback by recursively calling itself using the Tkinter after method.

Additionally, the class provides methods for applying various image processing techniques such as Gaussian blur, mean blur, median blur, bilateral filtering, non-local means denoising, anisotropic diffusion, total variation denoising, Wiener filter, adaptive thresholding, and wavelet transform to the video frames. These methods are invoked based on user selections from a combobox.

Furthermore, the class incorporates functionality for updating histogram plots and calculating hash values for the processed video frames, which are displayed alongside the processed frames in the GUI. Finally, the main function creates an instance of the VideoPlayerEdge class and starts the Tkinter event loop to run the application.

Importing Libraries

```
import tkinter as tk
from tkinter import ttk
from tkinter import filedialog
from PIL import Image, ImageTk
import imageio
import matplotlib.pyplot as plt
from matplotlib.backends.backend_tkagg import FigureCanvasTkAgg
import hashlib
import numpy as np
import cv2
import re
import pywt
from skimage.restoration import denoise_tv_chambolle
```

This code snippet imports several Python libraries commonly used for GUI development, image processing, and data visualization:
- tkinter: This is the standard Python interface to the Tk GUI toolkit.
- ttk: This module provides access to the Tk themed widget set.
- filedialog from tkinter: It provides dialogs for opening and saving files.
- PIL.Image and ImageTk from PIL: These modules provide support for opening, manipulating, and saving many different image file formats.
- imageio: This library provides an easy interface to read and write a wide range of image data.
- matplotlib.pyplot and FigureCanvasTkAgg from matplotlib.backends.backend_tkagg: These modules are used for data visualization and creating interactive plots embedded within Tkinter applications.
- hashlib: This module provides a common interface to many secure hash and message digest algorithms.

- numpy: This is the fundamental package for scientific computing with Python. It provides support for large, multi-dimensional arrays and matrices, along with a collection of mathematical functions to operate on these arrays.
- cv2 (OpenCV): OpenCV is a library of programming functions mainly aimed at real-time computer vision. It provides tools for image and video analysis, object detection, machine learning, and more.
- re: This module provides support for regular expressions (also called regexes) in Python.
- pywt: This library provides functions for 1D and 2D Discrete Wavelet Transform (DWT).
- skimage.restoration.denoise_tv_chambolle: This function performs Total Variation denoising on an image using the Chambolle algorithm, which is implemented in the scikit-image library.

These libraries are commonly used in applications involving GUI development, image processing, and scientific computing. They provide a wide range of functionalities for creating interactive applications, processing and analyzing image data, and visualizing results.

Class and Its Constructor

```
class VideoPlayerFiltering:
    def __init__(self, master):
        self.master = master
        self.master.title("FRAME FILTERING---VIVIAN SIAHAAN & RH.SIANIPAR")

        self.video = None
        self.video_path = None
        self.paused = False
        self.zoom_scale = tk.IntVar(value=1)
        self.frame_index = 0
        self.start_x = None
        self.start_y = None
        self.current_x = 0
        self.current_y = 0
        self.photo = None   # Save object reference to PhotoImage globally

        self.create_widgets()
```

The VideoPlayerFiltering class is designed to create a video player application with filtering capabilities using Tkinter. Let's break down the initialization and key attributes:
- __init__(self, master): This is the constructor method for the VideoPlayerFiltering class. It initializes the instance variables and sets up the initial state of the application.
- self.master = master: Stores a reference to the master widget, typically the root window of the Tkinter application.

- self.master.title("FRAME FILTERING---VIVIAN SIAHAAN & RH.SIANIPAR"): Sets the title of the application window to "FRAME FILTERING---VIVIAN SIAHAAN & RH.SIANIPAR".
- self.video, self.video_path: These variables store information about the video being displayed, including the video object itself (self.video) and the file path of the video (self.video_path). They are initialized to None until a video is loaded.
- self.paused: A boolean flag indicating whether the video playback is paused (True) or not (False). It is initially set to False.
- self.zoom_scale: An instance of tk.IntVar that stores the zoom scale value. It is initially set to 1.
- self.frame_index: Stores the index of the currently displayed frame in the video. It is initially set to 0.
- self.start_x, self.start_y: These variables store the coordinates of the starting position when dragging the video canvas. They are used for implementing dragging functionality and are initially set to None.
- self.current_x, self.current_y: Variables that store the current position of the video canvas. They are used for updating the position when dragging the canvas.
- self.photo: Stores the PhotoImage object representing the current frame being displayed. It is used to update the canvas with the latest frame.
- self.create_widgets(): Calls a method to create the GUI widgets for the video player.

Overall, the VideoPlayerFiltering class sets up the initial state of the video player application and prepares it for displaying videos with filtering capabilities. The next step would be implementing methods to load videos, play/pause, stop, and filter frames based on user input.

Creating Widgets

```python
def create_widgets(self):
    # Panel for video display
    video_panel = tk.Frame(self.master)
    video_panel.grid(row=0, column=0, padx=10, pady=10, sticky="nsew")
    
    # Canvas to display the video
    canvas_width = 800
    canvas_height = 600
    self.canvas = tk.Canvas(video_panel, width=canvas_width, height=canvas_height)
    self.canvas.pack(side="top", fill="both", expand=True)
    self.canvas.bind("<MouseWheel>", self.on_mousewheel)
    self.canvas.bind("<ButtonPress-1>", self.on_press)
    self.canvas.bind("<B1-Motion>", self.on_drag)
```

```python
        # Scrollbar
        self.scrollbar = tk.Scrollbar(video_panel, orient="horizontal", 
command=self.on_scroll)
        self.scrollbar.pack(side="bottom", fill="x")

        self.canvas.configure(xscrollcommand=self.scrollbar.set)

        # Panel for control buttons
        control_panel = tk.Frame(self.master)
        control_panel.grid(row=1, column=0, padx=10, pady=(0, 10), sticky="ew")

        # Button to open a video file
        self.open_button = tk.Button(control_panel, text="Open Video", 
command=self.open_video)
        self.open_button.grid(row=0, column=0, padx=10, pady=5)

        # Combobox for selecting zoom scale
        self.zoom_combobox = ttk.Combobox(control_panel, 
textvariable=self.zoom_scale, values=list(range(1, 11)))
        self.zoom_combobox.grid(row=0, column=1, padx=10, pady=5)
        self.zoom_combobox.bind("<<ComboboxSelected>>", self.update_zoom)

        # Label and entry for specifying time
        self.time_label = tk.Label(control_panel, text="Jump to Time (s):")
        self.time_label.grid(row=0, column=2, padx=10, pady=5, sticky="e")
        self.time_entry = ttk.Entry(control_panel)
        self.time_entry.grid(row=0, column=3, padx=10, pady=5, sticky="w")
        self.time_entry.bind("<Return>", lambda event: self.jump_to_time())

        # Button to jump to specified time
        self.jump_button = tk.Button(control_panel, text="Jump to Time", 
command=self.jump_to_time)
        self.jump_button.grid(row=0, column=4, padx=10, pady=5)

        # Button to play/pause the video
        self.play_button = tk.Button(control_panel, text="Play/Pause", 
command=self.toggle_play_pause)
        self.play_button.grid(row=0, column=5, padx=10, pady=5)

        # Button to stop the video
        self.stop_button = tk.Button(control_panel, text="Stop", 
command=self.stop_video)
        self.stop_button.grid(row=0, column=6, padx=10, pady=5)

        # Button to extract frame
        self.extract_button = tk.Button(control_panel, text="Extract Frame", 
command=self.extract_frame)
```

```
        self.extract_button.grid(row=1, column=0, padx=10, pady=5)

        # Label and entry for frame number
        self.frame_label = tk.Label(control_panel, text="Frame Number:")
        self.frame_label.grid(row=1, column=1, padx=10, pady=5, sticky="e")
        self.frame_entry = ttk.Entry(control_panel)
        self.frame_entry.grid(row=1, column=2, padx=10, pady=5, sticky="w")
        self.frame_entry.bind("<Return>", lambda event: self.extract_frame())

        # Button to open another instance of the application
        self.open_another_button = tk.Button(control_panel, text="Open Another Video Player", command=self.open_another_player)
        self.open_another_button.grid(row=2, column=0, columnspan=7, padx=10, pady=5)
```

The create_widgets() method of the VideoPlayerFiltering class is responsible for creating various GUI elements for the video player application. Let's break down each part:

1. Video Display Panel:
   - Creates a frame video_panel to contain the video display canvas.
   - Creates a canvas self.canvas inside video_panel to display the video.
   - Binds events for mouse wheel scrolling ("<MouseWheel>"), left button press ("<ButtonPress-1>"), and left button drag ("<B1-Motion>") to corresponding event handlers.
2. Scrollbar:
   - Adds a horizontal scrollbar self.scrollbar to enable scrolling when the video width exceeds the canvas width.
   - Configures the canvas to respond to horizontal scrolling events.
3. Control Panel:
   - Creates another frame control_panel to contain control buttons.
   - Adds buttons for:
     - Opening a video file (self.open_button).
     - Selecting zoom scale using a combobox (self.zoom_combobox).
     - Jumping to a specified time in the video (self.time_label, self.time_entry, self.jump_button).
     - Playing/pausing the video (self.play_button).
     - Stopping the video (self.stop_button).
     - Extracting frames (self.extract_button, self.frame_label, self.frame_entry).
     - Opening another instance of the application (self.open_another_button).

These widgets provide the user interface for controlling the video playback and interacting with the application. The associated event bindings and commands enable user interaction with the video player.

Opening, Playing, Stopping, and Toggling Video

```
def open_video(self):
    self.video_path = filedialog.askopenfilename(filetypes=[("Video files",
"*.mp4;*.avi;*.mkv")])
    if self.video_path:
        self.video = imageio.get_reader(self.video_path)
        self.play_video()

def play_video(self):
    if self.video:
        self.paused = False
        self.show_frame()

def stop_video(self):
    self.paused = True
    self.frame_index = 0
    self.current_x = 0
    self.current_y = 0  # Reset the current position
    self.show_frame()

def toggle_play_pause(self):
    self.paused = not self.paused
    if not self.paused:
        self.play_video()
```

These methods control the playback of the video:
1. open_video():
    - Opens a file dialog to select a video file (*.mp4, *.avi, *.mkv).
    - If a file is selected, it uses imageio.get_reader to initialize a video reader object (self.video) for the selected file.
    - Calls play_video() to start playing the video.
2. play_video():
    - If a video is loaded (self.video is not None), sets self.paused to False and calls show_frame to display the frames.
3. stop_video():
    - Stops the video playback by setting self.paused to True.
    - Resets self.frame_index to 0 to restart the video from the beginning.
    - Resets self.current_x and self.current_y to 0 to reset the current position.
    - Calls show_frame() to display the frame at the current index.
4. toggle_play_pause:
    - Toggles the play/pause state of the video.
    - If the video is currently paused, it resumes playback by calling play_video().
    - If the video is currently playing, it pauses the playback by setting self.paused to True.

Showing Frame

```
def update_zoom(self, event=None):
    self.show_frame()

def show_frame(self):
    if self.video:
        if not self.paused:
            self.frame_index += 1
            if self.frame_index >= len(self.video):
                self.frame_index = 0  # Reset frame index if it exceeds the maximum index
        if 0 <= self.frame_index < len(self.video):  # Check if frame index is within range
            try:
                frame = self.video.get_data(self.frame_index)
                frame = Image.fromarray(frame)
                frame = frame.resize((frame.width * self.zoom_scale.get(), frame.height * self.zoom_scale.get()))
                photo = ImageTk.PhotoImage(frame)
                self.photo = photo  # Save object reference to PhotoImage globally
                self.canvas.delete("video")  # Delete previous image
                self.canvas.create_image(self.current_x, self.current_y, anchor="nw", image=photo, tags="video")
                if not self.paused:
                    self.canvas.after(30, self.show_frame)
            except Exception as e:
                print("Error:", e)
```

The update_zoom() method and the show_frame() method work together to display video frames with zoom functionality:

1. update_zoom():
    - Called when the zoom scale is updated.
    - Calls show_frame() to update the displayed frame according to the new zoom scale.
2. show_frame():
    - Checks if a video is loaded (self.video is not None).
    - If the video is not paused, increments the frame index (self.frame_index) to move to the next frame.
    - If the frame index exceeds the maximum index, it resets it to 0 to loop back to the beginning of the video.
    - Checks if the frame index is within the range of available frames.
    - Tries to retrieve the frame from the video using self.video.get_data(self.frame_index).
    - Converts the frame to a PIL Image object (Image.fromarray(frame)).
    - Resizes the frame according to the current zoom scale (self.zoom_scale.get()).
    - Creates a PhotoImage object (photo) from the resized frame.

- Updates self.photo to store a reference to the PhotoImage.
- Deletes the previous image displayed on the canvas (self.canvas.delete("video")).
- Creates a new image on the canvas with the updated frame, position, and tags it as "video".
- If the video is not paused, schedules the show_frame method to be called again after a delay of 30 milliseconds using self.canvas.after(30, self.show_frame). This allows for smooth playback.

Handling Mouse Events

```
def on_mousewheel(self, event):
    direction = event.delta // 120
    current_value = int(self.zoom_scale.get())
    if direction == 1 and current_value < 10:
        current_value += 1
    elif direction == -1 and current_value > 1:
        current_value -= 1
    self.zoom_scale.set(current_value)
    self.update_zoom()

def on_press(self, event):
    self.start_x = event.x
    self.start_y = event.y

def on_drag(self, event):
    if self.start_x and self.start_y:
        x_offset = event.x - self.start_x
        y_offset = event.y - self.start_y
        self.current_x += x_offset  # Update current position
        self.current_y += y_offset  # Update current position
        self.canvas.move("video", x_offset, y_offset)
        self.start_x = event.x
        self.start_y = event.y

def on_scroll(self, *args):
    scroll_pos = self.scrollbar.get()
    self.current_x = -scroll_pos * self.canvas.winfo_width()
    self.canvas.xview_moveto(scroll_pos)
    self.frame_index = int(scroll_pos * len(self.video))  # Update frame index
    self.show_frame()
```

The on_mousewheel(), on_press(), on_drag(), and on_scroll() methods handle different interactions with the video player interface:
1. on_mousewheel():
    - Called when the mouse wheel is scrolled.
    - Determines the direction of the scroll (direction).
    - Updates the zoom scale (self.zoom_scale) based on the scroll direction.

- Calls update_zoom() to update the displayed frame with the new zoom scale.
2. on_press():
    - Called when a mouse button is pressed on the canvas.
    - Records the starting position (self.start_x, self.start_y) of the mouse pointer.
3. on_drag():
    - Called when the mouse is dragged (moved with the button pressed) on the canvas.
    - Calculates the offset of the mouse position from the starting position (x_offset, y_offset).
    - Updates the current position (self.current_x, self.current_y) based on the offset.
    - Moves the video frame on the canvas accordingly using self.canvas.move.
    - Updates the starting position (self.start_x, self.start_y) to the current position.
4. on_scroll():
    - Called when the scrollbar is scrolled.
    - Retrieves the current scroll position (scroll_pos) of the scrollbar.
    - Updates the current x-position of the video frame based on the scroll position.
    - Moves the canvas view (self.canvas.xview_moveto) to the corresponding position.
    - Calculates the frame index based on the scroll position to synchronize with the video.
    - Calls show_frame() to update the displayed frame accordingly.

Extracting and Showing Frame

```
def extract_frame(self):
    frame_number_str = self.frame_entry.get()
    try:
        frame_number = int(frame_number_str)
        if 0 <= frame_number < len(self.video):
            frame = self.video.get_data(frame_number)
            self.show_extracted_frame(frame, frame_number)
    except ValueError:
        pass

def show_extracted_frame(self, frame, frame_number):
    self.extracted_frame_window = tk.Toplevel(self.master)
    self.extracted_frame_window.title(f"EXTRACTED FRAME (Frame {frame_number}) --- VIVIAN SIAHAAN & RH.SIANIPAR")
    
    extracted_frame_label = tk.Label(self.extracted_frame_window, text=f"Frame yang Diekstraksi (Frame {frame_number})")
```

```python
        extracted_frame_label.pack()

        height, width, _ = frame.shape  # Get dimensions of the frame
        extracted_photo = ImageTk.PhotoImage(image=Image.fromarray(frame))

        # Create a panel for the frame and edge detection canvas
        frame_panel = tk.Frame(self.extracted_frame_window)
        frame_panel.pack(side="top")

        extracted_frame_canvas = tk.Canvas(frame_panel, width=width, height=height)
        extracted_frame_canvas.pack(side="left")
        extracted_frame_canvas.create_image(0, 0, anchor="nw", image=extracted_photo)
        extracted_frame_canvas.image = extracted_photo

        # Canvas for edge detection result
        self.edge_canvas = tk.Canvas(frame_panel, width=width, height=height)
        self.edge_canvas.pack(side="right")

        # Create a panel for histogram plots and hash values
        hist_hash_panel = tk.Frame(self.extracted_frame_window)
        hist_hash_panel.pack(side="bottom", fill="both", expand=True)

        # Plot histogram for each RGB channel
        fig, axs = plt.subplots(1, 3, figsize=(20, 3))
        colors = ['red', 'green', 'blue']
        for i, color in enumerate(['R', 'G', 'B']):
            hist, bins, _ = axs[i].hist(frame[:,:,i].ravel(), bins=64, range=(0, 255), color=colors[i], alpha=0.7)
            axs[i].set_title(f"Histogram of {color} Channel (Frame {frame_number})", fontsize=14, fontweight='bold', color='blue')
            axs[i].set_xlabel("Pixel Value", fontsize=12)
            axs[i].set_ylabel("Frequency", fontsize=12)
            axs[i].grid(True, linestyle='--', linewidth=0.5, color='gray', alpha=0.5)
            axs[i].tick_params(axis='both', which='major', labelsize=10)

            # Add frequency values above each bar
            for bar, frequency in zip(hist, bins[1:]):
                if bar > 0:
                    axs[i].annotate(f'{frequency:.0f}', xy=(bins[np.where(hist == bar)[0][0]] + (bins[1] - bins[0]) / 2, bar),
                                    xytext=(0, 3), textcoords='offset points', ha='center', va='bottom', fontsize=8)

        # Ensure the canvas is updated to display the histogram plots
        plt.tight_layout()
        fig.canvas.draw()

        # Display the histogram plots on a Tkinter canvas
```

```python
        self.histogram_canvas = FigureCanvasTkAgg(fig, master=hist_hash_panel)
        self.histogram_canvas.get_tk_widget().pack(side=tk.TOP, fill=tk.BOTH, expand=True)
        self.histogram_canvas.draw()

        # Calculate multiple hash values of the frame
        hash_algorithms = ['md5', 'sha1', 'sha256', 'sha224', 'sha384', 'sha512', 'blake2b', 'ripemd160']
        hash_values = {}
        for algorithm in hash_algorithms:
            hash_obj = hashlib.new(algorithm)
            hash_obj.update(frame.tobytes())
            hash_value = hash_obj.hexdigest()
            hash_values[algorithm] = hash_value

        # Edge detection combobox
        edge_detection_label = tk.Label(hist_hash_panel, text="Edge Detection Method:")
        edge_detection_label.pack()

        self.filtering_method = ttk.Combobox(hist_hash_panel, values=["None", "Gaussian", "Mean",
            "Median", "Bilateral Filtering", "Non-local Means Denoising", "Anisotropic Diffusion",
            "Total Variation Denoising", "Wiener Filter", "Adaptive Thresholding", "Wavelet Transform"])
        self.filtering_method.pack()
        self.filtering_method.current(0)  # Set default method
        self.filtering_method.bind("<<ComboboxSelected>>", self.apply_filtering)

        # Display hash values
        self.hash_listbox = tk.Listbox(hist_hash_panel, height=8, width=40, font=("Arial", 13), bg="crimson", fg="white")
        self.hash_listbox.pack(fill=tk.BOTH, expand=True)

        # Add horizontal scrollbar if needed
        scrollbar = tk.Scrollbar(hist_hash_panel, orient=tk.HORIZONTAL, command=self.hash_listbox.xview)
        scrollbar.pack(side=tk.BOTTOM, fill=tk.X)
        self.hash_listbox.config(xscrollcommand=scrollbar.set)

        for algorithm, value in hash_values.items():
            self.hash_listbox.insert(tk.END, f"{algorithm}: {value}")
```

The extract_frame() method is responsible for extracting and displaying a specific frame from the video based on the frame number entered by the user. If a valid frame number is provided, it retrieves the corresponding frame using self.video.get_data(frame_number) and calls the show_extracted_frame() method to display the frame along with additional information.

The show_extracted_frame() method creates a new window (self.extracted_frame_window) to display the extracted frame, its histogram, edge detection canvas, and hash values. Here's a breakdown of its functionality:
1. Display Extracted Frame:
    - The extracted frame is displayed using a Canvas widget (extracted_frame_canvas) with the help of ImageTk.PhotoImage.
2. Display Histogram:
    - Histograms for each RGB channel of the frame are plotted using matplotlib. The histograms are displayed on a FigureCanvasTkAgg widget (histogram_canvas) embedded within the GUI.
3. Calculate Hash Values:
    - Multiple hash values of the frame are calculated using different hashing algorithms (hashlib) and displayed in a Listbox widget (hash_listbox).
4. Edge Detection Method Selection:
    - Users can select different edge detection methods from a Combobox widget (filtering_method). The selected method triggers the apply_filtering() method when changed.
5. Scrollbar:
    - If the content exceeds the size of the hash_listbox, a horizontal scrollbar is added to scroll through the hash values.

Overall, the show_extracted_frame() method provides a comprehensive display of information related to the extracted frame, including visual representation, histogram analysis, hash values, and edge detection options.

Gaussian Filtering

```
# Define functions for filtering methods
def apply_gaussian_blur(self, frame, kernel_size=(5, 5), sigma_x=0, sigma_y=0):
    """
    Apply Gaussian blur to each channel of the input frame.

    Args:
        frame: Input image frame.
        kernel_size: Size of the Gaussian kernel. Default is (5, 5).
        sigma_x: Standard deviation in X direction. Default is 0.
        sigma_y: Standard deviation in Y direction. Default is 0.

    Returns:
        List of blurred images for each channel.
```

```
        """
        blurred_frames = []
        for i in range(3):  # Iterate over each color channel
            blurred_frame = cv2.GaussianBlur(frame[:,:,i], kernel_size, sigma_x,
sigma_y)
            blurred_frames.append(blurred_frame)
        return blurred_frames
```

The apply_gaussian_blur() function applies Gaussian blur to each color channel of an input image frame. Here's a breakdown of its functionality:

1. Arguments:
    - frame: Input image frame.
    - kernel_size: Size of the Gaussian kernel. It defines the width and height of the kernel, which determines the amount of blur. The default is set to (5, 5).
    - sigma_x and sigma_y: Standard deviations in the X and Y directions. These parameters control the spread of the Gaussian distribution along the X and Y axes, respectively. The default values are set to 0, which means they are calculated based on the kernel size.
2. Returns:
    - blurred_frames: A list containing the blurred images for each color channel.
3. Implementation:
    - The function iterates over each color channel (R, G, B) of the input frame.
    - For each channel, it applies Gaussian blur using cv2.GaussianBlur.
    - The resulting blurred frames for each channel are stored in the blurred_frames list.

This function allows for the application of Gaussian blur with customizable kernel size and standard deviations, providing flexibility in adjusting the amount of blur applied to the image.

Mean Filtering

```
    def apply_mean_blur(self, frame, kernel_size=(5, 5)):
        """
        Apply mean blur to each channel of the input frame.

        Args:
            frame: Input image frame.
            kernel_size: Size of the kernel. Default is (5, 5).

        Returns:
            List of blurred images for each channel.
        """
        blurred_frames = []
        for i in range(3):  # Iterate over each color channel
            blurred_frame = cv2.blur(frame[:,:,i], kernel_size)
```

```
            blurred_frames.append(blurred_frame)
    return blurred_frames
```

The apply_mean_blur() function applies mean blur to each color channel of an input image frame. Below is an explanation of its functionality:
1. Arguments:
    - frame: Input image frame.
    - kernel_size: Size of the kernel used for mean blur. It determines the area over which the mean value is calculated. The default size is (5, 5).
2. Returns:
    - blurred_frames: A list containing the blurred images for each color channel.
3. Implementation:
    - The function iterates over each color channel (R, G, B) of the input frame.
    - For each channel, it applies mean blur using cv2.blur.
    - The resulting blurred frames for each channel are stored in the blurred_frames list.

Mean blur is a simple and effective method for blurring an image. It replaces each pixel's value with the mean value of its neighboring pixels within the kernel. This function provides a straightforward way to apply mean blur to an image, allowing customization of the kernel size for different blurring effects.

Median Filtering

```
def apply_median_blur(self, frame, kernel_size=5):
    """
    Apply median blur to each channel of the input frame.

    Args:
        frame: Input image frame.
        kernel_size: Size of the kernel. Default is 5.
    Returns:
        List of blurred images for each channel.
    """
    blurred_frames = []
    for i in range(3):  # Iterate over each color channel
        blurred_frame = cv2.medianBlur(frame[:,:,i], kernel_size)
        blurred_frames.append(blurred_frame)
    return blurred_frames
```

The apply_median_blur() function applies median blur to each color channel of an input image frame. Below is an explanation of its functionality:

1. Arguments:
    - frame: Input image frame.
    - kernel_size: Size of the kernel used for median blur. It specifies the aperture linear size, which should be odd and greater than 1. The default size is 5.
2. Returns:
    - blurred_frames: A list containing the blurred images for each color channel.
3. Implementation:
    - The function iterates over each color channel (R, G, B) of the input frame.
    - For each channel, it applies median blur using cv2.medianBlur.
    - The resulting blurred frames for each channel are stored in the blurred_frames list.

Median blur is a nonlinear filter that replaces each pixel's value with the median value of its neighboring pixels within the kernel. It is effective at removing salt-and-pepper noise while preserving edges better than mean blur. This function provides a way to apply median blur to an image, allowing customization of the kernel size for different blurring effects.

Bileteral Filtering

```
def apply_bilateral_filtering(self, frame, d=9, sigma_color=75, sigma_space=75):
    """
    Apply bilateral filtering to each channel of the input frame.

    Args:
        frame: Input image frame.
        d: Diameter of each pixel neighborhood. Default is 9.
        sigma_color: Filter sigma in the color space. Default is 75.
        sigma_space: Filter sigma in the coordinate space. Default is 75.

    Returns:
        List of filtered images for each channel.
    """
    filtered_frames = []
    for i in range(3):  # Iterate over each color channel
        filtered_frame = cv2.bilateralFilter(frame[:,:,i], d, sigma_color, sigma_space)
        filtered_frames.append(filtered_frame)
    return filtered_frames
```

The apply_bilateral_filtering() function applies bilateral filtering to each color channel of an input image frame. Below is an explanation of its functionality:
1. Arguments:
    - frame: Input image frame.
    - d: Diameter of each pixel neighborhood. This parameter determines the size of the pixel neighborhood around each pixel. The default value is 9.

- sigma_color: Filter sigma in the color space. This parameter controls how much influence the color difference between the central pixel and its neighbors should have on the filtering process. A higher value means that colors farther away from the central color will be included in the filtering. The default value is 75.
- sigma_space: Filter sigma in the coordinate space. This parameter controls how much influence the spatial distance between the central pixel and its neighbors should have on the filtering process. A higher value means that pixels farther away from the central pixel will be included in the filtering. The default value is 75.

2. Returns:
    - filtered_frames: A list containing the filtered images for each color channel.
3. Implementation:
    - The function iterates over each color channel (R, G, B) of the input frame.
    - For each channel, it applies bilateral filtering using cv2.bilateralFilter.
    - The resulting filtered frames for each channel are stored in the filtered_frames list.

Bilateral filtering is a nonlinear filter that smooths images while preserving edges. It considers both the spatial distance and the intensity difference when performing smoothing, making it effective at reducing noise while preserving important image features. This function provides a way to apply bilateral filtering to an image, allowing customization of parameters for different filtering effects.

Non-Local Means Denoising

```
    def apply_non_local_means_denoising(self, frame, h=10, templateWindowSize=7, searchWindowSize=21):
        """
        Apply Non-local Means Denoising to each channel of the input frame.

        Args:
            frame: Input image frame.
            h: Parameter regulating filter strength. Larger 'h' value removes noise effectively but removes details of image also.
                Smaller 'h' value preserves details but also preserves noise. Default is 10.
            templateWindowSize: Size in pixels of the template patch. Recommended value is 7. Default is 7.
            searchWindowSize: Size in pixels of the window for the search. Recommended value is 21. Default is 21.

        Returns:
            List of denoised images for each channel.
        """
        denoised_frames = []
```

```
    for i in range(3):  # Iterate over each color channel
        denoised_frame = cv2.fastNlMeansDenoising(frame[:,:,i], None, h=h,
templateWindowSize=templateWindowSize, searchWindowSize=searchWindowSize)
        denoised_frames.append(denoised_frame)
    return denoised_frames
```

The apply_non_local_means_denoising() function applies Non-local Means Denoising to each color channel of an input image frame. Here's an explanation of its parameters and functionality:

1. Arguments:
    - frame: Input image frame.
    - h: Parameter regulating filter strength. A larger h value effectively removes noise but may also remove image details. Conversely, a smaller h value preserves details but also preserves noise. The default is 10.
    - templateWindowSize: Size in pixels of the template patch. A larger templateWindowSize may capture more image details but may also increase processing time. The recommended value is 7, and the default is 7.
    - searchWindowSize: Size in pixels of the window for the search. A larger searchWindowSize considers more pixels during the denoising process, potentially leading to better results at the cost of increased computation time. The recommended value is 21, and the default is 21.
2. Returns:
    - denoised_frames: A list containing the denoised images for each color channel.
3. Implementation:
    - The function iterates over each color channel (R, G, B) of the input frame.
    - For each channel, it applies Non-local Means Denoising using cv2.fastNlMeansDenoising.
    - The resulting denoised frames for each channel are stored in the denoised_frames list.

Non-local Means Denoising is a technique used to reduce noise in images while preserving image details. It works by averaging the intensities of similar patches in the image, thus effectively removing noise. This function provides a way to apply Non-local Means Denoising to an image, allowing customization of parameters for different denoising effects. Adjusting the h, templateWindowSize, and searchWindowSize parameters can fine-tune the denoising process based on the characteristics of the input image and the desired output quality.

Anisotropic Diffusion

```
    def apply_anisotropic_diffusion(self, frame, iterations=1, delta_t=0.25,
kappa=10):
        """"
```

```
            Apply Anisotropic Diffusion to each channel of the input frame.

            Args:
                frame: Input image frame.
                iterations: Number of iterations for diffusion. Default is 1.
                delta_t: Time step. Default is 0.25.
                kappa: Perona-Malik diffusion coefficient. Default is 10.

            Returns:
                List of processed frames after applying Anisotropic Diffusion to each
channel.
            """
            diffusion_frames = []
            for i in range(3):  # Iterate over each color channel
                # Copy the input frame channel to avoid modifying the original frame
                img = frame[:,:,i].astype(float)

                # Define the 4-neighbour mask
                mask = np.array([[0, 1, 0],
                                 [1, 0, 1],
                                 [0, 1, 0]], dtype=np.float32)

                # Perform Anisotropic Diffusion for the specified number of iterations
                for _ in range(iterations):
                    # Add padding to the image
                    img_padded = cv2.copyMakeBorder(img, 1, 1, 1, 1, cv2.BORDER_REFLECT)

                    # Compute gradients using central differences
                    dx = cv2.filter2D(img_padded, -1, np.array([[-1, 0, 1]]))
                    dy = cv2.filter2D(img_padded, -1, np.array([[-1], [0], [1]]))

                    # Resize gradients to match the size of the image
                    dx = cv2.resize(dx, img.shape[::-1])
                    dy = cv2.resize(dy, img.shape[::-1])

                    # Compute gradient magnitude squared
                    mag = np.square(dx) + np.square(dy)

                    # Compute diffusion coefficients
                    c = 1 / (1 + (mag / kappa ** 2))

                    # Update image using the diffusion equation
                    img += delta_t * (c * cv2.filter2D(dx, -1, mask) +
                                      c * cv2.filter2D(dy, -1, mask))

                # Append the processed channel to the list of diffusion frames
                diffusion_frames.append(np.clip(img, 0, 255).astype(np.uint8))

            return diffusion_frames
```

The apply_anisotropic_diffusion() function applies Anisotropic Diffusion to each color channel of an input image frame. Here's a breakdown of its parameters and functionality:
1. Arguments:
    - frame: Input image frame.
    - iterations: Number of iterations for diffusion. Default is 1.

- delta_t: Time step. Default is 0.25.
- kappa: Perona-Malik diffusion coefficient. Default is 10.
2. Returns:
    - diffusion_frames: A list containing the processed frames after applying Anisotropic Diffusion to each channel.
3. Implementation:
    - The function iterates over each color channel (R, G, B) of the input frame.
    - For each channel, it performs Anisotropic Diffusion using the Perona-Malik equation.
    - Anisotropic Diffusion is a technique used for image smoothing while preserving edges. It achieves this by diffusing pixel intensities while considering the local image gradients.
    - The diffusion process is iterated for the specified number of iterations.
    - Within each iteration:
        - Gradients of the image are computed using central differences.
        - Gradient magnitude squared is calculated.
        - Diffusion coefficients are computed based on the gradient magnitude and the Perona-Malik coefficient.
        - The image is updated using the diffusion equation, which takes into account the diffusion coefficients and the local gradients.
        - The processed channel is then appended to the list of diffusion_frames.

Anisotropic Diffusion is particularly effective for denoising images while preserving edges and fine details. Adjusting the iterations, delta_t, and kappa parameters allows for control over the strength and extent of the smoothing process. By customizing these parameters, one can achieve different degrees of denoising and edge preservation in the output images.

Total Variation Denoising

```
def apply_total_variation_denoising(self, frame, weight=0.7, eps=0.05):
    """
    Apply Total Variation Denoising to each channel of the input frame.

    Args:
        frame: Input image frame.
        weight: Denoising weight. Default is 0.7.
        eps: Denoising regularization parameter. Default is 0.05.

    Returns:
        List of denoised frames for each channel.
    """
    denoised_frames = []
    for i in range(3):  # Iterate over each color channel
```

```
        denoised_frame = denoise_tv_chambolle(frame[:,:,i], weight=weight, eps=eps)
        # Scale the result to the range 0 to 255
        scaled_denoised_frame = ((denoised_frame - denoised_frame.min()) * (255 / (denoised_frame.max() - denoised_frame.min()))).astype(np.uint8)
        denoised_frames.append(scaled_denoised_frame)
    return denoised_frames
```

The apply_total_variation_denoising() function applies Total Variation Denoising (TV denoising) to each color channel of an input image frame. Here's an overview of its parameters and functionality:
1. Arguments:
    - frame: Input image frame.
    - weight: Denoising weight. Default is 0.7.
    - eps: Denoising regularization parameter. Default is 0.05.
2. Returns:
    - denoised_frames: A list containing the denoised frames for each channel.
3. Implementation:
    - The function iterates over each color channel (R, G, B) of the input frame.
    - For each channel, it applies the Total Variation Denoising algorithm using the denoise_tv_chambolle function from scikit-image.
    - Total Variation Denoising is a technique used for image denoising while preserving edges. It achieves this by minimizing the total variation of the image, effectively smoothing regions with homogeneous intensity while preserving edges and fine details.
    - After denoising, the result is scaled to the range 0 to 255 to ensure it can be properly displayed as an image.
    - The denoised channel is then appended to the list of denoised_frames.

Total Variation Denoising is widely used for removing noise from images while preserving important structures, making it suitable for various image processing tasks, including medical imaging, computer vision, and photography. Adjusting the weight and eps parameters allows for control over the denoising strength and regularization, enabling customization according to specific requirements or characteristics of the input images.

Wiener Filtering

```
    def apply_wiener_filter(self, frame, kernel_size=(3, 3), noise_variance=0.1):
        """
        Apply Wiener Filter to each channel of the input frame.

        Args:
```

```
            frame: Input image frame.
            kernel_size: Size of the Gaussian kernel for blurring. Default is (3, 3).
            noise_variance: Variance of the noise. Default is 0.1.

        Returns:
            List of images after applying Wiener Filter to each channel.
        """
        filtered_frames = []
        for i in range(3):  # Iterate over each color channel
            blurred_frame = cv2.GaussianBlur(frame[:,:,i], kernel_size, 0)
            filtered_frame = cv2.fastNlMeansDenoising(blurred_frame, None, h=noise_variance)
            filtered_frames.append(filtered_frame)
        return filtered_frames
```

The apply_wiener_filter() function applies the Wiener filter to each color channel of an input image frame. Below is a breakdown of its parameters and functionality:

1. Arguments:
   - frame: Input image frame.
   - kernel_size: Size of the Gaussian kernel for blurring. Default is (3, 3).
   - noise_variance: Variance of the noise. Default is 0.1.
2. Returns:
   - filtered_frames: A list containing the filtered images for each channel.
3. Implementation:
   - The function iterates over each color channel (R, G, B) of the input frame.
   - For each channel, it applies Gaussian blurring to reduce noise and create a reference image. Gaussian blurring helps in estimating the noise present in the image.
   - The Wiener filter is then applied using the cv2.fastNlMeansDenoising function with the blurred frame and the noise variance as parameters.
   - The resulting filtered frame for each channel is appended to the filtered_frames list.

The Wiener filter is a popular method for noise reduction in images. It is particularly effective in scenarios where the characteristics of the noise are known or can be estimated. By adjusting parameters such as kernel_size and noise_variance, the filter's performance can be fine-tuned to suit the specific characteristics of the noise present in the image.

Adaptive Filtering

```
    def apply_adaptive_thresholding(self, frame, max_value=255,
adaptive_method=cv2.ADAPTIVE_THRESH_GAUSSIAN_C, threshold_type=cv2.THRESH_BINARY,
block_size=11, constant=2):
        """
        Apply Adaptive Thresholding to each channel of the input frame.

        Args:
            frame: Input image frame.
            max_value: Maximum intensity value. Default is 255.
            adaptive_method: Adaptive thresholding method. Default is
cv2.ADAPTIVE_THRESH_GAUSSIAN_C.
            threshold_type: Thresholding type. Default is cv2.THRESH_BINARY.
            block_size: Size of the local region. Default is 11.
            constant: Constant subtracted from the mean. Default is 2.

        Returns:
            List of images after applying Adaptive Thresholding to each channel.
        """
        thresholded_frames = []
        for i in range(3):  # Iterate over each color channel
            thresholded_frame = cv2.adaptiveThreshold(frame[:,:,i], max_value,
adaptive_method, threshold_type, block_size, constant)
            thresholded_frames.append(thresholded_frame)
        return thresholded_frames
```

The apply_adaptive_thresholding() function applies adaptive thresholding to each color channel of an input image frame. Here's a breakdown of its parameters and functionality:

1. Arguments:
    - frame: Input image frame.
    - max_value: Maximum intensity value. Default is 255.
    - adaptive_method: Adaptive thresholding method. Default is cv2.ADAPTIVE_THRESH_GAUSSIAN_C.
    - threshold_type: Thresholding type. Default is cv2.THRESH_BINARY.
    - block_size: Size of the local region. Default is 11.
    - constant: Constant subtracted from the mean. Default is 2.
2. Returns:
    - thresholded_frames: A list containing the thresholded images for each channel.
3. Implementation:
    - The function iterates over each color channel (R, G, B) of the input frame.
    - For each channel, it applies adaptive thresholding using cv2.adaptiveThreshold function.

- Adaptive thresholding computes the threshold value for each pixel based on the local region around it, which helps in handling varying illumination conditions across the image.
- The max_value, adaptive_method, threshold_type, block_size, and constant parameters are used to customize the adaptive thresholding process.
- The resulting thresholded frame for each channel is appended to the thresholded_frames list.

Adaptive thresholding is useful for segmenting images with non-uniform lighting conditions or varying background intensities. It adapts to the local characteristics of the image, making it particularly effective in scenarios where global thresholding methods may not perform well.

Wavelet Filtering

```python
def apply_wavelet_transform(self, frame, wavelet='haar', level=1):
    """
    Apply Wavelet Transform to each channel of the input frame.

    Args:
        frame: Input image frame.
        wavelet: Type of wavelet. Default is 'haar'.
        level: Decomposition level. Default is 1.

    Returns:
        List of images after applying Wavelet Transform to each channel.
    """
    transformed_frames = []
    for i in range(3):  # Iterate over each color channel
        coeffs = pywt.wavedec2(frame[:,:,i], wavelet, level=level)
        # Reconstruct the image from the coefficients
        reconstructed_img = pywt.waverec2(coeffs, wavelet)
        transformed_frames.append(reconstructed_img)

    return transformed_frames
```

The apply_wavelet_transform() function applies the Wavelet Transform to each color channel of the input image frame. Here's a detailed explanation:
1. Arguments:
    - frame: Input image frame.
    - wavelet: Type of wavelet. Default is 'haar'.
    - level: Decomposition level. Default is 1.
2. Returns:
    - transformed_frames: A list containing the images after applying the Wavelet Transform to each channel.
3. Implementation:

- The function iterates over each color channel (R, G, B) of the input frame.
- For each channel, it computes the 2D Discrete Wavelet Transform using pywt.wavedec2.
- The wavelet parameter specifies the type of wavelet to be used, with the default being the Haar wavelet.
- The level parameter determines the level of decomposition.
- After obtaining the wavelet coefficients, the function reconstructs the image from these coefficients using pywt.waverec2.
- The reconstructed image for each channel is appended to the transformed_frames list.

The Wavelet Transform is useful for various image processing tasks, including denoising, compression, and feature extraction. It decomposes the image into different frequency components, allowing for efficient representation and analysis of both coarse and fine details.

Applying Filters

```
def apply_filtering(self, event=None):
    # Get selected method from combobox
    method = self.filtering_method.get()

    # Get the current frame number from the title of the tkinter window
    title = self.extracted_frame_window.title()
    frame_numbers = re.findall(r'\d+', title)
    if frame_numbers:
        self.frame_number = int(frame_numbers[-1])  # Extract the last numerical value
    else:
        self.frame_number = 0  # Default frame number if no numerical value is found

    frame = self.video.get_data(self.frame_number)

    # Initialize filtered to None
    filtered = None

    # Apply edge detection method based on selected method
    if method == "Gaussian":
        filtered = self.apply_gaussian_blur(frame)
    elif method == "Mean":
        filtered = self.apply_mean_blur(frame)
    elif method == "Median":
        filtered = self.apply_median_blur(frame)
```

```python
elif method == "None":
    filtered = [frame[:,:,i].copy() for i in range(3)]
elif method == "Bilateral Filtering":
    filtered = self.apply_bilateral_filtering(frame)
elif method == "Non-local Means Denoising":
    filtered = self.apply_non_local_means_denoising(frame)
elif method == "Anisotropic Diffusion":
    filtered = self.apply_anisotropic_diffusion(frame)
elif method == "Total Variation Denoising":
    filtered = self.apply_total_variation_denoising(frame)
elif method == "Wiener Filter":
    filtered = self.apply_wiener_filter(frame)
elif method == "Adaptive Thresholding":
    filtered = self.apply_adaptive_thresholding(frame)
elif method == "Wavelet Transform":
    filtered = self.apply_wavelet_transform(frame)

# Display edge detection result
if filtered is not None:
    # Combine channels into a single image
    combined_image = self.combine_channels_to_image(filtered)

    # Convert the combined image to a PIL Image
    pil_image = Image.fromarray(np.uint8(combined_image))

    # Convert PIL Image to Tkinter PhotoImage
    edge_photo = ImageTk.PhotoImage(image=pil_image)

    # Display the image in the canvas
    self.edge_canvas.create_image(0, 0, anchor="nw", image=edge_photo)
    self.edge_canvas.image = edge_photo

    # Update histogram and hash values
    self.update_histogram_and_hashes(frame, filtered)
```

The apply_filtering() method is responsible for applying various filtering techniques to the extracted frame based on the selected method from the combobox. Here's a breakdown of its functionality:

1. Method Retrieval:
    - Retrieves the selected filtering method from the combobox.
2. Frame Retrieval:
    - Retrieves the frame data corresponding to the current frame number from the video.
3. Filtering Application:

- Applies the selected filtering method to the frame:
    - If the method is one of the predefined filters (e.g., Gaussian blur, mean blur, etc.), the corresponding filtering function is called.
    - If the method is "None," the original frame is copied for each channel.
    - If the method is "Wavelet Transform," the wavelet transform is applied.
    - For each filtering method, the appropriate function from the class is called with the frame as input.
4. Displaying Filtered Image:
    - Combines the filtered channels into a single image.
    - Converts the combined image to a PIL Image.
    - Converts the PIL Image to a Tkinter PhotoImage.
    - Displays the filtered image in the edge_canvas canvas.
5. Updating Histogram and Hash Values:
    - Calls the update_histogram_and_hashes() method to update the histogram and hash values based on the original frame and the filtered frame.

This method provides a modular and flexible approach to apply various filters to the extracted frame, allowing for easy comparison and analysis of different filtering techniques.

Combining Image Channels

```
def combine_channels_to_image(self, filtered):
    """
    Combine filtered channels into a single image.

    Args:
        filtered: List of filtered images for each channel.

    Returns:
        Combined image.
    """
    # Convert each filtered channel to numpy array
    filtered_arrays = [np.array(channel) for channel in filtered]

    # Stack the filtered channels along the last axis to form the combined image
    combined_image = np.stack(filtered_arrays, axis=-1)

    return combined_image
```

The combine_channels_to_image() method takes a list of filtered images, where each image represents the result of applying a specific filter to one color channel of the original frame. It then merges these filtered channels back into a single image.

Here's a breakdown of its functionality:

1. Conversion to Numpy Arrays: Iterate through the list of filtered images and convert each image into a Numpy array.
2. Stacking Channels: Stack these arrays along the last axis to form the combined image, effectively merging the separate filtered channels.
3. Return: Return the combined image, now ready for display in the Tkinter canvas.

This method ensures that the visual representation of the filtered frame accurately reflects the effects of the applied filters across all color channels.

Updating Histogram and Hash Values

```python
def update_histogram_and_hashes(self, frame, filtered):
    # Update histogram
    for i, ax in enumerate(self.histogram_canvas.figure.get_axes()):
        ax.clear()
        colors = ['red', 'green', 'blue']
        channel = filtered[i]  # Memilih saluran warna yang sesuai dengan indeks
        hist, bins = np.histogram(channel.ravel(), bins=32, range=(0, 255))
        ax.bar(bins[:-1], hist, color=colors[i], alpha=0.7, width=6)  # Menyesuaikan lebar batang histogram
        ax.set_title(f"Histogram of {colors[i]} Channel (Frame {self.frame_number})", fontsize=14, fontweight='bold', color='blue')
        ax.set_xlabel("Pixel Value", fontsize=12)
        ax.set_ylabel("Frequency", fontsize=12)
        ax.grid(True, linestyle='--', linewidth=0.5, color='gray', alpha=0.5)
        ax.tick_params(axis='both', which='major', labelsize=10)
        # Add frequency values above each bar
        for bar, frequency in zip(hist, bins[1:]):
            if bar > 0:
                ax.annotate(f'{frequency:.0f}', xy=(bins[np.where(hist == bar)[0][0]] + (bins[1] - bins[0]) / 2, bar),
                            xytext=(0, 3), textcoords='offset points',
                            ha='center', va='bottom', fontsize=8)
    self.histogram_canvas.draw()

    # Update hash values
    hash_algorithms = ['md5', 'sha1', 'sha256', 'sha224', 'sha384', 'sha512', 'blake2b', 'ripemd160']
    hash_values = {}
    for algorithm in hash_algorithms:
        hash_obj = hashlib.new(algorithm)
        for channel in filtered:
            hash_obj.update(channel.tobytes())  # Update hash values based on edge-detected image
        hash_value = hash_obj.hexdigest()
        hash_values[algorithm] = hash_value

    self.hash_listbox.delete(0, tk.END)  # Clear existing hash values
    for algorithm, value in hash_values.items():
        self.hash_listbox.insert(tk.END, f"{algorithm}: {value}")
```

The update_histogram_and_hashes() method is responsible for updating both the histogram plot and the hash values displayed in the application's interface based on the currently filtered frame. Here's what it does:
1. Update Histogram:
    - Iterate over each color channel in the filtered frame.
    - Calculate the histogram of pixel intensities for each channel using np.histogram.
    - Clear the existing histogram plot axes and redraw it with updated data for each channel.
    - Display the histogram title, axis labels, and annotate bars with frequency values.
    - Redraw the histogram canvas to reflect the changes.
2. Update Hash Values:
    - Iterate over a list of hash algorithms.
    - For each algorithm, update the hash value based on the filtered frame's pixel data.
    - Display the hash values in the application's interface, showing the algorithm name and corresponding hash value.

Overall, this method ensures that both the visual representation of the histogram and the displayed hash values accurately reflect the characteristics of the currently filtered frame.

Showing Filtering Result

```
def show_filterinng_result(self, filtered):
    # Combine channels into a single image
    combined_image = self.combine_channels_to_image(filtered)

    # Convert the combined image to a PIL Image
    pil_image = Image.fromarray(np.uint8(combined_image))

    # Convert PIL Image to Tkinter PhotoImage
    edge_photo = ImageTk.PhotoImage(image=pil_image)

    # Display the image in the canvas
    self.edge_canvas.create_image(0, 0, anchor="nw", image=edge_photo)
    self.edge_canvas.image = edge_photo
```

The show_filtering_result() method is responsible for displaying the result of a filtering operation on the canvas. Here's what it does:
1. Combine Channels: It combines the filtered channels into a single image using the combine_channels_to_image method.
2. Convert to PIL Image: It converts the combined image, represented as a NumPy array, to a PIL Image object.
3. Convert to Tkinter PhotoImage: It converts the PIL Image to a Tkinter PhotoImage object, which can be displayed in a Tkinter canvas.

4. Display Image: It creates an image item on the edge_canvas with the converted PhotoImage, ensuring it starts from the top-left corner (northwest anchor). Finally, it updates the reference to the image object held by the canvas.

This method ensures that the filtered result is correctly displayed on the canvas for visualization.

Entry Point for Application

```
def main():
    root = tk.Tk()
    app = VideoPlayerFiltering(root)
    root.mainloop()

if __name__ == "__main__":
    main()
```

The main function serves as the entry point of the program. Here's what it does:
1. Create Tkinter Root Window: It creates a Tkinter root window using tk.Tk(), which serves as the main window of the application.
2. Instantiate VideoPlayerFiltering: It creates an instance of the VideoPlayerFiltering class, passing the root window as its master.
3. Start the Tkinter Event Loop: It starts the Tkinter event loop by calling root.mainloop(), which listens for events such as user input and updates the GUI accordingly.
4. Conditional Execution: The if __name__ == "__main__": block ensures that the main function is only executed if the script is run directly, not if it is imported as a module into another script. This is a common Python idiom to allow a script to be both executable and importable as a module.

Running Program

Run program and click on Open Video button. Then, choose a video file.

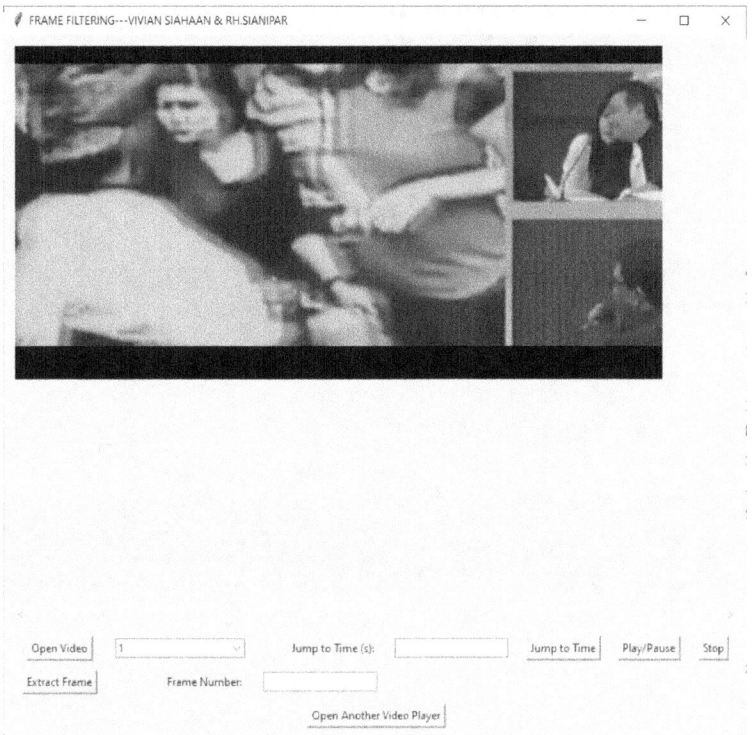

Type a specific number of frame number. Then, push ENTER key.

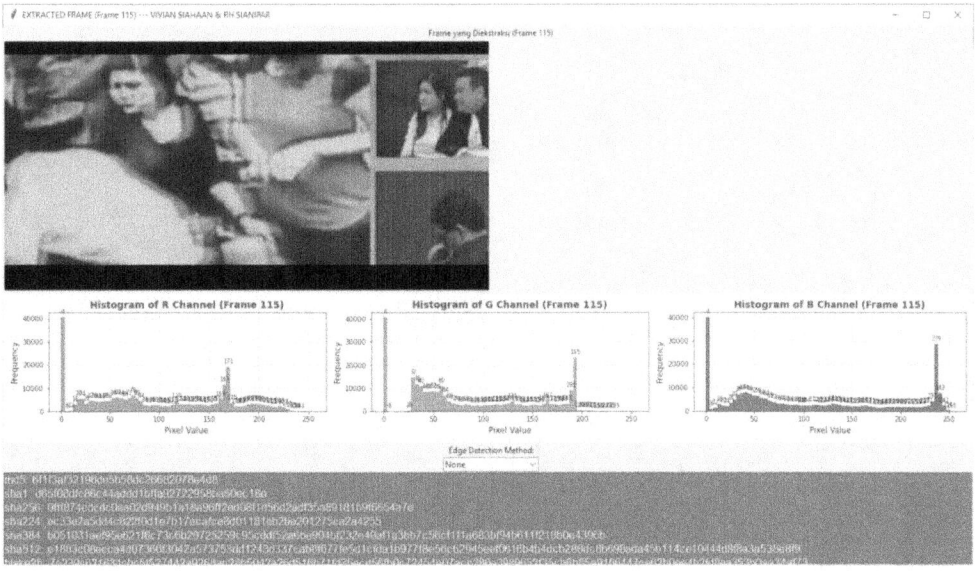

Type another specific number of frame number. Then, push ENTER key.

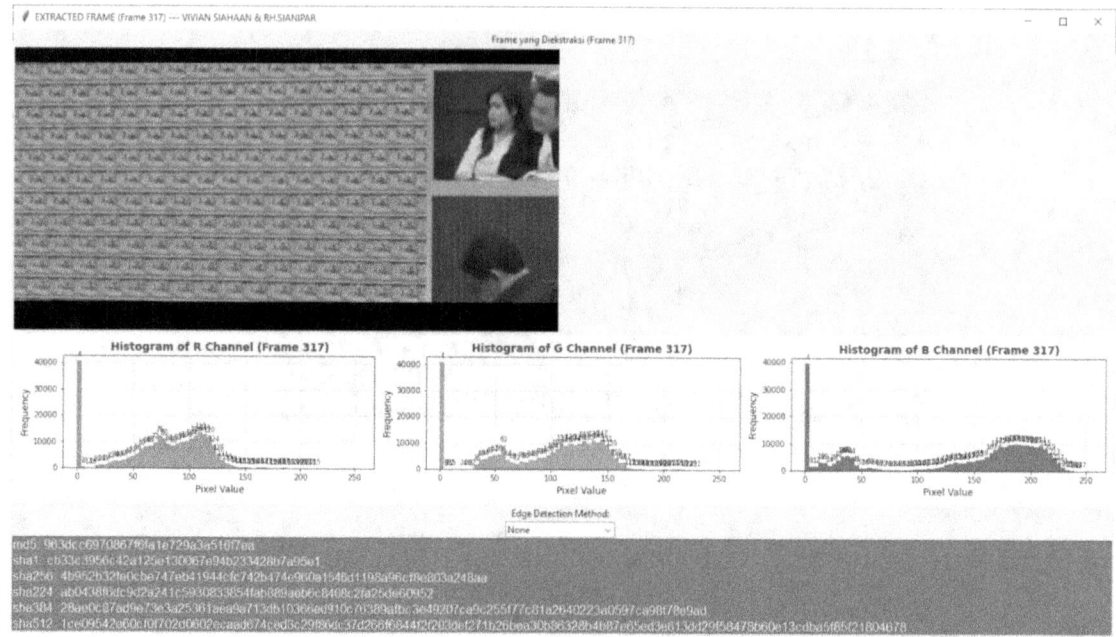

Full Source Code

```
import tkinter as tk
from tkinter import ttk
from tkinter import filedialog
from PIL import Image, ImageTk
import imageio
import matplotlib.pyplot as plt
from matplotlib.backends.backend_tkagg import FigureCanvasTkAgg
import hashlib
import numpy as np
import cv2
import re
import pywt
from skimage.restoration import denoise_tv_chambolle

class VideoPlayerFiltering:
    def __init__(self, master):
        self.master = master
        self.master.title("FRAME FILTERING---VIVIAN SIAHAAN & RH.SIANIPAR")
        
        self.video = None
        self.video_path = None
```

```python
        self.paused = False
        self.zoom_scale = tk.IntVar(value=1)
        self.frame_index = 0
        self.start_x = None
        self.start_y = None
        self.current_x = 0
        self.current_y = 0
        self.photo = None  # Save object reference to PhotoImage globally

        self.create_widgets()

    def create_widgets(self):
        # Panel for video display
        video_panel = tk.Frame(self.master)
        video_panel.grid(row=0, column=0, padx=10, pady=10, sticky="nsew")

        # Canvas to display the video
        canvas_width = 800
        canvas_height = 600
        self.canvas = tk.Canvas(video_panel, width=canvas_width, height=canvas_height)
        self.canvas.pack(side="top", fill="both", expand=True)
        self.canvas.bind("<MouseWheel>", self.on_mousewheel)
        self.canvas.bind("<ButtonPress-1>", self.on_press)
        self.canvas.bind("<B1-Motion>", self.on_drag)

        # Scrollbar
        self.scrollbar = tk.Scrollbar(video_panel, orient="horizontal", command=self.on_scroll)
        self.scrollbar.pack(side="bottom", fill="x")

        self.canvas.configure(xscrollcommand=self.scrollbar.set)

        # Panel for control buttons
        control_panel = tk.Frame(self.master)
        control_panel.grid(row=1, column=0, padx=10, pady=(0, 10), sticky="ew")

        # Button to open a video file
        self.open_button = tk.Button(control_panel, text="Open Video", command=self.open_video)
        self.open_button.grid(row=0, column=0, padx=10, pady=5)

        # Combobox for selecting zoom scale
        self.zoom_combobox = ttk.Combobox(control_panel, textvariable=self.zoom_scale, values=list(range(1, 11)))
        self.zoom_combobox.grid(row=0, column=1, padx=10, pady=5)
        self.zoom_combobox.bind("<<ComboboxSelected>>", self.update_zoom)
```

```python
        # Label and entry for specifying time
        self.time_label = tk.Label(control_panel, text="Jump to Time (s):")
        self.time_label.grid(row=0, column=2, padx=10, pady=5, sticky="e")
        self.time_entry = ttk.Entry(control_panel)
        self.time_entry.grid(row=0, column=3, padx=10, pady=5, sticky="w")
        self.time_entry.bind("<Return>", lambda event: self.jump_to_time())

        # Button to jump to specified time
        self.jump_button = tk.Button(control_panel, text="Jump to Time", command=self.jump_to_time)
        self.jump_button.grid(row=0, column=4, padx=10, pady=5)

        # Button to play/pause the video
        self.play_button = tk.Button(control_panel, text="Play/Pause", command=self.toggle_play_pause)
        self.play_button.grid(row=0, column=5, padx=10, pady=5)

        # Button to stop the video
        self.stop_button = tk.Button(control_panel, text="Stop", command=self.stop_video)
        self.stop_button.grid(row=0, column=6, padx=10, pady=5)

        # Button to extract frame
        self.extract_button = tk.Button(control_panel, text="Extract Frame", command=self.extract_frame)
        self.extract_button.grid(row=1, column=0, padx=10, pady=5)

        # Label and entry for frame number
        self.frame_label = tk.Label(control_panel, text="Frame Number:")
        self.frame_label.grid(row=1, column=1, padx=10, pady=5, sticky="e")
        self.frame_entry = ttk.Entry(control_panel)
        self.frame_entry.grid(row=1, column=2, padx=10, pady=5, sticky="w")
        self.frame_entry.bind("<Return>", lambda event: self.extract_frame())

        # Button to open another instance of the application
        self.open_another_button = tk.Button(control_panel, text="Open Another Video Player", command=self.open_another_player)
        self.open_another_button.grid(row=2, column=0, columnspan=7, padx=10, pady=5)

    def open_video(self):
        self.video_path = filedialog.askopenfilename(filetypes=[("Video files", "*.mp4;*.avi;*.mkv")])
        if self.video_path:
            self.video = imageio.get_reader(self.video_path)
            self.play_video()

    def play_video(self):
        if self.video:
```

```python
            self.paused = False
            self.show_frame()

    def stop_video(self):
        self.paused = True
        self.frame_index = 0
        self.current_x = 0
        self.current_y = 0  # Reset the current position
        self.show_frame()

    def toggle_play_pause(self):
        self.paused = not self.paused
        if not self.paused:
            self.play_video()

    def update_zoom(self, event=None):
        self.show_frame()

    def show_frame(self):
        if self.video:
            if not self.paused:
                self.frame_index += 1
                if self.frame_index >= len(self.video):
                    self.frame_index = 0  # Reset frame index if it exceeds the maximum index
            if 0 <= self.frame_index < len(self.video):  # Check if frame index is within range
                try:
                    frame = self.video.get_data(self.frame_index)
                    frame = Image.fromarray(frame)
                    frame = frame.resize((frame.width * self.zoom_scale.get(), frame.height * self.zoom_scale.get()))
                    photo = ImageTk.PhotoImage(frame)
                    self.photo = photo  # Save object reference to PhotoImage globally
                    self.canvas.delete("video")  # Delete previous image
                    self.canvas.create_image(self.current_x, self.current_y, anchor="nw", image=photo, tags="video")
                    if not self.paused:
                        self.canvas.after(30, self.show_frame)
                except Exception as e:
                    print("Error:", e)

    def on_mousewheel(self, event):
        direction = event.delta // 120
        current_value = int(self.zoom_scale.get())
        if direction == 1 and current_value < 10:
            current_value += 1
```

```python
        elif direction == -1 and current_value > 1:
            current_value -= 1
        self.zoom_scale.set(current_value)
        self.update_zoom()

    def on_press(self, event):
        self.start_x = event.x
        self.start_y = event.y

    def on_drag(self, event):
        if self.start_x and self.start_y:
            x_offset = event.x - self.start_x
            y_offset = event.y - self.start_y
            self.current_x += x_offset  # Update current position
            self.current_y += y_offset  # Update current position
            self.canvas.move("video", x_offset, y_offset)
            self.start_x = event.x
            self.start_y = event.y

    def on_scroll(self, *args):
        scroll_pos = self.scrollbar.get()
        self.current_x = -scroll_pos * self.canvas.winfo_width()
        self.canvas.xview_moveto(scroll_pos)
        self.frame_index = int(scroll_pos * len(self.video))  # Update frame index
        self.show_frame()

    def jump_to_time(self):
        time_str = self.time_entry.get()
        try:
            time_seconds = float(time_str)
            if 0 <= time_seconds:
                self.frame_index = int(time_seconds * self.video.get_meta_data()['fps'])
                self.show_frame()
        except ValueError:
            pass

    def extract_frame(self):
        frame_number_str = self.frame_entry.get()
        try:
            frame_number = int(frame_number_str)
            if 0 <= frame_number < len(self.video):
                frame = self.video.get_data(frame_number)
                self.show_extracted_frame(frame, frame_number)
        except ValueError:
            pass

    def show_extracted_frame(self, frame, frame_number):
```

```python
        self.extracted_frame_window = tk.Toplevel(self.master)
        self.extracted_frame_window.title(f"EXTRACTED FRAME (Frame {frame_number}) --
- VIVIAN SIAHAAN & RH.SIANIPAR")

        extracted_frame_label = tk.Label(self.extracted_frame_window, text=f"Frame 
yang Diekstraksi (Frame {frame_number})")
        extracted_frame_label.pack()

        height, width, _ = frame.shape  # Get dimensions of the frame
        extracted_photo = ImageTk.PhotoImage(image=Image.fromarray(frame))

        # Create a panel for the frame and edge detection canvas
        frame_panel = tk.Frame(self.extracted_frame_window)
        frame_panel.pack(side="top")

        extracted_frame_canvas = tk.Canvas(frame_panel, width=width, height=height)
        extracted_frame_canvas.pack(side="left")
        extracted_frame_canvas.create_image(0, 0, anchor="nw", image=extracted_photo)
        extracted_frame_canvas.image = extracted_photo

        # Canvas for edge detection result
        self.edge_canvas = tk.Canvas(frame_panel, width=width, height=height)
        self.edge_canvas.pack(side="right")

        # Create a panel for histogram plots and hash values
        hist_hash_panel = tk.Frame(self.extracted_frame_window)
        hist_hash_panel.pack(side="bottom", fill="both", expand=True)

        # Plot histogram for each RGB channel
        fig, axs = plt.subplots(1, 3, figsize=(20, 3))
        colors = ['red', 'green', 'blue']
        for i, color in enumerate(['R', 'G', 'B']):
            hist, bins, _ = axs[i].hist(frame[:,:,i].ravel(), bins=64, range=(0, 
255), color=colors[i], alpha=0.7)
            axs[i].set_title(f"Histogram of {color} Channel (Frame {frame_number})", 
fontsize=14, fontweight='bold', color='blue')
            axs[i].set_xlabel("Pixel Value", fontsize=12)
            axs[i].set_ylabel("Frequency", fontsize=12)
            axs[i].grid(True, linestyle='--', linewidth=0.5, color='gray', alpha=0.5)
            axs[i].tick_params(axis='both', which='major', labelsize=10)

            # Add frequency values above each bar
            for bar, frequency in zip(hist, bins[1:]):
                if bar > 0:
                    axs[i].annotate(f'{frequency:.0f}', xy=(bins[np.where(hist == 
bar)[0][0]] + (bins[1] - bins[0]) / 2, bar),
                                    xytext=(0, 3), textcoords='offset points',
ha='center', va='bottom', fontsize=8)
```

```python
        # Ensure the canvas is updated to display the histogram plots
        plt.tight_layout()
        fig.canvas.draw()

        # Display the histogram plots on a Tkinter canvas
        self.histogram_canvas = FigureCanvasTkAgg(fig, master=hist_hash_panel)
        self.histogram_canvas.get_tk_widget().pack(side=tk.TOP, fill=tk.BOTH, expand=True)
        self.histogram_canvas.draw()

        # Calculate multiple hash values of the frame
        hash_algorithms = ['md5', 'sha1', 'sha256', 'sha224', 'sha384', 'sha512', 'blake2b', 'ripemd160']
        hash_values = {}
        for algorithm in hash_algorithms:
            hash_obj = hashlib.new(algorithm)
            hash_obj.update(frame.tobytes())
            hash_value = hash_obj.hexdigest()
            hash_values[algorithm] = hash_value

        # Edge detection combobox
        edge_detection_label = tk.Label(hist_hash_panel, text="Edge Detection Method:")
        edge_detection_label.pack()

        self.filtering_method = ttk.Combobox(hist_hash_panel, values=["None", "Gaussian", "Mean",
            "Median", "Bilateral Filtering", "Non-local Means Denoising", "Anisotropic Diffusion",
            "Total Variation Denoising", "Wiener Filter", "Adaptive Thresholding", "Wavelet Transform"])
        self.filtering_method.pack()
        self.filtering_method.current(0)  # Set default method
        self.filtering_method.bind("<<ComboboxSelected>>", self.apply_filtering)

        # Display hash values
        self.hash_listbox = tk.Listbox(hist_hash_panel, height=8, width=40, font=("Arial", 13), bg="crimson", fg="white")
        self.hash_listbox.pack(fill=tk.BOTH, expand=True)

        # Add horizontal scrollbar if needed
        scrollbar = tk.Scrollbar(hist_hash_panel, orient=tk.HORIZONTAL, command=self.hash_listbox.xview)
        scrollbar.pack(side=tk.BOTTOM, fill=tk.X)
        self.hash_listbox.config(xscrollcommand=scrollbar.set)

        for algorithm, value in hash_values.items():
```

```python
            self.hash_listbox.insert(tk.END, f"{algorithm}: {value}")

    # Define functions for filtering methods
    def apply_gaussian_blur(self, frame, kernel_size=(5, 5), sigma_x=0, sigma_y=0):
        """
        Apply Gaussian blur to each channel of the input frame.

        Args:
            frame: Input image frame.
            kernel_size: Size of the Gaussian kernel. Default is (5, 5).
            sigma_x: Standard deviation in X direction. Default is 0.
            sigma_y: Standard deviation in Y direction. Default is 0.

        Returns:
            List of blurred images for each channel.
        """
        blurred_frames = []
        for i in range(3):  # Iterate over each color channel
            blurred_frame = cv2.GaussianBlur(frame[:,:,i], kernel_size, sigma_x, sigma_y)
            blurred_frames.append(blurred_frame)
        return blurred_frames

    def apply_mean_blur(self, frame, kernel_size=(5, 5)):
        """
        Apply mean blur to each channel of the input frame.

        Args:
            frame: Input image frame.
            kernel_size: Size of the kernel. Default is (5, 5).

        Returns:
            List of blurred images for each channel.
        """
        blurred_frames = []
        for i in range(3):  # Iterate over each color channel
            blurred_frame = cv2.blur(frame[:,:,i], kernel_size)
            blurred_frames.append(blurred_frame)
        return blurred_frames

    def apply_median_blur(self, frame, kernel_size=5):
        """
        Apply median blur to each channel of the input frame.

        Args:
            frame: Input image frame.
            kernel_size: Size of the kernel. Default is 5.
```

```python
    Returns:
        List of blurred images for each channel.
    """
    blurred_frames = []
    for i in range(3):  # Iterate over each color channel
        blurred_frame = cv2.medianBlur(frame[:,:,i], kernel_size)
        blurred_frames.append(blurred_frame)
    return blurred_frames

def apply_bilateral_filtering(self, frame, d=9, sigma_color=75, sigma_space=75):
    """
    Apply bilateral filtering to each channel of the input frame.

    Args:
        frame: Input image frame.
        d: Diameter of each pixel neighborhood. Default is 9.
        sigma_color: Filter sigma in the color space. Default is 75.
        sigma_space: Filter sigma in the coordinate space. Default is 75.

    Returns:
        List of filtered images for each channel.
    """
    filtered_frames = []
    for i in range(3):  # Iterate over each color channel
        filtered_frame = cv2.bilateralFilter(frame[:,:,i], d, sigma_color, sigma_space)
        filtered_frames.append(filtered_frame)
    return filtered_frames

def apply_non_local_means_denoising(self, frame, h=10, templateWindowSize=7, searchWindowSize=21):
    """
    Apply Non-local Means Denoising to each channel of the input frame.

    Args:
        frame: Input image frame.
        h: Parameter regulating filter strength. Larger 'h' value removes noise effectively but removes details of image also.
            Smaller 'h' value preserves details but also preserves noise. Default is 10.
        templateWindowSize: Size in pixels of the template patch. Recommended value is 7. Default is 7.
        searchWindowSize: Size in pixels of the window for the search. Recommended value is 21. Default is 21.

    Returns:
        List of denoised images for each channel.
    """
```

```python
        denoised_frames = []
        for i in range(3):  # Iterate over each color channel
            denoised_frame = cv2.fastNlMeansDenoising(frame[:,:,i], None, h=h, 
templateWindowSize=templateWindowSize, searchWindowSize=searchWindowSize)
            denoised_frames.append(denoised_frame)
        return denoised_frames

    def apply_anisotropic_diffusion(self, frame, iterations=1, delta_t=0.25, 
kappa=10):
        """
        Apply Anisotropic Diffusion to each channel of the input frame.

        Args:
            frame: Input image frame.
            iterations: Number of iterations for diffusion. Default is 1.
            delta_t: Time step. Default is 0.25.
            kappa: Perona-Malik diffusion coefficient. Default is 10.

        Returns:
            List of processed frames after applying Anisotropic Diffusion to each 
channel.
        """
        diffusion_frames = []
        for i in range(3):  # Iterate over each color channel
            # Copy the input frame channel to avoid modifying the original frame
            img = frame[:,:,i].astype(float)

            # Define the 4-neighbour mask
            mask = np.array([[0, 1, 0],
                             [1, 0, 1],
                             [0, 1, 0]], dtype=np.float32)

            # Perform Anisotropic Diffusion for the specified number of iterations
            for _ in range(iterations):
                # Add padding to the image
                img_padded = cv2.copyMakeBorder(img, 1, 1, 1, 1, cv2.BORDER_REFLECT)

                # Compute gradients using central differences
                dx = cv2.filter2D(img_padded, -1, np.array([[-1, 0, 1]]))
                dy = cv2.filter2D(img_padded, -1, np.array([[-1], [0], [1]]))

                # Resize gradients to match the size of the image
                dx = cv2.resize(dx, img.shape[::-1])
                dy = cv2.resize(dy, img.shape[::-1])

                # Compute gradient magnitude squared
                mag = np.square(dx) + np.square(dy)
```

```python
            # Compute diffusion coefficients
            c = 1 / (1 + (mag / kappa ** 2))

            # Update image using the diffusion equation
            img += delta_t * (c * cv2.filter2D(dx, -1, mask) +
                              c * cv2.filter2D(dy, -1, mask))

        # Append the processed channel to the list of diffusion frames
        diffusion_frames.append(np.clip(img, 0, 255).astype(np.uint8))

    return diffusion_frames

def apply_total_variation_denoising(self, frame, weight=0.7, eps=0.05):
    """
    Apply Total Variation Denoising to each channel of the input frame.

    Args:
        frame: Input image frame.
        weight: Denoising weight. Default is 0.7.
        eps: Denoising regularization parameter. Default is 0.05.

    Returns:
        List of denoised frames for each channel.
    """
    denoised_frames = []
    for i in range(3):  # Iterate over each color channel
        denoised_frame = denoise_tv_chambolle(frame[:,:,i], weight=weight, eps=eps)
        # Scale the result to the range 0 to 255
        scaled_denoised_frame = ((denoised_frame - denoised_frame.min()) * (255 / (denoised_frame.max() - denoised_frame.min()))).astype(np.uint8)
        denoised_frames.append(scaled_denoised_frame)
    return denoised_frames

def apply_wiener_filter(self, frame, kernel_size=(3, 3), noise_variance=0.1):
    """
    Apply Wiener Filter to each channel of the input frame.

    Args:
        frame: Input image frame.
        kernel_size: Size of the Gaussian kernel for blurring. Default is (3, 3).
        noise_variance: Variance of the noise. Default is 0.1.

    Returns:
        List of images after applying Wiener Filter to each channel.
    """
    filtered_frames = []
    for i in range(3):  # Iterate over each color channel
```

```python
            blurred_frame = cv2.GaussianBlur(frame[:,:,i], kernel_size, 0)
            filtered_frame = cv2.fastNlMeansDenoising(blurred_frame, None, h=noise_variance)
            filtered_frames.append(filtered_frame)
        return filtered_frames

    def apply_adaptive_thresholding(self, frame, max_value=255, adaptive_method=cv2.ADAPTIVE_THRESH_GAUSSIAN_C, threshold_type=cv2.THRESH_BINARY, block_size=11, constant=2):
        """
        Apply Adaptive Thresholding to each channel of the input frame.

        Args:
            frame: Input image frame.
            max_value: Maximum intensity value. Default is 255.
            adaptive_method: Adaptive thresholding method. Default is cv2.ADAPTIVE_THRESH_GAUSSIAN_C.
            threshold_type: Thresholding type. Default is cv2.THRESH_BINARY.
            block_size: Size of the local region. Default is 11.
            constant: Constant subtracted from the mean. Default is 2.

        Returns:
            List of images after applying Adaptive Thresholding to each channel.
        """
        thresholded_frames = []
        for i in range(3):  # Iterate over each color channel
            thresholded_frame = cv2.adaptiveThreshold(frame[:,:,i], max_value, adaptive_method, threshold_type, block_size, constant)
            thresholded_frames.append(thresholded_frame)
        return thresholded_frames

    def apply_wavelet_transform(self, frame, wavelet='haar', level=1):
        """
        Apply Wavelet Transform to each channel of the input frame.

        Args:
            frame: Input image frame.
            wavelet: Type of wavelet. Default is 'haar'.
            level: Decomposition level. Default is 1.

        Returns:
            List of images after applying Wavelet Transform to each channel.
        """
        transformed_frames = []
        for i in range(3):  # Iterate over each color channel
            coeffs = pywt.wavedec2(frame[:,:,i], wavelet, level=level)
            # Reconstruct the image from the coefficients
            reconstructed_img = pywt.waverec2(coeffs, wavelet)
```

```python
            transformed_frames.append(reconstructed_img)

        return transformed_frames

    def apply_filtering(self, event=None):
        # Get selected method from combobox
        method = self.filtering_method.get()

        # Get the current frame number from the title of the tkinter window
        title = self.extracted_frame_window.title()
        frame_numbers = re.findall(r'\d+', title)
        if frame_numbers:
            self.frame_number = int(frame_numbers[-1])  # Extract the last numerical value
        else:
            self.frame_number = 0  # Default frame number if no numerical value is found

        frame = self.video.get_data(self.frame_number)

        # Initialize filtered to None
        filtered = None

        # Apply edge detection method based on selected method
        if method == "Gaussian":
            filtered = self.apply_gaussian_blur(frame)
        elif method == "Mean":
            filtered = self.apply_mean_blur(frame)
        elif method == "Median":
            filtered = self.apply_median_blur(frame)
        elif method == "None":
            filtered = [frame[:,:,i].copy() for i in range(3)]
        elif method == "Bilateral Filtering":
            filtered = self.apply_bilateral_filtering(frame)
        elif method == "Non-local Means Denoising":
            filtered = self.apply_non_local_means_denoising(frame)
        elif method == "Anisotropic Diffusion":
            filtered = self.apply_anisotropic_diffusion(frame)
        elif method == "Total Variation Denoising":
            filtered = self.apply_total_variation_denoising(frame)
        elif method == "Wiener Filter":
            filtered = self.apply_wiener_filter(frame)
        elif method == "Adaptive Thresholding":
            filtered = self.apply_adaptive_thresholding(frame)
        elif method == "Wavelet Transform":
            filtered = self.apply_wavelet_transform(frame)

        # Display edge detection result
```

```python
        if filtered is not None:
            # Combine channels into a single image
            combined_image = self.combine_channels_to_image(filtered)

            # Convert the combined image to a PIL Image
            pil_image = Image.fromarray(np.uint8(combined_image))

            # Convert PIL Image to Tkinter PhotoImage
            edge_photo = ImageTk.PhotoImage(image=pil_image)

            # Display the image in the canvas
            self.edge_canvas.create_image(0, 0, anchor="nw", image=edge_photo)
            self.edge_canvas.image = edge_photo

            # Update histogram and hash values
            self.update_histogram_and_hashes(frame, filtered)

    def combine_channels_to_image(self, filtered):
        """
        Combine filtered channels into a single image.

        Args:
            filtered: List of filtered images for each channel.

        Returns:
            Combined image.
        """
        # Convert each filtered channel to numpy array
        filtered_arrays = [np.array(channel) for channel in filtered]

        # Stack the filtered channels along the last axis to form the combined image
        combined_image = np.stack(filtered_arrays, axis=-1)

        return combined_image

    def update_histogram_and_hashes(self, frame, filtered):
        # Update histogram
        for i, ax in enumerate(self.histogram_canvas.figure.get_axes()):
            ax.clear()
            colors = ['red', 'green', 'blue']
            channel = filtered[i]  # Memilih saluran warna yang sesuai dengan indeks
            hist, bins = np.histogram(channel.ravel(), bins=32, range=(0, 255))
            ax.bar(bins[:-1], hist, color=colors[i], alpha=0.7, width=6)  # Menyesuaikan lebar batang histogram
            ax.set_title(f"Histogram of {colors[i]} Channel (Frame {self.frame_number})", fontsize=14, fontweight='bold', color='blue')
            ax.set_xlabel("Pixel Value", fontsize=12)
            ax.set_ylabel("Frequency", fontsize=12)
```

```python
            ax.grid(True, linestyle='--', linewidth=0.5, color='gray', alpha=0.5)
            ax.tick_params(axis='both', which='major', labelsize=10)
            # Add frequency values above each bar
            for bar, frequency in zip(hist, bins[1:]):
                if bar > 0:
                    ax.annotate(f'{frequency:.0f}', xy=(bins[np.where(hist == bar)[0][0]] + (bins[1] - bins[0]) / 2, bar),
                                xytext=(0, 3), textcoords='offset points',
                                ha='center', va='bottom', fontsize=8)
            self.histogram_canvas.draw()

            # Update hash values
            hash_algorithms = ['md5', 'sha1', 'sha256', 'sha224', 'sha384', 'sha512', 'blake2b', 'ripemd160']
            hash_values = {}
            for algorithm in hash_algorithms:
                hash_obj = hashlib.new(algorithm)
                for channel in filtered:
                    hash_obj.update(channel.tobytes())  # Update hash values based on edge-detected image
                hash_value = hash_obj.hexdigest()
                hash_values[algorithm] = hash_value

            self.hash_listbox.delete(0, tk.END)  # Clear existing hash values
            for algorithm, value in hash_values.items():
                self.hash_listbox.insert(tk.END, f"{algorithm}: {value}")

    def show_filterinng_result(self, filtered):
        # Combine channels into a single image
        combined_image = self.combine_channels_to_image(filtered)

        # Convert the combined image to a PIL Image
        pil_image = Image.fromarray(np.uint8(combined_image))

        # Convert PIL Image to Tkinter PhotoImage
        edge_photo = ImageTk.PhotoImage(image=pil_image)

        # Display the image in the canvas
        self.edge_canvas.create_image(0, 0, anchor="nw", image=edge_photo)
        self.edge_canvas.image = edge_photo

    def open_another_player(self):
        # Open another instance of the application
        root = tk.Toplevel(self.master)
        app = VideoPlayerFiltering(root)

def main():
    root = tk.Tk()
```

```
    app = VideoPlayerFiltering(root)
    root.mainloop()

if __name__ == "__main__":
    main()
```

Bibliography

Vivian Siahaan and Rismon Hasiholan Sianipar. *TKINTER, DATA SCIENCE, AND MACHINE LEARNING*. North Sumatera: Balige Publishing, 2023.

Vivian Siahaan and Rismon Hasiholan Sianipar. *DATA VISUALIZATION, TIME-SERIES FORECASTING, AND PREDICTION USING MACHINE LEARNING WITH TKINTER*. North Sumatera: Balige Publishing, 2023.

Vivian Siahaan and Rismon Hasiholan Sianipar. *TIME-SERIES WEATHER FORECASTING AND PREDICTION USING MACHINE LEARNING WITH TKINTER*. North Sumatera: Balige Publishing, 2023.

Vivian Siahaan and Rismon Hasiholan Sianipar. DATA VISUALIZATION, TIME-SERIES FORECASTING, AND PREDICTION USING MACHINE LEARNING WITH TKINTER. North Sumatera: Balige Publishing, 2023.

Vivian Siahaan and Rismon Hasiholan Sianipar. START FROM SCRATCH DIGITAL SIGNAL PROCESSING WITH TKINTER. North Sumatera: Balige Publishing, 2023.

Vivian Siahaan and Rismon Hasiholan Sianipar. START FROM SCRATCH DIGITAL IMAGE PROCESSING WITH TKINTER. North Sumatera: Balige Publishing, 2023.

Vivian Siahaan and Rismon Hasiholan Sianipar. START FROM SCRATCH DIGITAL IMAGE PROCESSING WITH TKINTER. North Sumatera: Balige Publishing, 2023.

Vivian Siahaan and Rismon Hasiholan Sianipar. IMAGE DENOISING, EDGE DETECTION, AND SEGMENTATION WITH TKINTER. North Sumatera: Balige Publishing, 2023.

www.ingramcontent.com/pod-product-compliance
Lightning Source LLC
Chambersburg PA
CBHW062103220526
45471CB00010B/3587